BY THE AUTO EDITORS OF CONSUMER GUIDE®

# BMW
## Bavaria's Driving Machines

JAN P. NORBYE

**BEEKMAN HOUSE**
New York

# CONTENTS

Manufactured in the United States of America
10 9 8 7 6 5 4 3 2 1

Library of Congress Catalog Card Number: 84-60309

ISBN: 0-517-42464-9

This edition published by:
Beekman House
Distributed by Crown Publishers, Inc.
One Park Avenue
New York, New York 10016

**Principal Author**
Jan P. Norbye

**Illustrator**
James R. Kust

**Photographers**
David Gooley
Bud Juneau

**Photo Credits**
AFN, Ltd.
Bayerische Motoren Werke,
   AG
BMW of North America, Inc.
Prof. Mihailo Borisavljevic
Bristol Cars, Ltd.
Thomas Knighten
Jan P. Norbye
Michael Schimpke
Halwart Schrader

Dirk Strassl
Ron Wakefield

Sincere thanks to the BMW owners who made their cars available for photography: Gregory Beemer (white 1963 Type 700 cabriolet), John Bentz (white 1971 Type 1600 Baur cabriolet), Edwina DeRousse (blue 1963 Type 700LS sedan), Franz Fechner (manila 1967 Type 2000 CS), Marilyn Felling (red 1957 BMW-Isetta 300), Armen Gasparian (black & green 1938 Type 327 coupe), Bill Hedberg (black 1983 Type 320i S), Tom Jervis (white 1971 Type 2800 CS), Donald Kamm (cream 1937 Type 328), Ray Korman (white 1977 630 CSi Twin Turbo), Guido Nagel (blue 1983 Type 320i Baur cabriolet), Tom Pathe (blue 1974 Type 1802 Baur cabriolet), Ivan Pato (black Hartge H5S sedan), James L. Roman (red 1957 Type 507), Carla Rouke (black 1981 Type 635 CSi), Stephen Rouke (silver 1973 Type 3.0 CSL), Dennis Ryan (orange 1972 2000 Touring), Rick and Miki Schug (light yellow 1971 Type 2002ti), Gilbert L. Steward, Jr. (silver Type 507), Ernest Weil (white 1938 racing Type 328). Special thanks to Tom Cobb for providing the handsome setting used for some of these cars.

# INTRODUCTION

*Above: Fifty years of BMW cars, represented by (l to r) the 1931-32 Dixi 3/15, 1933-36 Type 303, 1936-41 Type 326, 1954-58 Type 502, 1971-75 1502, and 1977-date 733i. Left: The inspiration for the BMW badge.*

All over the world, BMW automobiles are known and respected primarily because they're built for one thing: driving pleasure. And they deliver. Perhaps more than any other, the cars bearing the famed blue-and-white logo are recognized as the very essence of speed and sport combined with great engineering originality, superb execution, and the sort of high-quality craftsmanship that has always seemed uniquely German. These qualities set BMWs—any BMW—apart from other cars in a manner not unlike the way a Leica stands apart from other cameras. In short, there's simply nothing else quite like them.

This image has not been easy to establish. Compared to, say, Mercedes-Benz, the BMW "phenomenon" and the company's most memorable cars are both fairly recent developments. American car connoisseurs have been taken with Bavaria's driving machines for only some two decades now, while the marque's reputation in Europe only began to be forged in the mid-Thirties. Today's high-technology BMWs are still making converts of people who take the wheel of a "Bimmer" for the first time, but that alone doesn't explain what makes these cars so outstanding or their owners so fiercely loyal.

An understanding of what BMW is all about is the prime focus of this book. The origins and evolution of the company and its products are at the very heart of BMW enthusiasm. These traditions are also essential for appreciating how the marque's enviable reputation came to be.

BMW was a successful motorcycle manufacturer long before it ventured into automobiles, and it remains so today. But the firm's heritage really began in aviation. The famed blue-and-white circular logo preserves this link with the past. It has nothing to do with wheels and bears no trace of antique heraldry. Rather, it is a commercial artist's rendering of a whirling air-

5

plane propeller seen from the front, its rotation stopped as if by a strobe light and highlighted with the state colors of Bavaria. As we shall see, aircraft engine production was BMW's first major activity, and it remained a vital part of the firm's business through World War II. But BMW's return to car manufacturing in the postwar era would not have been possible without its motorcycle business. It's instructive to realize that it was not until the early Sixties that the firm began producing the kind of cars we admire so much today—and then only after several false starts.

It's amusing to reflect that if history had taken a slightly different course, you might be admiring a Rapp or a Dixi instead of a BMW. There was nothing pretentious or extraordinary about the firm's early cars. On the contrary, they were rather primitive contraptions with a design that was already outmoded when they first appeared. Yet within 10 short years they had changed dramatically. By the start of World War II, BMW was competing strongly against even the best established

and most respected German marques, with exciting cars that were widely acknowledged as among the world's best. The firm's spectacular climb up the automotive "social ladder," its tragic fate in the aftermath of war, and its remarkable recovery in the Fifties and Sixties is a story filled with drama and intrigue.

BMW, of course, stands for Bayerische Motoren Werke—Bavarian Motor Works—and that prideful region of Germany has probably been as important to the firm's history as the achievements of its leaders. Its headquarters have always been in the state capital of Munich, medieval seat of The Dukes of Wittelsbach, prestigious center of cultural life and higher education, and beer capital of western Europe. Though BMW was first financed by sources from Berlin and Austria, and although its first leader was Austrian by birth, the company has always operated as a Bavarian concern under Bavarian laws, and has thus acquired a genuine Bavarian character. Naturally, this influence has permeated the cars themselves, even though they

were not actually built in Bavaria up to 1945 but rather in Thuringia, further north. Yet the Bavarian landscape, with its flatlands and long, straight roads in the north and the demanding Alps in the south, is undeniably responsible for the brilliant all-around performance associated with the marque. Over the years, engines, steering, brakes, and suspensions have all been designed to excel in these diverse regional driving conditions, something that has become part of the BMW mystique. Another factor in shaping Bavaria's driving machines has been the keen, long-standing competition between BMW and another car company in the rival state of Swabia, Daimler-Benz.

BMW is not the largest German automaker. Though its output has increased tenfold in the space of 25 years, it has never really engaged in a production "race" with D-B or Audi. Instead, the company remains committed to building the best cars it knows how in a variety of sizes—automobiles consistent with traditional BMW ideals on the one hand and the rising expectations of an ever-growing

clientele on the other. That is no easy task, but one drive in any modern BMW should be enough to convince you that the people in Munich continue to succeed in a way that is unique in the automotive world.

With photographer Julius Weitmann at my side, I first set foot inside BMW headquarters one day in February 1963. We had an assignment to road test the "New Class" 1500 sedan then recently announced, and were received by Dr. C. T. Hoepner, chief of the press department. We drove the car on all sorts of roads from fast *Autobahnen* to mountain passes, ran the Rossfeld hillclimb course, and stopped for photography at Berchtesgaden. On our return to Milbersthofen the next day, we were given a factory tour and saw how the 1500 was built. I came away thoroughly impressed and fully assured about BMW's

future, which in those days was not nearly as rosy as it is today.

I wish Weitmann and Hoepner were still alive to receive my renewed thanks for this splendid introduction to BMW. Since that time, I have been a frequent visitor, following the firm's products and its fortunes, and have met most of its executives and engineers. The information they have shared with us over the years has been indispensable in compiling this book.

In particular, we have relied heavily on the BMW Archives, and we wish to express our gratitude to Dirk Henning Strassl, Michael Schimpke, Peter Zollner, and Rita Strothjohann. Herr Senf from the Volkseigene Betrieb Automobilwerk Eisenach provided valuable research assistance from the East German organization. A special word of thanks to Halwart Schrader and Professor Mihailo Borisavljevic, both of whom supplied rare ma-

terial from their private collections. We also appreciate the advice and assistance of Peter von Mantueffel of the Verband der Automobilindustrie, John Weinthal and Janet Wilkinson of the Society of Motor Manufacturers and Traders in Great Britain, T. A. D. Crook of Bristol Cars, Ltd., and J. T. Aldington of A. F. N. Ltd. Finally, the editors gratefully acknowledge Thomas Knighten at BMW of North America public relations for acting as our transatlantic liaison, as well as for his enthusiastic support.

With its highly individual, supremely capable cars backed by a tradition of innovation and a dedication to excellence, BMW today stands in the first rank of the world's automakers. The story of its great success and the many struggles and achievements that made it possible is a fascinating one, yet it has not often been told in its entirety. We hope you find it as rewarding to read as we have in telling it.

Jan P. Norbye
January, 1984

*Then and now: the fabulous racing M1 and a late-1920s Dixi 3/15 sedan.*

BMW DIXI

# THE ORIGINS OF BMW: FROM FLYING MACHINES TO DRIVING MACHINES

A motorcycle was the first product to carry the BMW badge—more than five years before an automobile would. The early history of several other equally famous marques has involved a process of graduation from bicycles to motorcycles to automobiles. Such was the case with Adler, NSU, and Opel in Germany, Minerva in Belgium, Darracq in France, and Puch in Austria, to name a few. But BMW had no antecedents in bicycle manufacturing, wheelrighting, wagon building, or any of the traditional stepping-stones to motor vehicle production. Instead, its roots are in the entrepreneurial supplier industries that got their start during the period of rearmament preceding World War I and that ultimately served the Prussian Kaiser's war machine.

It was not unusual for weapons manufacturers to go into automaking in those years, usually as a peacetime sideline. Among the better-known examples are Hotchkiss in France, Skoda in what is now Czechoslovakia, Steyr in Austria, and BSA in England. And Krupp in Germany built military trucks for many years. But the predecessor

*The 500cc shaft-drive R-32 was BMW's first successful venture into motorcycles. Here, a delightful period view of the Munich factory, circa 1924.*

companies of BMW did not produce guns, cannon, ammunition, or other weaponry. They were in the transport business. Remember that World War I was the first motorized war, and trucks, tanks and airplanes were important new tactical tools. The conflict saw the first applications of aerial bombardment, though at first the main military use for aircraft was as observation plat-forms overlooking the battlefield. Later, planes would be used for reconnaissance.

No matter how they were used, airplanes needed engines. Pioneer firms such as Bleriot, DeWoitine, Fokker, Roe, Morane, Junkers, Dornier, Farman, Voisin, Sopwith, Blackburn, and Handley-Page were mainly air-frame builders, so they naturally looked to the motor industry for engines. Europe's car companies, led by Sunbeam, Hispano-Suiza, Daimler Motoren Gesellschaft, Panhard-Levassor, Wolseley, Fiat and Renault, thus became the main suppliers to the fledgling aviation industry. There were also some new firms organized expressly for developing and producing aircraft engines. The most prominent in England was Bentley. In Germany it was a

Left: Besides aero engines, BMW also built marine engines during WWI. Here, workers pose with two completed units ready for delivery in 1918. Above: Max Friz, master engineer in BMW's early years. Top: Pilot Zeno Diemer set a world altitude record in 1919 with this WWI Fokker biplane powered by the six-cylinder BMW Type IV engine.

firm that would soon operate under the initials BMW.

The story begins when Karl Friedrich Rapp, an engineer and one-time director of Flugwerk Deutschland GmbH (located in Brand outside Aachen), went to Munich to raise capital for starting an engine company. With 200,000 marks he founded Rapp Motoren Werke on October 28, 1913, and began operations

in a plant at Schleissheimer Strasse 288 in the Munich suburb of Milbertshofen. This site was chosen because it was conveniently near the Gustav Otto Flugmaschinenfabrik, with which Rapp had secured substantial contracts. Now Gustav Otto was the son of Nikolaus August Otto, inventor of the four-stroke internal-combustion engine and founder of Gas-

motorenfabrik Deutz. The aircraft concern had been established in 1911 with a factory on Lerchenauer Strasse 76, opposite Munich's Oberwiesenfelde airfield. After four years of operation, the company was reorganized, and in January 1915 adopted the title of Otto Werke, Gustav Otto, München. Rapp's contact called for him to supply the Otto firm with four-cylinder water-cooled engines. His company also produced a line of marine power units. Both were his own designs.

Meantime, the Hapsburg empire had belatedly decided to constitute an air force, and one of its main suppliers, Austro-Daimler, suddenly found itself hopelessly short of production capacity to meet the demand. To take up the slack, A-D began looking around for a subcontractor for its V-12 aircraft engines and ended up on Rapp's doorstep. The man who negotiated this agreement was a young Austrian engineer, Franz Josef Popp. Before the war, he had worked for the Vienna branch of Berlin's giant electrical engineering combine, AEG (Allgemeine Elektrizitäts Gesellschaft). Now he was in procurement for the Austro-

Hungarian government. Popp's influence was to be far wider than the authority of his office, for he was also well connected in Vienna's financial world. On the strength of this lucrative new business, Rapp Motoren Werke was transformed into Bayerische Motoren Werke GmbH, with a capital stock of 1.2 million marks, on March 7, 1916. It was the official birth of BMW. That same day, the Otto Werke became Bayerische Flugzeugwerke AG. Though there was close collaboration between the two firms at the operations level, they remained separate for the time being.

Popp must have wondered occasionally whether he had chosen the right outfit, for BMW was really not well equipped for the task of building the Austro-Daimler V-12s. Contradictory as it may seem, Rapp had tried to expand his business too quickly. As a result, he had run short of working capital and, by this time, settling bills from suppliers and meeting the payroll were overwhelming problems.

Popp now approached a powerful friend, Camillo Castiglioni, chief of the Wiener Bankverein and board member of several

large industrial corporations. Castiglioni put up the money necessary to raise BMW's capital reserves, and he and Popp stepped in as stockholders. Rapp abruptly left the company in the summer of 1917. Under the new regime, total capital was increased tenfold, to 12 million marks. New incorporation papers were filed for Bayerische Motoren Werke AG on August 13, 1918, and the GmbH was dissolved. The distinction between GmbH (Gesellschaft mit beschränkter Haftung) and AG (Aktiengesellschaft) lies in the statutes of incorporation. AG denotes a company with publicly owned and traded stock, while GmbH merely specifies "limited responsibility" with regard to the amount of capital. The Vienna-born Popp, then only 32 and armed with mechanical and electrical engineering degrees from the Brunn (Brno) Technical University, took over the management of BMW AG. Prominent among the new firm's stockholders was Fritz Neumeyer, president of Zündapp in Nuremberg, a company that would later be a strong rival for BMW in the motorcycle field. Hjalmar Schacht, who later became fa-

mous as Hitler's financial wizard, joined the supervisory board. A new and very large plant was now erected at the north end of the Oberwiesenfelde airfield, with a total of 3400 employees working in shifts.

By this time, BMW also had a new product, the first engine to bear those initials. This was the Type IIIa, a water-cooled six-cylinder aircraft engine designed by 35-year-old Max Ernst Friz. Neither Bavarian nor Austrian, Friz was a true Swabian, hailing from Urach in Württemberg. His career was unusual for this period. After completing business school he became an apprentice at a steam engine factory, then went on to the Royal School of Civil Engineering in Esslingen. He joined Daimler Motoren Werke in 1906, where he suggested that firm should build engines for sports airplanes. Friz also assisted in development of the 4.5-liter Mercedes four-cylinder engine that powered the car Christian Lautenschlager drove to victory in the French Grand Prix at Lyon in the summer of 1914. He worked on Daimler fighter-plane engines from the outbreak of the war until he left the Stuttgart

area at the end of 1916. He moved into his office at BMW on the first working day of 1917.

Friz was not only a good engineer but a shrewd salesman as well. Once he went to the Air Ministry in Berlin with nothing but a briefcase full of blueprints—and returned to BMW with an order for 2000 of the new engines. But things were not rosy for long, as the government cancelled all its aircraft and engine contracts with the end of hostilities in 1919. No more than 70 of the Type IIIa engines were delivered. Worse, German industry was expressly forbidden by the Treaty of Versailles to build military aircraft, and there was little demand for civilian planes in postwar Germany. As a result, both BMW AG and Bayerische Flugzeug were forced to turn to new lines of business—which brought up the question of what to do about money.

The answer came at the beginning of 1919, when Castiglioni sold his BMW holdings for 28 million marks to Johannes Philipp Vielmetter of Berlin, chief of Knorr Bremsen AG. Within weeks, this firm placed an order for compressed-air brakes to be used on railway cars, and BMW delivered no fewer than 10,000 sets before the end of the year. At the same time, Bayerische Flugzeug began turning out motorcycles, workbenches, office furniture, and other goods. But no lasting solution was in sight, and it took the ambition and imagination of Franz Josef Popp to formulate a long-term scheme for corporate survival. He wanted to make cars, and he saw the motorcycle not only as the best way to accomplish that but also as a logical companion product.

Once more he looked to Castiglioni for financial aid. And to ensure adequate facilities, he would combine the engine concern with the aircraft company. The merger was duly arranged by Castiglioni, who purchased all the assets of BMW AG from Knorr Bremsen, which held about 90 percent of the shares, for 75 million marks on May 20, 1922. At the same time he paid 4 million marks for complete ownership of Bayerische Flugzeug, including its plant on Lerchenauer Strasse. The BMW operation on Moosacher Strasse that had been recently retooled for brake production was split off and reorganized as Suddeutsche Bremsen AG, becoming a wholly owned subsidiary of Knorr Bremsen.

Popp's plan would not be easy to execute. The country was in a social upheaval, and inflation was rampant in the early years after WWI. But he had made a start, and many factors were in his favor. Even so, he didn't have much to work with. The only engine BMW had designed up to this point was the Type IIIa, and the firm had inherited little original technology from the previous Rapp company. The

four-cylinder Rapp aero engine was hardly an engineering masterpiece, and its performance in the air was mediocre. Installed in a typical German military biplane, its speed was barely adequate for reconnaissance duties, and it was hopelessly outclassed for combat.

In their quest for more power, Rapp and his engineers had tried to make a six out of the four, but instead of adding one cylinder at each end to make an inline unit they added two separate cylinders, standing vertically alongside the four-cylinder crankcase on the side of the valvegear. This arrangement necessitated a separate two-throw crankshaft geared to the main crankshaft. The result was conveniently short, it presumably had the expected power, and no serious problems cropped up in bench tests. But when installed it was found to suffer such severe vibration that it literally shook the plane apart. The first flight test came to an end when the entire tail, rudder and ailerons fell off as the machine rumbled down the runway. Reinforcing the airframe was obviously not the practical solution because of the added weight.

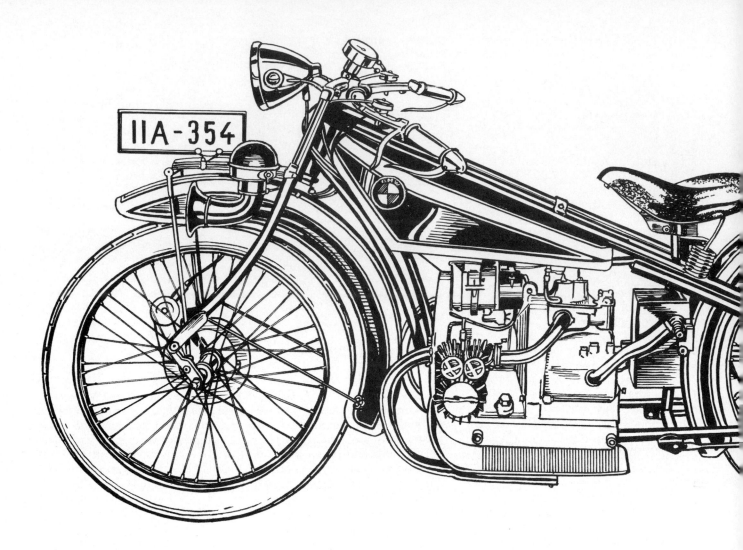

What Rapp needed was a better engine.

Rapp still hoped Max Friz could fix the four-plus-two design. But Friz wasted few words in explaining that this was no way to power an airplane. Even a partial redesign would have been so major that it was just as easy to go back to the drawing board and start all over. That wouldn't be necessary, though, for Friz had in his briefcase a complete set of drawings for a modern water-cooled six. Interestingly, it bore definite Mercedes influence, which wasn't surprising since Friz had developed some of his ideas while on the staff under Paul Daimler, son of that company's founder.

The new Friz design mounted the six cylinders vertically and in line, bolted to a two-piece, horizontally split aluminum crankcase. The cylinders were separate and made of cast iron, with integral cylinder heads and water jackets. Each cylinder had two overhead valves splayed at a narrow angle (about 27 degrees) and operated by rocker arms from a single overhead camshaft. The camshaft drive took the form of a vertical shaft geared to the rear of the crankshaft, with skew gears at the camshaft end. The vertical shaft extended down below the crankshaft center to drive both an oil pump and a water pump. Near its center, it was worm-geared to a horizontal jackshaft that carried an ignition distributor on each end. Together these sparked two plugs per cylinder, timed for simultaneous firing. With a massive displacement of 19 liters (1159 cubic inches), this was the unit that became the BMW Type IIIa. Rated at 185 horsepower, it received its airworthiness certificate after flight tests in a Fokker DVII biplane (normally powered by a 160-bhp Daimler-Benz unit).

The first planes to use BMW's first engine were allocated to the squadron commanded by none other than the infamous Baron Von Richthofen. Installed in an all-metal Junkers Ju F13 in 1919, it set a world altitude record of 6750 meters (22,500 feet) with eight persons aboard. This flight was the first of many claims BMW would make to supremacy in the art of aero engine engineering. Franz Josef Popp may have had other ambitions, but the feat demonstrated that BMW was first and foremost an engine builder.

Under pressure from Popp and others for even more perfor-

mance, Friz developed the IIIa into the BMW IV, a 22-liter (1342-cid) unit with initial output of 250 bhp. Power was later boosted to about 320 bhp. While this engine was undergoing static tests, someone noticed that a wartime Fokker biplane had been left behind at Oberwiesenfelde, and the engineers couldn't wait to install their newest power unit in this aircraft. A pilot was needed for the flight test, someone willing to risk his life by taking the untried engine as high as it would go. Like the airplane, Oberleutnant Zeno Diemer had been overlooked by demobilization, but he would not be forgotten. In his first flight on May 9, 1919, he flew to an altitude of 9700 meters (32,333 feet), well above the expected ceiling of an unsupercharged engine. He made a second trial on June 17, climbing to a full 9760 meters (32,535 feet) and setting a new world altitude record. Germany was not then part of the FAI, the international governing body for air sports, so the record was never official. But the plane was equipped with two barographs (altimeters), and the local director of meteorology certified the readings.

Production of the BMW IV was cut short by the Allied Control Commission, which ordered the company to hand over all completed units as well as the engineering drawings after the war. Spare parts were to be destroyed. The action was not unexpected, however, and both Popp and Friz had time to make certain preparations. Before the end of 1919, BMW began producing a truck engine called the "Bayern Motor," officially the Type M4 Al. An updated version of the IIIa, it was also suitable for farm tractors and marine and industrial applications. Like the IIIa it had a single overhead camshaft driven by vertical shaft and skew gears. But here the four cylinders were cast in pairs, which lowered production costs. With a bore of 120mm (4.72 in.) and stroke of 180mm (7.08 in.) it had a capacity of 8143cc (497 cid) and weighed 728 pounds. Power output ranged from 45 to 60 bhp, depending on application. The Bayern Motor made a big contribution to the revival of German road transport in the post-WWI era, as well as spurring farm mechanization, motorized travel on inland waterways, and the mining and power generating industries.

That same year, BMW began production of a second Bayern Motor for Victoria Werke AG in Nuremberg. Another Max Friz creation, it was a 6.5-bhp air-cooled flat twin of 500cc (30 cid). Initially intended as a portable industrial engine, it found its main use on Victoria motorcycles. Before it was melded in with BMW AG, Bayerische Flugzeug was also building motorcycles, and used this same M2 B15 unit in its Helios two-wheelers. (The firm was also producing a motorized bicycle, a forerunner of the moped, called the Flink, with a tiny two-stroke single-cylinder unit supplied by Curt Halfland of Berlin.) After the merger, Franz Josef Popp asked Friz to go over and look at the Helios and to tell him what he thought. Though its designer remains blissfully anonymous, the Helios bore all the hallmarks of makeshift construction. Politely but firmly, Friz suggested that the best thing Popp could do was to dump it in the nearest lake. Specifically, Friz felt his engine shouldn't have been mounted with the crankshaft in the transverse plane, because this left one cylinder with plenty of cooling and the other with very little. Of course, the Helios had it this way in order to simplify the gearbox for use with the usual chain drive. A test ride convinced Friz that the bike also had atrocious steering, roadholding, and brakes.

Though Popp respected Friz's judgment and generally took his advice, he couldn't afford to adopt the suggestion about the lake: he had too many Helios machines in stock. So, he and Friz came up with a two-step plan. First, Friz would redesign the worst parts of the Helios to make it more saleable, at least for a while. This task would take him no more than a week. As a second step, he would create a completely new design. It would be the first motorcycle to carry the BMW badge.

Designated R-32, the new bike debuted at the Paris show in the autumn of 1923. Compared with the Helios it was shorter, lower, and lighter. The frame was a rigid tubular structure with one end curving around the front fender arch and the other looping around at the rear wheel hub

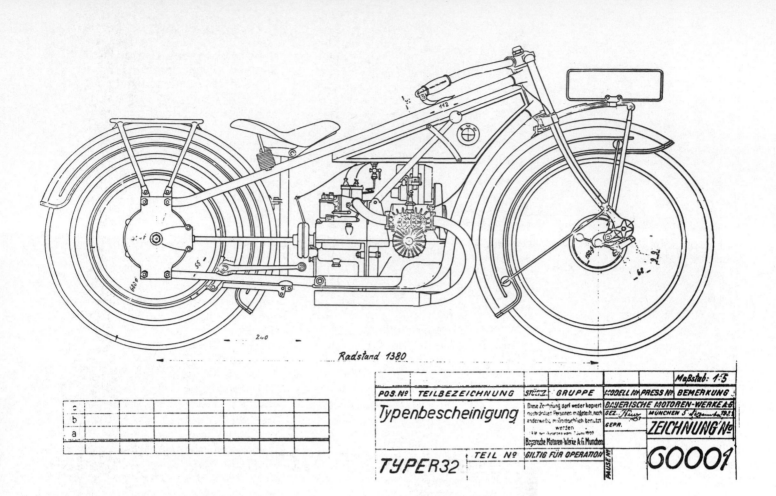

Radstand 1380

| POS.Nº | TEILBEZEICHNUNG | STÜCZ. | GRUPPE | MODELL Nº | PRESS Nº | BEMERKUNG | Maßstab: 1:5 |
| --- | --- | --- | --- | --- | --- | --- | --- |
| | Typenbescheinigung | | Diese Zeichnung darf weder kopiert noch dritten Personen mitgeteilt, noch anderweitig, mißbräuchlich benutzt werden. Lt. der Anordnung vom 7. Juni 1922 Bayerische Motoren-Werke A.G. München | | | BAYERISCHE MOTOREN-WERKE A.G. GEZ. Huy MÜNCHEN 5 Dezember 1923 GEPR. | ZEICHNUNG Nº |
| | TYPE R32 | | TEIL Nº | GILTIG FÜR OPERATION | PAUSE Nº | | 60001 |

IIA-453

casing. There was a brake and leaf-spring cantilever suspension at the front. But the real news was Friz's powertrain innovations. He mounted the 8.5-bhp 500cc twin with the cylinder axes set across the frame—that is, with a longitudinal crankshaft—which gave equal cooling for both cylinders. The gearbox pinions turned in the transverse plane, as Friz had wisely rejected the idea of bevel gears to turn the direction of rotation through a 90-degree angle as would be required for chain drive. His solution was more elegant: a flexible coupling on the gearbox output shaft and a straight shaft with a pinion on its rear end to match a ring gear in the rear wheel hub. Thus was born the shaft-drive motorcycle, a concept still employed by BMW today.

With the R-32, Friz and BMW leaped into the vanguard of the motorcycle art. And, indeed, it was art. He had succeeded in combining many functional elements into a single, harmonious whole by simple, elegant means. Over the next five years he would go on to create nine more models along this basic theme. The R-39, introduced in 1925, had a 6.5-bhp 250cc single-cylinder engine mounted vertically and combined with shaft drive. Like the R-32 twin, this was a side-valve unit. For the R-37 sports model of 1925, Friz developed a 500cc overhead-valve flat twin. With 16 bhp available at 4000 rpm and a weight of only 275 pounds, the R-37 had outstanding performance. In its very first year it won the German Grand Prix, ridden by Paul Koppen, plus 90

other races. Josef Stelzer won the GP for BMW the next year. In 1927, victory again went to Stelzer, this time mounted on a new 750cc bike, the R-63. Emmerich Nagy won the Austrian Grand Prix that season with an R-37, while Stelzer won the 1.0-liter class in the Grand Prix of Luxembourg with his R-63. A young engineer named Rudolf Schleicher had joined BMW in 1923, and contributed greatly to the development of motorcycles and motorcycle engines. In 1926 he decided to enter an R-37 in the International Six Days Trial in England. He came back with a gold medal.

From then on, BMW cycles were potential winners wherever they went: in road racing, on closed tracks, and in straightline speed events. Their victories are too numerous to repeat here, but the total was 573 in the 1923-28 period.

Big changes were made with the 1929 models. The R-11 and R-16 had weight-saving pressed-steel frames of tremendous stiffness, plus innovative styling. By the end of 1927, BMW had sold 27,875 motorcycles, and the company was solvent, profitable, and full of hope for the future. But it didn't neglect other product areas. Expansion of the factory at Lerchenauer Strasse had been started in 1922, and included an aluminum foundry, machine shops, and mechanical test laboratories.

The runaway inflation that plagued Germany after WWI confuses BMW's financial picture in these years, but a few events stand out. In a "sanitation" move, the firm's capital stock was written down from 160 million to only 3 million marks in late 1924. Castiglioni was now chairman of the supervisory board as well as majority stockholder. The following year, a new block of shares was issued, bringing 2 million marks in new funds and raising capital reserves to 5 million. This money was raised by A. E. Wassermann of Berlin, and among the new

shareholders were Daimler Motoren Gesellschaft and Benz und Cie. Why would these automakers be interested in a motorcycle company? Mainly because of BMW's tremendously successful line of aircraft engines. When Daimler and Benz completed their merger in 1926, Franz Josef Popp was asked to sit on the supervisory board of the new Daimler-Benz AG. Soon, BMW shares were being traded on the Berlin stock exchange, and in 1927 a new block issue boosted the firm's capital to 10 million marks.

BMW had resumed aircraft engine production in 1925 with a revived Type IV. It also introduced a new and far more ambitious design, again in the work of Max Friz. Called the BMW VI, it was a water-cooled V-12 giving 700 bhp for takeoff and 550 bhp for sustained operation. The new engine successfully passed a 200-hour test in 1924, and was then tried in a Dornier Merkur seaplane. In addition to setting eight world records for speed and altitude, the Merkur flew from Lake Constance to the Caspian Sea at an average speed of 185 km/h (115 mph) and the 20,000km from Zurich to Cape Town in South Africa with a flying time of 97 hours. Three of these engines were fitted to a Rohrbach Roland seaplane in 1927, which set 22 world records for speed, acceleration, altitude, and duration. By 1930, BMW had delivered 1000 examples of the Type VI, which would remain in production until 1939.

Despite its early difficulties and the chaos of the post-WWI years, BMW was firmly established as one of Germany's leading industrial powers by the mid-Twenties. The firm had achieved high success in both aviation and the motorcycle field. Its prospects were bright, its outlook optimistic. It seemed like a good time to consider new challenges and new ventures. Franz Josef Popp was more than willing. BMW was about to enter the car business.

# BMW BUILDS A CAR: DIXI AND THE AUSTIN CONNECTION

If a prosperous industrial firm wants to build cars, and if it has multifaceted operations with plants capable of tackling the most diverse engineering projects, it usually becomes an automaker through one of three different methods. The first and most obvious is to design and develop its own car. That usually means hiring a leading engineer away from another company, followed by a few years of testing, tooling, and solving unexpected problems before production begins. It also means making heavy investments for several years, even as the basic design is growing older. This approach had been successful for firms as diverse as the small Voisin aircraft works, which converted to car production after World War I, and the giant Ansaldo shipbuilding yards, which set up a car division at about the same time. The other methods would be to purchase a license to produce an existing model of proven quality—and, preferably, sales—or to take over a small car company with a promising product. These were the choices facing Franz Josef Popp around 1926. He had decided that BMW should get into the car business.

Historically, commercial and financial considerations have probably been more important than technical matters in deciding which method to use. Whatever route Popp chose, it would have to be approved by BMW's supervisory board, which was composed mainly of bankers. The car BMW would build would have to be one that could find a ready market. It also had to be free of inherent design bugs, because basic reliability problems could kill a new make of car— and its maker. With BMW's spectacular growth since 1922, Popp was in a sanguine mood about the future of the German economy and the car market in general. However, this optimism was tempered by the realism of those bankers. And his freedom of choice in what sort of car to produce was restricted by the need to steer clear of any overt competition against Daimler-Benz, which was then a major BMW stockholder.

Consequently, the new car from Munich was more or less destined to be positioned down-market from the various Mercedes models. It would be smaller in size and lower in price, which also implied a broader buyer group and potentially higher profits. Popp and his general manager, Richard Voigt, began looking into the German small car market. At that time it was dominated by Hanomag, which had an original and intelligent design that was

*The snazziest of the early license-built Dixi cars was the DA-3 Wartburg, offered in 1930-31. Just 150 were built. Note the cut-down body, sidemount spare, and minimal rear overhang. Mechanicals were derived from the Austin Seven and shared with other 3/15 models.*

perhaps too basic in its execution, and by Opel, which fielded what was more or less a copy of the Citroën 5CV.

Popp was enough of an opportunist to avoid excluding any possibilities out of hand, and wondered whether BMW should go with the conventional or set a more progressive course for its first automobile. He was an engineer, remember, and this explains his attraction to a prototype built in 1924 for Schwabische Hüttenwerke (Swabian Steel Works) in Boblingen. It was designed by Professor Wunibald Kamm of the Stuttgart Technical University, who would win fame in the Thirties for his pioneer work in applying aerodynamics to automobiles. Max Friz was also impressed with the SHW car. It was a radical, highly advanced machine with seating for four in a very compact package that bristled with technical innovation: all-aluminum unit body/chassis construction, all-independent coil-spring suspension, front-wheel drive and—no doubt to Friz's delight—a 20-bhp 1030cc (63-cid) flat twin, designed by Oskar Kurtz.

Should BMW buy production rights to this design? The idea made a certain amount of sense. It would, presumably, catch the imagination of technically minded buyers and give BMW what we would now call a "high-tech" image. The new model might even set the standards for ride comfort and roadholding in the small car field. It would certainly be economical to operate and, thanks to its lightweight construction, would have an unusual performance reserve for a 20-bhp car. But it certainly wouldn't be easy to produce or to sell at a profit. Aluminum was much more expensive than steel, and many of the basic design's technical advances would require precision machining and great assembly skill, both of which would only aggravate the cost problem. There was also a time factor. A single new system

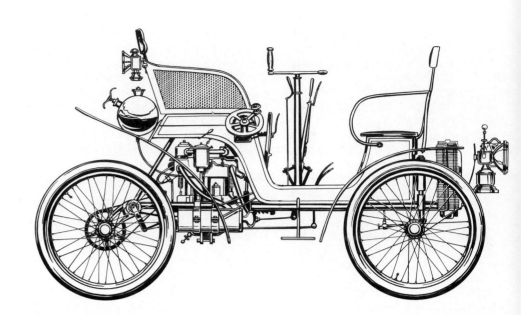

Dixi 5/14 P.S. 1919/2

*The ancestors of the first BMWs were built by Fahrzeugfabrik Eisenach, which later became the Dixi Automobil Werke. Here, a quartet of cars built by that firm, which BMW acquired in 1927. Opposite page, top: Built under license, this 1899-1900 Wartburg was a virtual duplicate of the French Decauville. Tiller steering, "vis-a-vis" seating, and a 4-bhp 1.0-liter two-cylinder engine were featured. Approximately 85 were built. Opposite page, bottom: The four-cylinder, chain-drive T 24 was one of several models to bear the Dixi name in 1904-07. Shown is a high-roof touring car from 1905. This page, top: A light tourer from the Dixi R 5 series of 1914-25, a 5/14 four-cylinder model. Above: A Dixi G 3 30-bhp rally car driven by Albert Kandt, director of Gothaer Waggonfabrik, in 1925.*

or subsystem for an existing design usually demands lengthy and thorough testing before its quality and dependability have been sufficiently proven to warrant production. Yet here was a car composed almost entirely of new and largely untried ideas, making the development phase a hundred times more difficult and time-consuming.

BMW's bankers listened to the arguments pro and con—and nixed any notions Popp might have had about building this car. They now urged him to come up with a more conventional proposal that could be readied with minimum lead time and having reasonable, known production costs. Thus, economic necessity compelled Popp to search for a simpler and more available automobile.

As it happened, events were unfolding that would give Popp precisely the car he needed. Sir Herbert Austin of England was looking for a German licensee to produce his tiny Austin Seven. Previously, Austin cars had been imported by Koch & Weichsel AG of Berlin, but Sir Herbert wasn't satisfied with the amount of business they generated. He also saw that international trade might be strangled by currency restrictions, tariffs, and import licenses, and figured it would be more profitable to sell manufacturing rights than to export a few cars and wait for them to be sold. One day in 1927 he met Jakob Schapiro. The owner and operator of an industrial investment and management empire in Germany, Schapiro, then 42, had been a meteoric success, beginning humbly as a poor immigrant from Odessa. His holdings included the Schebera Karosserie Werke in Berlin, NSU in Neckarsulm, Gothaer Waggonfabrik, Nordgummi Werke (tires), Chillingworth (steel pressings), Georg Grauert (iron foundry and machine works), Panzer AG (foundry and machine works), and Metrum Instruments. In addition, he held large blocks of stock in Daimler-

21

Benz and sat on its supervisory board—as did Franz Josef Popp.

Sir Herbert mentioned his idea to Schapiro, who immediately recognized it as a golden opportunity for one of his companies. Gothaer Waggonfabrik had a subsidiary in Eisenach, some 530 miles to the north and northwest of Munich, the Dixi Automobil Werke AG. In Schapiro's analysis, Dixi needed a new small car. At the time, it had only two models, both designed by Leonhard C. Grass. One was a 1.6-liter car with a side-valve four that dated from 1920. Built on a long 111.8-inch wheelbase and fitted with heavy bodies, it sold in the 6800-7800 mark range. The other was a 3.5-liter (215-cid) six, new in 1926, sharing its Ambi-Budd steel bodies with the Adler Standard Six. Unfortunately, both Dixi models were too large and costly to attract many buyers in the hyperinflated economy of post-WWI Germany. The company needed a more saleable product—and in a hurry.

Dixi had been established as Fahrzeugfabrik Eisenach in late 1896, with a capital stock of 1.25 million gold marks. Along with a banking consortium, it was founded by Heinrich Ehrhardt, the owner of Rheinmetall, then second only to Krupp in the German arms industry. It is likely that Ehrhardt was interested in the automobile mainly for its military potential, but he became a manufacturer by securing a license to produce a most inoffensive vehicle, the French Decauville. Originally built in Bordeaux by two engineers named Cornilleau and Guesdon, this was a light (485-pound) car powered by a 494cc vertical twin mounted at the rear and delivering 3.75 bhp at 1200 rpm. The most unusual aspect about this design was its independent front suspension, via sliding pillars and enclosed coil springs.

After Ehrhardt had secured the Decauville license for Germany, Orio & Marchard of Pia-

*Above: The first BMW-built Dixi 3/15s were designated DA-1 and had left- instead of right-hand drive. Cabriolet shown was an extremely rare body style. Right: The 3/15 was powered by this tiny 750cc Austin-based four. Opposite page, top: A Dixi racer driven by Bobby Kohlrausch in 1926. Bottom: Side hood louvers marked the improved DA-2 model, issued in mid-1929.*

cenza purchased the Italian rights. Interestingly, the Decauville also served as the basis for Henry Royce's first car, before he teamed with Charles Rolls. Ehrhardt called his version the Wartburg in honor of the historic castle that overlooks Eisenach and famous as the seat of Hermann I of Thuringia at the start of the 13th century. His license took effect in September 1898. At the Dusseldorf Fair that month, Fahrzeugfabrik Eisenach displayed three motor vehicles. One was the Wartburg, the second a three-wheeler intended for military use, and the third an electric. These were the creations of Arthur Rebling, who revised the Decauville and also introduced four-cylinder models based on newer French designs in 1903. Up to that time, about 400 Wartburgs had been built.

Ehrhardt suddenly withdrew

from Fahrzeugfabrik Eisenach in 1903, taking his financial support and the Decauville license with him. He tooled up one of his arms factories at Zella St. Blasii to continue its production. Without any cars it could build

legally, the Eisenach company was now forced to create its own. A young and imaginative engineer named Willy Seck took over as technical director in 1903, but left after creating this new product, the first to bear the name Dixi. Replacing Seck was Oberingenieur Schwartz, who expanded the new 1904 Dixi S.12 into a whole range of cars, one of which remained in production up to 1925.

Fahrzeugfabrik Eisenach

prospered in the years before WWI. It branched out into marine engines in 1909, then to aircraft engines the following year. It also moved into the truck field beginning in 1907. Soon the company was selling its cars outside Germany—in France under the name "Regina" and in England with the "Leander" label. A few were even sent to the U.S. where they were known as the "Cosmobile." (Incidentally, this marks the first direct link between BMW and the American market.) The expansion continued during the war, largely the result of fat military contracts. But this only made the conversion to peacetime production more difficult. Soon the company was teetering on the brink of bankruptcy, and in 1920 it was taken over by Gothaer Waggonfabrik. By 1926 it was again in difficulty, and Schapiro began grasping for solutions. That's why he was so quick to act on Sir Herbert Austin's proposal.

Gothaer had the cash on hand to secure the Austin license, which gave Dixi the exclusive manufacturing rights to the Seven for Germany and Eastern Europe—provided it used only German raw materials. Gothaer committed to building 2000 cars the first year on a budget of 6 million marks, secured from a group of banks, but the original plan was for 300 cars a week or about 12,500 a year. Actual production fell between these extremes. The first 50 units were assembled strictly from parts supplied by Austin from Longbridge. All had right-hand drive and were completed in September 1927 by the 1200-strong Eisenach workforce. The older Dixi models were not immediately phased out, and Grass remained as technical director with prime responsibility for production. By December the plant was turning out a slightly different variant named 3/15 PS, reflecting its taxable/actual horsepower. This first local model, with left-hand drive and styling needlessly faithful to the British original, was given the type designation DA-1, with DA denoting Deutsche Ausführung (German version), and a total of 9307 were completed within 10 months. Both engines and chassis were manufactured at Eisenach, but the standard bodies came from, of all places, the Daimler-Benz facility at Sindelfingen. A few chassis are also known to have received special bodywork. Final assembly for all units took place at Eisenach.

Schapiro felt he had saved Dixi with this move and believed he could sell the German Seven at a profit. Though he wasn't a company "savior" in the sense that, say, Lee Iacocca is today, he did have an uncanny ability for identifying companies that were basically sound but in temporary difficulties, picking the right moment to buy them at his own price, and then nursing them along until they were profitable once more. With his banking and industry connections, Schapiro

was quite well informed about what went on in the German auto business. To some extent, therefore, he was aware of BMW's situation before he spoke privately to Franz Josef Popp about selling Dixi and its Austin license. Schapiro might have made an even better deal had Popp been in a position to clinch it on the spot. Popp saw in Dixi and the Seven everything his bankers wanted, and Schapiro quite likely knew it.

However, formal negotiations for the sale were opened by Camillo Castiglioni on BMW's behalf. Simultaneously, he maneuvered to increase the firm's capital holdings from 6 to 16 million marks and secured a line of credit from the Disconto Gesellschaft for a cash payment to Schapiro. The final selling price was 15 million marks. But Dixi owed its banks 11 million, so what Schapiro actually got was 200,000 marks in cash and 800,000 shares of BMW stock. As of October 1, 1928, Dixi Automobil Werke AG of Eisenach officially became a branch of Bayerische Motoren Werke AG, and on November 18 the Dixi company ceased to exist as a corporate entity. With this single transaction, BMW jumped into the German industry as the second largest producer of small cars, acquiring a 32 percent share of a market that accounted for 40,000 units a year.

As a first car, the Austin Seven was clearly a compromise choice for BMW. It was hardly a machine of advanced engineering, high performance, or appeal for sporting motorists. Rather, it was a child of British road and traffic conditions, British legislation, and the British market, where light cars and cyclecars abounded in 1923. Five years later, when BMW acquired it, the Seven was unmistakably old, a holdover from an earlier era and definitely not a fresh, forward-looking product. Popp, however, embraced the Dixi-built Austin, and for very good reasons. It was already in produc-

tion and its manufacturing costs were known. Acquisition of the Eisenach plant gave BMW a second, complementary production facility. And though the cost was high, Dixi was an instant revenue producer that was expected to pay for itself in short order. Also, the Austin was a proven design, with thousands of them running on British roads after more than five years of production. Finally, the engineering was not without technical merit. Indeed, it would prove to have surprising development potential.

How competitive was the Seven in the German market? The answer lies in a comparison with its direct rivals. The main ones were the Opel 4/12, nicknamed the "Laubfrosch" (tree frog), and the Hanomag 2/10, also known as the "Kommissbrot" (literally, military hardtack bread). Both were two-seaters, while the Austin had a rear area suitable for children, though it was too small for adults. The Hanomag was the most recent design, dating from 1924, while the Opel was a copy of a Citroën model planned in 1920-21. With its low build, lightweight construction, and the general appearance of a scaled-down large car rather than an overgrown cyclecar, the Austin was unique.

Interestingly, the Seven also found a place on the west side of the Rhine. Encouraged by his deal with Schapiro, Sir Herbert began looking for a French connection. He found one in Lucien Rosengart, a tremendously wealthy industrialist who had made his fortune in automotive accessories and also served at one time as financial advisor to both Citroën and Peugeot. In 1927, Rosengart was helping his

*Top: A trio of 3/15s poses in front of the Eisenach factory after winning the 1929 International Alpine Rally. It was BMW's first major competition victory. Bottom left: BMW built its 25,000th car in September 1931. Total 3/15 production was 25,325. Only a handful survive today. Bottom right: Two-seat sports tourer was a popular 3/15 body style.*

DER
25 000.
0,75 ltr. 3/15 PS
B.M.W.
WAGEN

friend Robert Bellanger keep his big car factory busy on Boulevard Dixmude in Paris. The two leased some factory space to Peugeot, and also got a chassis assembly contract from De Dion Bouton. When that expired, it looked like the end of the road for Bellanger, who threw in the towel and left the whole mess to Rosengart. Providentially, Rosengart met Sir Herbert at this crucial moment. A wily "gamin" who had grown up in the streets of Paris, Rosengart talked Austin into settling for easy terms and, armed with the license, transformed the Bellanger company into Automobiles L. Rosengart. His chief engineer was Jules Salomon, who had designed the first-generation Citroëns and had then gone on to Peugeot. The French Seven, called the Rosengart 5CV, made its debut at the Paris Salon in the autumn of 1928. Its early success made Rosengart the fourth largest automaker in France by 1930, and the firm continued to offer Austin-based models right up to 1940.

Sir Herbert saw the Seven as the ideal solution to the problem of cheap personal transport anywhere in the world, and sent envoys to the U.S. and Japan at an early date. They spent some 2½ years trying to find an American licensee, and in mid-1929 they found one: former General Motors executive Arthur J. Brandt. He signed an agreement, established the American Austin Car Company, bought an idle plant at Butler, Pennsylvania, from the Standard Pressed Steel Car Company, and tooled up for 100 cars a day. The American Austin was displayed at the New York Automobile Show in January 1930, and orders flowed in. But only 8558 units were completed that year, followed by a mere 1279 in 1931. The company shut down, only to be revived as Bantam Motor Car Company in 1936. Though dramatically restyled, this firm's offerings, called American Bantam, were still technically re-

lated to the original Austin Seven. This firm would be equally short-lived, a victim of the consolidation in the U.S. industry in the aftermath of World War II. Today, of course, American Bantam is best remembered as the company that developed the prototype for what became the Jeep.

It was not until 1933 that Austin would conclude a pact with the Japanese. The licensee was Jidosha Seizo Company Ltd. of Yokohama, which called its version the Datsun. The firm was reorganized as Nissan Motor Company, Ltd. in 1934, and mass production of a modernized Datsun began the next year. The Austin-based model was Nissan's only offering up to 1937, when a line of larger cars was added.

But it was the German-built Dixi more than these transatlantic and oriental ventures that proved the validity of the Austin Seven concept. In essence, the Dixi pushed both its rivals off the market, the Kommissbrot disappearing in 1928 and the Laubfrosch the next year. Hanomag then came out with a 3/16 model that resembled the Dixi 3/15, while Opel abandoned the low end of the market entirely for its upscale 4/20 PS. DKW also jumped into the small car fray with its two-cylinder two-stroke P-Type in 1928, while it took Brennabor until 1931 to get its little D-Type into production. The following year, Ford began building the 21-bhp Y-series cars at Cologne, and Fiat followed with the 20-bhp Type 508 "Balilla" produced locally at Heilbronn. By that time, however, BMW would be rid of its Austin shackles and preparing to move upmarket.

Nevertheless, without the Seven there likely would not have been a BMW car until several years later—and perhaps none at all. For Popp, as for Rosengart, it was a good choice. But just why was this little box so successful all over Europe at a time when so many other cars

failed? Price was naturally a big factor. Anthony Bird once remarked that the British Seven "cost little more than a Morgan three-wheeler and considerably less than the two-seater twin-cylinder air-cooled Rover." But the real secret of its success was simplicity, which made it easy to control the production costs that determine selling price. In a very real sense, the Seven did for Europe what the Ford Model T had done for America: provide reliable transportation at a price almost anyone could afford.

Just what sort of a car was it? Well, it was no performance machine and it was certainly no style-setter. Dennis May, as he so often did, described it best: "the dinky little family runabout which Sir Herbert Austin designed with cue chalk on the green felt of a pool table one night in 1922." Calling it primitive would not be accurate. It would be closer to the truth to say that it was a big Austin reduced to its essential minimum. But it was not exactly a scaled-down version of a larger model. Sir Herbert realized that smaller dimensions, lighter weight, and lower payload would allow him to simplify construction, and he went as far as common, low-cost materials would allow.

Accordingly, the Seven was built on a steel frame with two channel-section side members that came closer together at the front than at the rear, tied together with flimsy cross-members. The front cross-member carried the forward engine mounts, radiator, and front suspension. A second cross-member provided mounts for the gearbox (bolted to the flywheel housing) and a rear anchorage point for the diagonal radius rods that served to locate the front axle. The frame came to its narrow end fractionally ahead of the front axle line. At the rear, the side members were cut off just behind the third cross-member, which supported a propeller shaft center bearing and provided an anchorage point for the front end of the short torque tube to the final drive unit. Quarter-elliptic leaf springs extended diagonally and rearwards from the side members to eyebolts on brackets mounted near the ends of the rear axle. The front axle was suspended by a transverse leaf spring not unlike that of Ford's Model T. To keep things as simple and cheap as possible, there were no shock absorbers at all. Worm-and-sector steering, quite popular at the time, was used, purchased from an outside supplier. Wheelbase was quite short, just 75 inches.

The Seven's engine was typical of British anvilwork in these years. It was a side-valve inline four with a detachable cast-iron cylinder head and a short cast-iron block mounted atop an aluminum crankcase. All valves were on the same side, the classic L-head layout, with a gear-driven camshaft in the upper side of the crankcase. The crankshaft was a spindly two-bearing affair with a roller bearing at the clutch end, and a roller bearing with a ball race for taking axial thrust was added at the front. There was no starter motor. As with a Tin Lizzy, you had to step outside and turn a crank handle. Magneto ignition was used up to 1929; on later models the plugs were fired by coil and distributor. The camshaft drove a vane-type oil pump, but there was no water pump and cooling depended entirely on the thermo-syphon effect.

Initially the little engine had a 55mm (2.165-in.) bore and a 75mm (2.95-in.) stroke for only 696cc (42.5 cid). Maximum output was a puny 9-9.5 bhp, which gave a piddling top speed of only 34 mph. This wasn't anywhere near good enough, and the block was quickly bored out to 56mm (2.2 in.). Combined with a longer-stroke crankshaft giving a 76.2mm (3.00-in.) stretch, displacement rose to 747.5cc (45.6cid) and power climbed a bit, to 10.5 bhp at 2400 rpm. Top speed was now a more respect-

able, but still hardly exciting, 38 mph.

The Seven's clutch was a single dry plate with an ultra-short separation between grip and slip, and the gate-change gearbox had three forward speeds predictably devoid of any synchronization. Third gear was direct (1.00:1 ratio), second gear was 1.82:1, and first 3.25:1. And there was also a reverse (4.28:1). Final drive ratio was 4.9:1, which seems excessively high until you realize that the car ran on 26 x 3.00 tires, so actual gearing was nearly 16 mph/1000 rpm in top, entirely reasonable for such a small engine in those days. Detachable wire wheels were standard, and tiny brake drums were employed front and rear with rod-and-lever actuation that suited the letter of the law if not its spirit. Out of concern for safety, British regulations specified that a car had to have two independent brake systems. Nothing was said about which should do what, so Austin felt perfectly justified in hooking up the front rods to the handbrake lever and the rear rods to the brake pedal. These binders have been described as "undernourished" (Dennis May) and

"terrible—though successive improvements made them less calamitous" (Anthony Bird). The complete car with standard four-seat tourer body tipped the scales at approximately 900 pounds, making it a real featherweight.

Before a Dixi version was planned, Austin made a couple of improvements to the Seven. An electric starter was fitted beginning with the 1924 model year, and wider 26 x 3.50 tires became standard for 1927. And that, basically, describes the car BMW found itself building in the latter months of 1928. The only difference was Dixi's adoption of Bosch shock absorbers, a real touch of luxury! Factory specifications show that the German engine ran with 5.6:1 compression and put out 15 bhp at 3000 rpm, slightly better than that year's British equivalent. Top speed was listed as 47 mph and average fuel consumption was 39 mpg.

Earlier in 1928, BMW had obtained manufacturing rights for

*Last of the 3/15s was the DA-4 of 1931-32. Standard two-door sedan body was supplied by Ambi-Budd of Berlin. Dixi name had long since disappeared.*

the Pratt & Whitney Hornet air-cooled radial aircraft engine, and began building it at Milbertshofen alongside the Type VI unit. This meant that the aircraft side of the business now ranked about evenly with the automobile and motorcycle branches in turnover, with the result that BMW was now on a firm, broad-based industrial tripod. The following year, Camillo Castiglioni sold his BMW stock and left his seat on the supervisory board. His holdings, valued at 5 million marks, were liquidated via a consortium headed by the Deutsche Bank. Schapiro is also believed to have sold his stock at about the same time. All these shares did not necessarily fall into new hands right away. In those days it was common for German banks to hold on to such blocks for years, especially if they bore dividends. In any case, Popp's control over the corporation was not threatened from any quarter.

And his automotive plans were going ahead full steam. Popp fully realized that BMW could not go on producing a mildly warmed-over Seven indefinitely, even after correcting the most glaring faults of its basic design. But the BMW 3/15, as it was now called, had to be improved to remain competitive in a more hotly contested and—after the Great Crash—depressed market.

Leonhard Grass's engineering staff duly went to work on the ex-Dixi car, and some synergistic benefits were realized through technical collaboration between the automobile and motorcycle departments. The result appeared in mid-April 1929 when the DA-2 model supplanted the DA-1. Though the engine remained unchanged, the Eisenach engineers had done well in other areas. First, the brake pedal now worked on all four wheels, while the handbrake still acted on the front wheels only. Larger 27 x 4.00 tires were fitted, and the final drive ratio was lowered to 5.35:1 for better top-gear performance. Top speed and fuel

consumption were practically unaffected. Besides the standard steel-bodied sedan, produced in collaboration with Ambi-Budd of Berlin, there was a new two-seat convertible and a delivery van.

After exploring the commercial market with his mini-van, Popp wanted to establish BMW in the sports car market. Austin had set the example when it entered a three-car team at Brooklands in 1923. These were not just stock Sevens stripped for racing. They had special engines with hotter camshafts and twin carburetors, a rear axle with longer gearing, and fabric bodies. "Small but potent scrappers," Dennis May called them. The Seven chassis became a favorite of independent coachbuilders such as Mulliners, Avon, and Swallow, who created

sporty bodywork of all sorts from the starkest to the most ornate. The first factory-built regular production roadster was the Ulster of 1930.

It was only natural that a BMW equivalent, appearing that same year, should bear a close resemblance to the Ulster, from its flat-face radiator to its boat-tail rear end. It also had a drop-center front axle to bring the frame closer to the ground, enhancing the ready-to-run look. Compression ratio was increased to 7.0:1, which raised maximum output to 18 bhp at 3500 rpm and top speed to a heady 53 mph. Average fuel mileage dropped to 36 mpg, a negligible sacrifice in view of how cheap gasoline was in those days. Transmission, steering and brakes remained unchanged

from the DA-2. The new sportster, officially designated DA-3, saw the revival of the honorable Wartburg name, but even that did not make the sales manager's job any easier. No doubt the timing was wrong, for the year when the reverberations from Wall Street hit Europe was hardly the best for a new model of such frivolous character. As for performance, the DA-3 was easily overshadowed by more potent, more civilized, and less expensive contenders from DKW, Amilcar, and Fiat. The bottom line was that only 150 of these Wartburgs found buyers.

In mid-February 1931, the DA-4 replaced the DA-2 on the Eisenach production line. BMW began breaking away from Austin engineering practice with this model, which featured inde-

*An improved successor to the original 3/15 appeared in March 1932 as the 3/20. Main alterations were a new ohv engine and redesigned frame with backbone-type construction and swing-axle suspension. Shown is the initial AM-1 (three-speed gearbox) two-seat convertible.*

pendent front suspension, something the British Seven would never have. In fact, ifs was something of a rarity for the day, offered in Europe only by such prestige marques as Lancia, Mercedes-Benz (one 1931 model), and Peugeot (optional for one model that year).

The DA-4 setup was not a copy of any existing design but BMW's own (a German patent was issued for it in 1931) and quite original. The principles and basic geometry were likely worked out by Max Friz, but the actual hardware was designed in

Eisenach under Leonhard Grass. The system seemed almost too simple, more like something from a motorcycle than an automobile, which makes sense as Friz was less auto engineer than motorcycle designer. The arrangement employed front wheel hubs shackled to a transverse leaf spring acting as a lower control arm. There were no upper arms, all other wheel location functions being handled by two diagonal leading arms obviously derived from those that supported the front axle on previous models. Though hefty, these arms were not up to the task of assuring parallel front wheel alignment, and wheel deflection produced excessive camber changes that seriously compromised steering accuracy. For a car with the BMW's speed potential, this flimsy suspension still performed tolerably well on the road—well enough to convince Popp that ifs was the way to go in the future. From here on, the rigid front axle was *verboten* at BMW.

In appearance, the DA-4 was still very Austin-like, but it was heavier than its predecessors at 1070 pounds for the base coupe and 1210 pounds for the sedan. To carry the extra weight, tire size was increased to 4.00-18. Engine and gearing, however, remained unchanged.

BMW car sales declined as the Depression set in, and the company's welfare now increasingly depended on revenues from the motorcycle and aircraft branches. Car output declined from 6792 units in 1930 to less than half—3326—in 1931. Understandably, Franz Josef Popp was eager to bring out a new model devoid of any Austin heritage in an attempt to reverse the situation, and, growing more and more insistent as time went on, badgered Friz to come up with a solution. Friz proposed a light, low-slung front-wheel-drive design powered by a two-cylinder two-stroke engine. Several prototypes were built and tested in 1931, but proved disappointing. In the aftermath of this effort, Friz resigned. He went on to be an engine consultant at Daimler-Benz for a few years, then returned to BMW in 1938 as technical chief for the aircraft engine plant in Eisenach. (He retired in 1945 to Tegernsee, a lovely lake in the Bavarian alps, where he died in 1966). Succeeding Friz as technical director was Karl Rech, who was given overall responsibility for engine, motorcycle, and car production. Alfred Böning became chief of the auto section in the drawing office. At the same time, the versatile and talented Rudolf Schleicher became chief of engine testing.

Böning's task was simple but hardly easy: design a completely new non-Austin model that would have none of the shortcomings of the 3/15. The worst of these had been perhaps high engine noise and low power, but there were also the uncomfortable ride and insufficient interior space to overcome. In a nutshell, BMW needed a bigger, quieter, faster car—and it needed one yesterday. In fact, Popp insisted it be ready in time for 1932 production startup, thus effectively cancelling his agreement with Austin way ahead of schedule (the license didn't expire until March 1932). This abbreviated timetable would have been inconceivable for a larger producer, involving design, testing, and development of all key elements, most of which would require new tooling and assembly methods. Delays were thus inevitable, as all the technical changes in the product had to be coordinated with Karl Rech and his manufacturing staff.

Naturally, Böning had to take every possible shortcut to make the deadline. Boring the engine for more displacement was prohibited by the tight cylinder spacing, so all he could do was lengthen stroke, which meant a new crankshaft. Roller bearings were discarded in favor of plain bearings. He would have preferred to add a center bearing,

too, but the block would not allow it and that put a limit on how much he could stretch stroke without the crankshaft becoming too "whippy." So, he settled for an 80mm (3.15-in.) stroke, which boosted capacity to 788cc (48 cid). Other alterations included the addition of a water pump, adoption of duplex chain drive for the camshaft, and different cam profiles. But the biggest change was the switch to overhead valvegear. Böning created an entirely new cylinder head, with rocker arms actuated by pushrods standing in the same slots formerly occupied by the side valves. The result was a 33 percent gain in output, still on the basic 5.6:1 compression ratio.

All this massaging boosted rated power on the little four to 20 bhp at 3500 rpm, and the new model was thus designated a 3/20. However, a new suffix was adopted, AM-1, symbolic of the break with Austin. The letters stood for Automobile München to emphasize the distinctiveness of this new local product. Unfortunately, the AM-1 was also considerably heavier—1433 pounds for the sedan—though this was inevitable because it was larger. Wheelbase was increased from 75 to 84.6 inches and overall length went from 122 inches to 126 inches. The new body was also wider, 56 inches compared with the previous 45.3, and the silhouette was considerably lower, overall height now 61 instead of 64 inches. A very rigid box-section backbone frame replaced the Austin A-shaped frame, with crossmembers to carry the mechanicals and provide body supports along the perimeter. The independent front suspension from the DA-4 was adapted to the wider track, and Böning threw in an independent *rear* suspension, too. This employed pendulum-type swing axles and a high-mounted transverse leaf spring much like the system used by Tatra since 1923 and Steyr since 1926. Diagonal

radius arms were fitted to take up driving thrust.

The AM-1 was offered in a choice of four body styles, all supplied by the D-B works. These were a four-seat sedan, sunroof sedan, four-seat cabriolet and two-seat convertible coupe. A few special sports bodies were also supplied for this chassis by Reutter in Stuttgart and by Weinberger in Munich. In appearance, the AM-1 remained as boxy as its Austin-based forebears, with a wheelbase that still seemed too short relative to overall length. But its general air was definitely continental and not British. Comparatively speaking it was squat, wide-stanced, well-proportioned, business-like and purposeful.

To provide acceptable top speed and acceleration, Böning picked a final drive of 5.90:1, tires sized at 4.50-17, and went from a 3.25 to a 4.00:1 first gear ratio. For the followup 1933 models he trotted out a four-speed gearbox with a 4.30:1 first gear, which enabled final drive to be raised slightly to 5.85:1. With its direct-drive top, the new four-speed had a 1.62:1 third gear and a 2.64:1 second gear. So equipped, this AM-2 could reach an even 50 mph and average 31.3 mpg, both reasonable figures for a subcompact four-seater.

With the AM-1, BMW made a decisive move toward being a fully independent automaker, and Austin engineers could have remarked that this new German small car was more comparable with their Ten than the Seven. BMW had indeed come a remarkably long way in a remarkably short time. From 1929 through the end of the 3/15 series, production totalled a respectable 18,976 units. The new 3/20 models would number 7215 through the AM-4 of 1934.

But all this was merely a prelude. The most romantic machines to bear the *blau-und-weiss* badge in the prewar years were just around the corner.

# COMING OF AGE: HEXAPARTITE POWER

The year is 1933, and Adolf Hitler comes to power as chancellor of Germany. As the Nazi rearmament begins, aircraft engine production accounts for a growing share of BMW's earnings. Goering's *Luftwaffe* places substantial orders for the locally built 525-bhp Hornet engine and, later, its Munich derivative, the BMW 132, both nine-cylinder air-cooled radials, plus the Type VI water-cooled V-12. Meanwhile, BMW's motorcycles are climbing faster than its automobiles in sales. The latter hit a new low in 1932, when only 2886 cars were delivered, including 480 leftover 3/15s. By contrast, motorcycle output was rapidly approaching 10,000 units annually, and BMW would produce its 100,000th bike just six years later. With all this, the firm's industrial triangle, which

*A cross-sectional view of the significant 2.0-liter six-cylinder engine introduced with the Type 326 in 1936. It would be the heart of BMW power for 20 years.*

had been neatly equilateral in 1929-30, now took on definite isosceles geometry, with automobiles on the short side.

Since both bikes and aircraft engines were manufactured in Munich, this imbalance tended to reinforce the influence of the Bavarian headquarters in overall company policy at the expense of the Eisenach-based car division. The auto arm, of course, needed to keep its factories busy to maintain income levels, so it tried something new: a vehicle that was a cross between a truck and a motorcycle.

Three-wheel delivery vehicles were quite popular in Germany from the mid-Twenties to the early Thirties. Usually they were laid out in a fashion almost opposite to that of a sidecar-equipped motorcycle: single rear driving wheel, two front wheels that steered, and a big cargo bin ahead of the driver's seat or cabin. Companies like Steigboy and Borgward (Blitzkarren) cashed in on the demand for these vehicles, which offered very low-cost transport for light

goods over short distances, important in the as-yet not fully recovered German economy of the day. BMW wanted a piece of this action, but it waited too long and the market was already disappearing when it introduced its own three-wheel delivery in 1932. The first model was driven by a vertically mounted single-cylinder motorcycle engine of 200cc (12.2 cid), which had insufficient power according to most users. A second version with a 400cc (24.4-cid) one-lunger had more satisfactory performance, but it still wasn't enough. BMW built no more than 600 of these little carts through 1934. The company would not be involved with miniature motor vehicles again until the Fifties, and under very different circumstances.

Fortunately for the auto division, Franz Josef Popp was growing more ambitious about the kind of car that should wear the BMW badge. He was frustrated by the lack of power inherent in the 3/15 and 3/20 models, and their Austin origins

*Above and right: The wartime Junkers JU 52 tri-motor aircraft was powered by the BMW 132, a nine-cylinder radial engine derived from the Pratt & Whitney Hornet powerplant built under license in Munich. Rated output was 550 horsepower. The 132 saw extensive service in the Luftwaffe during World War II.*

offended his sense of pride. What he now had in mind was the sort of middle-class family car that Wanderer, Steyr, NAG, and Adler were starting to field, with elegant and modern coachwork, low and wide, and engines ranging from 1.5 to 2.3 liters (92 to 140 cid). While this idea met with applause from the sales department, it garnered only groans from the accountants. With car sales already lackluster, BMW was hardly in a position to undertake a complete new-model program. Cash reserves were gone and, in March 1932, the firm's capital stock had been written down from 16 million to only 1 million marks. At the same time, Popp's bankers added insult to injury by giving Wilhelm Kissel, the dynamic president of Daimler-Benz, a

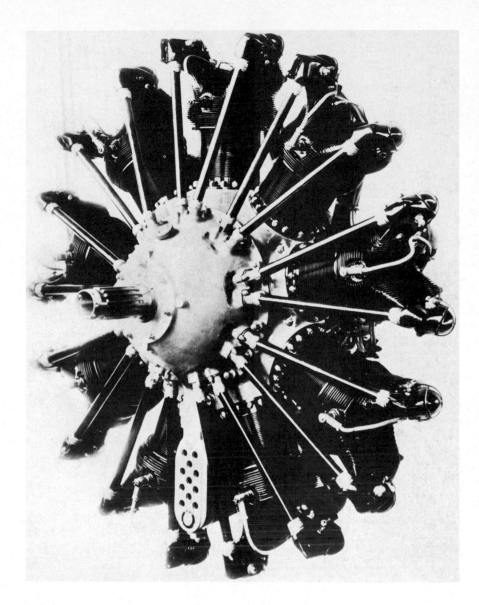

motive history, the decision to proceed with a six-cylinder BMW—a potential competitor with low end of the Mercedes lineup—came not in Eisenach nor at the BMW headquarters in Munich, but in D-B's own offices in Stuttgart! No doubt it was the right choice, based on honest, expert, collegial advice. For, lovely though Friz's engine might have been, it seems certain that its development and tooling would have demanded more time and money than BMW's resources would have allowed.

Overall design responsibility for the new six-cylinder model was given to Fritz Fiedler, an experienced 33-year-old Austrian-born engineer who would be a key figure in BMW fortunes for the next three decades. He was a close friend of Schleicher, who had urged Fiedler to follow him to Munich. His first engineering job was with Stoewer in Stettin. He then moved on to Horch in Zwickau in 1924, but left as chief engineer when that company was blended into the Auto Union organization under the aegis of DKW. Fiedler thus joined BMW in the summer of 1932. Alfred Böning remained chief of the Eisenach drawing office, Grass was now in charge of production, and Schleicher was named head of the motorcycle testing department in Munich.

Output at Eisenach improved in 1933 to 5839 cars. Of these, 1383 were the new six-cylinder Type 303. With this model, BMW adopted a new numbering system, abandoning horsepower designations such as 3/20 (3 taxable/20 brake horsepower) in favor of a serial approach. The 303 was considered the first production model of the 3rd series, hence the first numeral. (The Austin-based DA-1 to DA-4 models were the 1st series and the 3/20 cars, AM-1 to AM-4, the 2nd series.) Why wasn't it named 301? Probably because the "01" and "02" designs didn't get beyond the prototype stage,

seat on the BMW supervisory board.

When Popp began insisting on more powerful auto engines, Max Friz began work on an all-new four-cylinder unit of advanced design with an expensive aluminum block. Popp wanted to go ahead with it, but hesitated. Then, at a crucial moment, someone made a counter-proposal. That someone was Rudolf Schleicher, who had become chief of engine testing in 1931 after four years at Horch, where he worked as an assistant to Fritz Fiedler. Schleicher, who had left BMW in 1927 after working on bike engines, thus returned to the company with four years of automotive engi-

neering experience under his belt—and probably an extra measure of credibility. His idea was simply to add two cylinders to the 3/20 four to create a six, which offered a distinct advantage in that it could be machined on the same equipment. It was a sensible alternative that won strong support from Leonhard Grass and his staff at Eisenach. But Popp still wasn't sure, so he called Wilhelm Kissel and asked for a meeting with the engineers at Untertürkheim. The problem was put before D-B's top design and production engineers, and they, too, came out in favor of Schleicher's solution. Thus, in one of the oddest and most amusing paradoxes in auto-

while the "03" was the first one that did. The new model was displayed in pre-production form at the Berlin auto show in February 1933, which indicates just how quickly the project was completed. Although Fiedler and Böning necessarily had to take a number of shortcuts, the results were, on balance, highly praiseworthy.

By the nature of Schleicher's formula, the 303's engine architecture was destined to follow that of the 3/20. This meant a chain-driven camshaft in the side of the block, plus pushrods and rocker arms to vertical overhead valves. The block was, however, physically different. It was still cast iron with a detachable cast-iron cylinder head and linerless bores, but Böning and Fiedler took advantage of the chance to move the cylinder centers further apart to provide sufficient room for possible bore increases in the future. Another reason was to provide space for more crankshaft main bearings. Bore and stroke dimensions were kept exactly the same at 56 x 80mm (2.20 x 3.15 in.), which yielded 1173cc (71.6 cid). The crankshaft ran in four plain bearings, one at each end and one between each pair of crank throws. The engine might have been quieter with seven bearings, but friction losses are lower with four, as are bearing loads (due to opposing forces on paired rods). Compression was kept at 5.6:1 as on the 3/20 four. The result was 30 bhp at 4000 rpm.

34

Though there were some four-cylinder models on the market with more power, such as the 35-bhp Wanderer W-20 (1695cc/103 cid) and the 45-bhp Fiat Ardita (1944cc/118 cid), none had the 303's silky six-cylinder smoothness. What's more, the new engine had a much higher specific output (bhp per liter/cubic inch) than the prevailing industry average, which gave the 303 a better-than-average power-to-weight ratio. It was a fast-revving little

motor too, and by virtue of its wide speed range, spared the driver from frequent shifting.

The gearbox employed for the 303 was the four-speed unit developed for the 3/20, with synchromesh on top and third. However, the final drive ratio was dropped numerically to 5.15:1, which made it advisable to alter the intermediate gearbox ratios. Thus, third gear was dropped to 1.65:1 and second moved up to 2.54:1 so as to narrow the gap between the two.

First gear, on the other hand, was dropped to 4.42:1 to mitigate the risk of clutch wear on starting from standstill. The shift pattern was unusual. Third (forward) and top (back) were on the usual right side of the H-pattern gate, but the left side had second gear (back) and reverse (forward), with first on a dogleg at the extreme left.

As noted previously, cramped interiors had been a literal shortcoming of both the 3/15 and 3/20, so the Type 303 was given

*Announced in 1933, the Type 303 was BMW's first "grown-up" car and can be considered the ancestor of today's six-cylinder models. Basic chassis design was shared with the four-cylinder Type 309 and the later six-cylinder 315 and 319. Far left: The front suspension with high-mount transverse leaf spring was very Ford-like. Near left: The Type 309's 845cc four-cylinder engine installation. Below: All these models employed an A-shaped tubular chassis with a live rear axle on semi-elliptic leaf springs. Below left: The intake side of the Type 309 four, which was derived from the Type 303 power unit.*

a roomier cabin, made possible by stretching wheelbase nearly a full 10 inches, now 94.5 versus the 84.6 inches of the previous AM-series cars. However, the overall proportions were still a bit odd, with the passenger compartment positioned well back on the chassis and the front wheel centerline almost even with the radiator. The minimal front overhang together with a relatively long hood gave the 303 an appearance that suggested a crouching jackrabbit, with muscular "hind quarters" that seemed to imply acceleration that was, well, jackrabbit quick.

Initial Type 303 body styles were a two-door sedan and four-window convertible, both supplied by the D-B coachworks at Sindelfingen. Later, Ambi-Budd of Berlin took over body production, and a sunroof sedan and a two-seat sports cabriolet were added. Special sports styles could also be ordered from houses like Reutter, Glaser, Wendler, and Autenrieth, and Weinberger of Munich, a BMW

dealer, built a number of convertibles on this chassis. One thing they all had in common was a new "face." Instead of the previous flat-nose front, the 303 wore a decorative split radiator design, still quite vertical but with a blunt, prow-like shape. It marked the first use of the "twin-kidney" motif that would become a BMW hallmark, and was probably the work of Peter Schimanowski of Grass's staff in Eisenach. It was distinctive enough that Rosengart in France copied it for his contemporary six-cylinder Super Cinq.

Compared with the 3/20 PS, which continued in production through 1934, the Type 303 jumped from the three-meter size class to the four-meter league, an enormous difference on the order of enlarging a minesweeper to become a destroyer. Overall length was 153.5 inches, and curb weight rose to 1808 pounds. The chassis was derived from the 3/20 layout, with tubular side members of 90mm (3.5-in.) diameter, plus a

number of box-section cross-members. Front and rear tracks were considerably widened: from 43.3 inches front and rear on the 3/20, the 303 went to 45.3 inches front and 48.0 inches rear. Proper suspension and steering geometry were assured by a new front end with the wheels carried on triangular lower control arms. A high-mounted transverse leaf spring and hydraulic shock absorbers completed the arrangement. Pressed-steel disc wheels were used, and tire size was 5.25-16 all around. The differential had spiral-bevel, semi-floating hub construction, and was suspended by semi-elliptic leaf springs. Steering was rack-and-pinion, geared at a high 11.2:1 to give only two turns of the wheel lock-to-lock. Chassis greasing was a frequent and troublesome task in those days, but automatic or "one-shot" lu-

brication systems were common only on high-price cars. BMW scored a first for this class by adopting Willy Vogel's one-shot system for the 303. Brakes on the new model were larger than its predecessors', but the system remained purely mechanical, with rods from the brake pedal to the four drums. The hand-brake worked cables to the rear drums.

The 303 went on sale at a very attractive price, just 3600 marks. By comparison, the next smallest six-cylinder car on the market, the Mercedes-Benz 170, listed at 4400 marks, and even a garden variety 1.2-liter four-cylinder Opel cost 2700 marks. Buyers may have liked the 303 for its six-cylinder smoothness, but most were undoubtedly disappointed by its lack of power. Despite their tiny size, the 303's six cylinders meant extra weight and higher fuel consumption

compared to most fours, including its Austin-based forebear. Thus, top speed was only 56 mph and average fuel consumption was an unimpressive 23.5 mpg. First gear would run out at only nine mph, second at 22 mph, third at 37 mph, and the 303 needed 10.6 seconds just to reach 30 mph from standstill. Above 40 mph or so, acceleration was quite limited, and almost nonexistent against a strong headwind or on a steep grade.

Despite its updated, "wide-track" chassis, the 303 was not exactly a thoroughbred when it came to ride and handling. The main reason was that the front and rear suspensions were not at all well matched. The front transverse leaf spring was comparatively soft, but the rear semi-elliptics were much stiffer in order to cope with load variations. As a result, ride suffered. The car tended to pitch at the

slightest provocation, and with a full load the front end would bob up and down merrily while the rear squatted close to the ground, the springs transmitting bumps to the occupants with achingly high fidelity. The 303 was also plagued by excessive understeer, again because of the large disparity in front and rear spring rates. There was partial compensation in the quick steering, and in the hands of an enterprising expert the car could be made to oversteer. But for ordinary drivers the safest thing to do was simply put up with the front-end plowing, which discouraged any cornering antics. Excess body roll was another problem, and only aggravated the understeer. By contrast, most cars of the period, tall as they were, had stiff springs mounted at frame height, giving excellent roll resistance with their rigid axles.

At some point during the 303's development, it occurred to BMW engineers that a four could be spun off from the new six, with a bigger bore and thus more power than the old 3/20 engine. BMW needed a successor to the 3/20 as it was not yet in a position to abandon the four-cylinder market. The problem was how to create this car as quickly and cheaply as possible.

The answer almost suggested itself: put the enlarged four into the Type 303. Popp approved, and ordered development to proceed without delay. As he saw it, four-cylinder buyers would care less that the new car's performance was no better than in the 3/20 than that they would be getting extra carrying capacity and more modern styling. And by sharing the complete chassis and many engine parts with the 303, the new four-cylinder model could be brought in at an extremely competitive price. This also meant greatly reduced lead time for design and tooling.

Thus was born the Type 309, which replaced the last of the 3/20 models, the AM-4, in February 1934. (We can only speculate about the nature and fate of projects 304 through 308.) A wider choice of body types was offered for this new price-leader. Apart from the standard two-door sedan, four-window convertible, and two-seat convertible shared with the 303, the 309 was also available as a two-door cabrio/sunroof sedan and as a four-seat two-door tourer. Styling was practically indistinguishable from that of the six-cylinder cars. The standard Type 309 sedan came in at 3200 marks (convertibles were more expensive). This was about 1000 marks more than the DKW F-3 with its 20-bhp two-stroke twin, but 500 marks below the Adler Trumpf Junior with its 25-bhp 995cc (60.7-cid) four.

Due to its lighter engine, the 309 was lighter overall than a comparable 303 (the base sedan, for example, tipped the scales at 1654 pounds), so it could get by with less power. The revised four, essentially a reconstituted 3/20 unit, had a 58mm (2.28-in.) bore and 80mm (3.15-in.) stroke, thus measuring 845cc (51.5 cid). Maximum power was 22 bhp (DIN) at 4000 rpm on the usual 5.6:1 compression. Because of its reduced power and torque, the 309 retained the 5.85:1 final

drive ratio of the 3/20. This gave a top speed of 50 mph and an overall fuel economy average of 27.6 mpg.

Popp was still power-hungry, so the development spotlight now turned again to the six-cylinder cars. While at Horch, Fiedler had worked mainly on large powerplants, including straight eights with capacities of 3.4, 4.0 and 4.5 liters (207, 244 and 274.5 cid). Answering Popp's continued prodding for more horses, he enlarged the BMW six, thus echoing the old Detroit slogan, "There's no substitute for cubic inches." The result was the new Type 315, which succeeded the 303 after it was phased out in April 1934. While the 303 and 309 designations were serial type numbers indicating the sequence in which their design projects had been started, the 315 introduced new model nomenclature. Here the designation referred not to number 15 in the 3rd series but a 3-series vehicle with a 1.5-liter engine.

The newly enlarged six naturally employed familiar parts and construction. It was created by simply boring out the 303 unit to 58mm (2.28 in.) as in the Type 309 four, while lengthening stroke to 94mm (3.70 in.). There were thus only two major component changes, crankshaft and connecting rods. Everything else was the same: block, head, pistons, valves, crankcase, and many accessories. The new cylinder dimensions not only increased total displacement to 1490cc (91 cid) but also involved something of a departure in engine character. It isn't that the six went from being a short-stroke to a long-stroke engine— it's just not that clear-cut. But stroke was suddenly longer, by a considerable 17 percent. The stroke/bore ratio went from 1.43:1 in the 303 unit to 1.62:1 for the 315. A stroke under 100mm (3.94 in.) was considered moderate in those days. And no one saw anything wrong with stretches up to 114.3mm (4.5 in.) or even 127mm (5.0 in.), particularly in large-displacement, slower-running units. With the now-customary 5.6:1 compression and twin Solex carburetors, the 315 engine delivered 34 bhp at 4000 rpm. Naturally, its main parts could be machined on existing tools alongside 309 components, and the assembly sequence was, of course, no different from that of the smaller six.

As for the chassis, the 315 was practically unchanged from 303 specifications. There was a new gearbox, however, manufactured by Hurth. It was still a four-speed unit, but had revised ratios of 1.52 on third, 2.35 on second, and 4.08:1 on first. With the same 5.15:1 final drive ratio as its predecessor, the 315 had an overall bottom-gear ratio of 21.0:1, which was adequate for moving off from rest up a 27 percent slope with a full load. Top speed improved to 62 mph, and acceleration times were correspondingly shorter than the 303's, with 50 mph coming up in 12 to 15 seconds from rest, depending on body style.

In appearance, the 315 was quite close to the 309, the most noticeable difference being in the configuration of the louvers on the side of the hood. The earlier models had a single long row of vertical slots, while the newer cars had two horizontal rows of short vertical louvers, arranged in groups of three. Body styles were the same, too. The two-seat sports convertible gained a new sloped tail that featured a round metal cover, hinged on the left, to conceal the spare tire. Only 242 examples of this model were built through 1937.

Over its two-year production life, the Type 303 had seen hundreds of detail changes in hardware and settings, and the 315 naturally benefited from these. Steering precision, ride quality, and handling finesse were all considerably better, and the car's character took a definite turn towards sportiness. Its race and rally potential was not lost on BMW engineers, and they came up with an even sportier version, the 315/1, with average speeds that surpassed even the most optimistic predictions.

This new roadster arrived shortly after the rest of the Type 315 line, being shown in prototype form at the 1935 Berlin auto show. Though it used the same 94.5-inch-wheelbase chassis, the 315/1 looked considerably more rakish thanks to its more steeply angled windshield, plus graceful cut-down doors that served to lower the car visually.

Also enhancing looks was a natty two-tone paint treatment, with the hood, cowl, and doors done in a lighter color to contrast with the black fenders and rear deck. A final touch was large semi-circular skirts (adorned with external hubcaps) that almost completely concealed the rear wheels. The sharply sloped tail was similar to that of the normal two-passenger convertible and featured the side-hinged spare tire cover. With the 315/1, designer Peter Schimanowski was clearly moving toward the streamlined look then gaining favor all over the world, balanced by traditional sports car elements.

Mechanically, the 315/1 used higher 6.8:1 compression and a new manifold with three horizontal Solex carburetors. This boosted maximum output to 40 bhp at 4000 rpm, still a modest figure, but the car was lighter, so its power-to-weight ratio was doubly improved. Tipping the scales at just 1654 pounds (compared with 1830 pounds for the standard two-door sedan), the 315/1 could see a top speed of 74.5 mph with 4.50:1 final drive, and 0-50 mph acceleration times came down to between 10 and 11 seconds. In all, it was a far cry from the Type 303 for performance and enthusiast appeal, and streets ahead of the old Austin-based Dixi 3/15s of just a few years earlier.

With the higher performance of the 315/1, BMW at last had a car that might make headlines in competition. Of course, the firm was no stranger to racing even at this early juncture, as we have seen, and Popp was well aware of how valuable speed record attempts and racing wins were to BMW's reputation as a motorcycle maker. The man who first suggested the firm try speed runs was Ernst Henne, a member of the factory motorcycle team since 1927. On September 9, 1929, he set a new absolute world record at 134.6 mph, and continued to take BMW bikes to new speed marks with monotonous regularity:

| 1930 | 137.5 mph |
| 1931 | 148.0 mph |
| 1932 | 151.8 mph |
| 1934 | 152.8 mph |
| 1935 | 159.0 mph |
| 1936 | 168.9 mph |
| 1937 | 173.6 mph |
| 1931 | 118.5 mph* |
| 1932 | 129.0 mph* |

* with sidecar

The list of successes grew longer with each season. A splendid highlight from 1933: Eduard Kratz won the 1.0-liter class in the German Grand Prix with a 750cc BMW, Josef Stelzer won the 500cc class, and Theo Schoth's BMW came home first in the sidecar category. Another factory rider, Ernst Loof, took the German championship eight times, the Spanish title three times.

BMW's motorcycle racing program and the many victories it produced would have a profound effect on the firm's engineering personnel. Loof, for example, later did valuable automotive development work for several years. And a young competitor named Alexander Freiherr von Falkenhausen would leave his long-lasting mark on all kinds of BMW machines in the Fifties and Sixties. Born in the Munich suburb of Schwabing in 1907, Von Falkenhausen was a young count who majored in automobile and aircraft engineering as a student at the Munich Technical University in the early Twenties. Interestingly, one of his teachers there was professor Willy Messerschmitt, who offered Alex a job at his airplane factory, if he wanted it. But Von Falkenhausen had already made up his mind: he had been racing motorcycles since the age of 19, and was set on working for the company that built them. Ultimately, he was hired by BMW, and reported to Rudi Schleicher at the engine drawing office on May 1, 1934. Schleicher, then chief of motorcycle development and an active racer himself, took a liking to the young nobleman, who quickly became a member of the factory team.

Motorsports would prove as valuable for BMW's car division as it had been for the motorcycle arm. But though there had been no organized factory support up to this point, BMW cars had been racing and winning for several years. They contested rally events as early as 1929, when Max Buchner, Albert Kandt, and W. Wagner drove to capture the cup at the International Alpine Trials. In 1931, Max Rudat drove a 3/15 in the fabled Monte Carlo Rally, ending up the highest-placed finisher in the under-750cc class. Rudat also drove in a three-car team that proved best in the under-2.0-liter category in the International 10,000-Kilometer Tour that same year. With the advent of the 315/1 roadster, Franz Josef Popp tentatively began supporting the most promising privateers. One result was BMW victories in the German 2000-Kilometer Tour and the International Alpine Trials in 1934. Ernst von Delius, now remembered mainly for his career with Auto Union (and his untimely death in a crash), was part of the three-car BMW team that took a team prize and the 1.5-liter class at the 1934 International Alpine Tour. Alex von Falkenhausen began campaigning a 315/1, and collected 35 first-place wins over two seasons.

Meanwhile, an interesting historical twist was in the making. In 1933, H. J. Aldington was at the wheel of a chain-drive Frazer-Nash in the Austrian Alpine Trials. Seeing for the first time what the little BMW sixes could do, he decided then and there to become the authorized BMW importer for Britain. His bid was successful, and in 1935 his Frazer-Nash factory at Isleworth in Middlesex began assembling a right-hand-drive version of the Type 319, a larger-engine derivative of the 315 (see next chapter). Events had now

Above: Fritz Fiedler, the guiding light of BMW engineering from 1932 through his retirement in 1966. Below: An exploded view of the significant 1971cc six from the Type 326. This engine would carry BMW to new heights in the Thirties.

come full circle. Instead of building minicars in Munich under a British license, BMW was now licensing rights to its own cars to a British company. About the same time, Ernst Loof began dividing his efforts between the car and the motorcycle departments. By 1936 he had been assigned to sports car development.

The 315/1 marked a turning point for BMW's fortunes as an automaker, just as the advent of hexapartite power had been a turning point for its cars. In the space of less than five years, its four-wheel machines had shed whatever remained of their Austin heritage, and by the mid-Thirties had matured into proper automobiles. If not the last word in performance or roadability, they at least offered design originality plus high value for the money. BMW was still far from "the ultimate driving machine," but it was moving toward that ideal with a swiftness matched only by that of its progressively quicker and more refined new models.

With its new six-cylinder engines, BMW—both the firm and its cars—truly came of age. There was still much more to do, of course, but this cocky newcomer was only too eager to get on with the job. More importantly, it showed every sign of success. Though it hardly seemed possible for a marque so new, BMW was about to enter the automotive big leagues with an impact that reverberates to this day. The glory years were at hand.

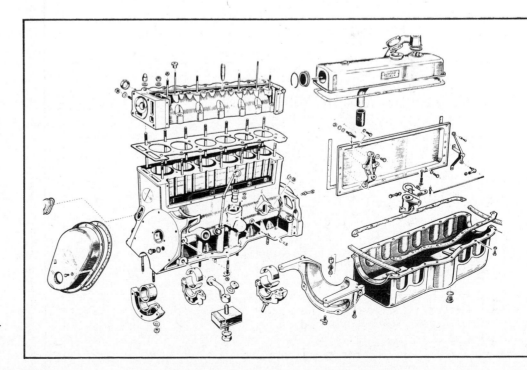

Life became easier for the German auto industry after Adolf Hitler came to power in 1933. *Der Führer* was an avid car enthusiast, and some of his earliest social and economic development programs unabashedly reflected this—and his desire to demonstrate German superiority in virtually every phase of human endeavor. Accordingly, the first stretches of *Autobahnen*, the world's first superhighways, had been opened by 1935, and the Third Reich was busy pushing the *Kraft durch Freude* (KdF) small car

project that would ultimately produce the Volkswagen Beetle. Naturally, Hitler also wanted to make Germany the dominant power in international motorsports, especially the prestigious Grand Prix, so he approved large government subsidies to support the racing team of his favored company, Daimler-Benz. A bit later, he pitted D-B against Auto Union in a canny strategy that achieved his goal perfectly.

The automotive arm of Bayerische Motoren Werke also found life a bit easier in the early years of the Nazi regime.

After bottoming out in 1932, BMW sales improved in 1933, mostly on the strength of the successful new Type 303 and its four-cylinder followup, the Type 309. Through 1936, combined production for these models totalled 8300-9210 units (sources disagree on exact numbers for the 303, though Type 309 output is generally pegged at 6000 cars). The more powerful six-cylinder Type 315 proved even more popular, with 9521 of the standard-body models built in 1934-37, plus another 242 examples of the slick-looking 315/1

# GLORY YEARS: A TALE OF TWO LITERS

sports roadster. In both its automotive designs and its market penetration, BMW seemed to be finding its way at last.

Hitler's pro-car policies prompted two key developments in the mid-Thirties that would lift BMW's fortunes still further—and pave the way for the most exciting and advanced automobiles to wear the blue-and-white badge in the immediate prewar era. The first of these was a task force headed by Colonel Adolf von Schell that was charged with rationalizing all German industry as part of the Nazi military buildup. In the space of just 20 months, this group managed to purge the nation's automakers of their bewildering array of non-interchangeable generators, starter motors, belts, hoses, and other parts, which resulted in fewer but more universally applicable parts. This move not only simplified servicing but also helped the industry come to grips with production costs and inventory control.

The second development had an even greater impact: the lifting of Germany's automobile tax in 1935. Previously, cars had been taxed on the basis of cylinder displacement, which encouraged the industry to develop small engines that had to rev like mad to give decent performance. Abolition of the tax reversed this situation, and carmakers were now free to develop the most efficient engines for their various models without worrying about fiscal penalties. The benefits of this change went far beyond the borders of the Third Reich, and demand for German cars began increasing rapidly in many export markets.

The new "anything goes" policy quickly led to two product changes at BMW. First, the firm immediately moved up a class in engine displacement with introduction of a new 2.0-liter six. Second, the firm initiated work on an even more ambitious 3.5-liter unit. The first of the new 2.0-liter models was dubbed 319 (a 3-series vehicle with a 1.9-liter engine), which started coming off the Eisenach assembly lines in early 1935. Ex-

*Factory cutaway shows the "in-wheelbase" seating of the Type 326.*

cept for its extra engine capacity, the new model was virtually identical to the Type 315, which was continued. The main external differentiation was in the 319's less ornate horizontal hood louvers, overlaid with triple chrome strips. Body styles were also shared. The engine, simply an enlarged version of the 1.5-liter unit, used the same block and head castings but had larger pistons and a new crankshaft having longer throws. Bore was increased to 65mm (2.56 in.) while stroke was stretched to 96mm (3.78 in.), raising displacement to 1911cc (116.6 cid).

Thoroughly tested in high-compression form in 1934, the new powerplant was also installed in a few—about 102—of the 315/1 roadsters, which were accordingly renamed 319/1. Compression ratio was unchanged at 6.8:1 and the three-carburetor setup was retained, but the carbs themselves were larger (30mm throats instead of 26mm). In this form, the 1.9 delivered a maximum of 55 bhp (DIN) at 4000 rpm. The twin-carburetor, low-compression (5.6:1) version specified for the rest of the line peaked at 3750 rpm with 45 bhp.

No chassis design changes were ordained in the transition from 315 to 319. However, the greater torque of the 1.9-liter six made it possible to revise gearing to reduce engine speed relative to road speed, and engineer Fritz Fiedler specified a 4.38:1 final drive for standard models and 4.50:1 for the 319/1. Gearbox ratios were rearranged accordingly, with a 1.51 third (1.38 in the 319/1), 2.07 second, and 3.63:1 first.

The 319 weighed 1874 pounds with the basic two-door sedan body, still supplied by Ambi-Budd, and had a top speed of 71.5 mph. Capacity of the fuel tank, located on the firewall as on the 315, was increased from 9.2 to 10.5 gallons to compensate for the increased fuel consumption, which worked out to an average of 21.4 mpg. Tank

capacity in the 319/1 was 13 gallons. Average mileage was a slightly thirstier 19.6 mpg, but the roadster was quicker, with an 81-mph top end. Price climbed to 5800 marks, compared with 5200 for the 315/1. The least expensive 319 sedan listed at 4150 marks, which was quite reasonable compared with the 1.7-liter four-cylinder Adler Trumpf (4100), the six-cylinder 2.2-liter Hanomag Sturm (4950), or the six-cylinder Mercedes-Benz 170 (4400), but it wasn't competitive against Opel's new 2.0-liter Six, priced at 3400 marks.

BMW production remained modest in 1934, reaching about 6500 units for the calendar year. Yet that was good enough to account for six percent of the German market. By contrast, Daimler-Benz had five percent, Opel had 21, and Auto Union 20 percent. The rest of the market was split mainly among Ford, Adler, Hanomag, Hansa, and NSU-Fiat. BMW might have done even better had it not been for the Eisenach plant, which had now reached the limit of its production capability. Yet there was no thought of expanding output by adding a second facility. Instead, Franz Josef Popp decided to move his cars up-market in size, price, and power, which would yield a higher profit margin per unit. It also fit in with his long-time aim of establishing BMW among Europe's most prestigious marques. Engineer Fiedler was ready to accommodate him with the sort of car he had created during his days with Horch.

Popp had declared that this largest and most expensive BMW yet should be ready in time for the Berlin auto show in February of 1936. Initial design work commenced in late 1934, with Fiedler and Alfred Böning

45

working against the calendar as usual. A new chassis took shape very quickly, while designer Peter Schimanowski was instructed to come up with an overall styling theme that would look fresh for years to come. Of course, there were constraints. The Eisenach plant was not equipped to build just anything, which meant no drastic conceptual changes in the product, its construction materials, or production methods. And although BMW was beginning to turn a healthy profit on its aircraft engine business (especially after Lufthansa airlines ordered a large quantity of nine-cylinder Hornet engines for its fleet of Junkers Ju-52 trimotor planes), Popp still had to watch his spending. He therefore decreed that the engine for the new car could not be all-new. A derivative of the existing six-cylinder design would have to do. The prototype for the new Type 326 was ready on time, but production startup was delayed until the middle of 1936. Chassis changes were extensive enough to warrant a 4-series type number, but for some reason the 300-series identification was retained.

You might think that the 326 was a 3-series vehicle with a 2.6-liter engine, but it wasn't. It was a 2.0-liter car, the "6" merely indicating its position in the lineup. However, displacement of the now-familiar BMW powerplant went up closer to the 2.0-liter mark, precisely 1971cc (120.2 cid). This was achieved by shaving off another millimeter in bore, to 66mm (2.60 in.). Stroke remained at 96mm (3.78 in.) for a stroke/bore ratio of 1.45:1. Compression ratio of the baseline engine was raised to 6.0:1, and with dual 26mm Solex carburetors it delivered a maximum 50 bhp (DIN) at 3750 rpm. The Hurth four-speed gearbox was also revised with a new freewheeling feature on first (3.85:1) and second (2.38:1) gears; third (1.54:1) and top (1:1) gears received syn-

chromesh engagement for the first time. In view of the size and weight of the 326—2481 pounds for the four-door sedan, BMW's first use of this body style—the final drive ratio was fixed at 4.875:1, which gave a top speed of 71.5 mph.

The 326 arrived with a newly conceived platform frame made up from deep box-section elements, a radical departure from earlier BMW practice. The 303/319/315 chassis had been hampered by its considerable flexibility, but this one was endowed with unusual stiffness, so that all suspension movement depended strictly on the springs, which made for more durable body mounts. Fiedler also developed a new form of rear suspension. He had been intrigued with Dr. Ferdinand Porsche's layout for the 1933 Mathis Emysix, which had an all-independent setup via torsion bars, and by the torsion-bar rear axle of the front-drive 1934 Citroën, an arrangement we would now call a "dead" axle. Fielder drew up his own version of the Citroën design, made some calculations, had it made up in hardware, and put it on a test car. After further development, it was adopted for the 326. The

BMW setup employed little crank levers near the ends of the axle casing, connected to long longitudinal torsion bars running below floor level. Short radius arms served to locate the axle relative to the frame. The 326's front suspension was also new, not unlike that of the 315 in principle but turned upside down. The transverse leaf spring was retained, but it was now positioned under the frame to serve as a lower control arm for both wheels. New upper control arms were attached to the top ends of the kingpins. Rack-and-pinion steering, with lower gearing than on preceding models, was used. Tires were 5.25-17 during 1936, going to 5.50-16 the following year. A notable safety feature new to BMW was four-wheel hydraulic brakes as standard equipment. Also for safety, the fuel tank was relocated to a less vulnerable position behind the rear axle.

In Germany as in the U.S., car size related directly with price, so this costliest BMW ever was also the biggest BMW to date. The 326 was large by the standards of the day, riding a 113-inch wheelbase and stretching out to 181 inches overall. The styling managed to retain the

*Opposite page: BMW turned its earlier front suspension upside down for the Type 326 so that the transverse leaf spring acted as lower control arms. This page: The initial version of the 2.0-liter six, shown here from its intake side.*

typical BMW proportions that suggested "muscles" in the rear quarter area by emphasizing overhang, while front overhang was minimal. But the greater size enabled Schimanowski to create new, smoothly flowing contours that were unique to BMW yet very much in line with design trends of the day. The vertical twin-kidney radiator shell was blended in gracefully with the curvatures of the surrounding sheetmetal, the fenderlines were rounded teardrop shapes, and the louvers on both sides of the engine compartment were shaped and outlined with chrome in a way that suggested the profile of a blimp. Standing apart from all its rivals, the 326—even the sedan—looked sprinty, speedy, and sporty. The two- and four-door cabriolets were even more pleasing, though in typical German fashion their heavily padded tops (complete with landau bars) looked awkwardly bulky when folded down.

With the demise of the Type 309 in 1936, BMW's lineup became exclusively six-cylinder. The 315 and 319 continued in production through the 1937 model year when they, too, disappeared. In their stead, BMW produced about 1200 examples of a curious crossbreed, the Type 329. Mechanically it was pure 319, with the short 94.5-inch-wheelbase chassis. It also looked much like the smaller models from the cowl back, but its front sheetmetal and fenders came from the 326. Offered only in two- and four-seat convertible form, the 329 was priced from 4950 to 5800 marks—a bit puzzling as the 326 sedan listed at 5500. Prices for the 326 cabriolets, which were added during 1937, were 6650 marks for the two-door and 7300 marks for the four-door.

Naturally, the 329 was just what it appeared to be: a stopgap. It was created due to a shortage in production capacity for the longer 326 chassis. That was partly remedied in 1937 with its replacement, the Type 320. This model was built on a chassis that combined the 326 platform frame, shortened a bit in wheelbase to 108.3 inches, with the 319 front and rear suspension. The engine was a 45-bhp single-carburetor version of the 1971cc six.

With the 326 and 320 established on the passenger-car side, it was time for BMW to do something about its sporting entries. The winsome 315/1 and its larger-capacity 319/1 spinoff had literally rewritten the sports car rulebook in Germany, even though they were built only in small numbers. These lithe, lovely, lightweight roadsters with their smooth, willing little six-cylinder engines proved that a sporting machine needn't be a big, heavy brute burdened by a locomotive-like powerplant to have good performance and stamina. Nevertheless, they were beginning to look dated by 1936, their last year of production, particularly next to the new 326/320. Franz Josef Popp wanted a more modern replacement of similar, more streamlined appearance and, as usual, he wanted it yesterday. Fiedler knew that the old chassis could not simply be rebodied and remain competitive either on the race tracks or in the showroom, so he decided to work up an entirely new two-seater. It was a big job given Popp's tight deadline, and though Böning could handle the drawing board end of it, Fiedler would need help with testing and development. Luckily, he was able to get Alex von Falkenhausen transferred to the car section from Rudi Schleicher's motorcycle engineering staff. A little later, Ernst Loof came on board. Without their help—Fiedler's fertile imagination and Böning's flawless draftsmanship notwithstanding—the new BMW 328 would not have been the sensation it turned out to be.

Prototype testing went beyond normal road conditions to open competition, and the 328 debuted at the *Eifelrennen,* held on the challenging Nürburgring circuit, in the spring of 1936. Ernst Henne drove it to a clear victory in the 2.0-liter class at an average speed of 63 mph over 70.8 miles.

*An extension of the 315/319 roadsters, the romantic Type 328 debuted in 1937 with a three-carb, 80-bhp version of the 2.0-liter six. It's shown above in an original 1938 photo. At the right is a restored car owned by BMW and shown in front of the company museum in Munich.*

Production of the 328 began in February, 1937. The single body style, a sensuously curvaceous two-seat roadster, bore only a hint of the traditional running boards and had a low, ground-hugging stance. The front end was dominated by a tall, slim interpretation of the twin-kidney grille motif, smoothly melded in with the front fenders and a long hood held down by leather straps. The large round head-lamps nestled in the "catwalk" areas between hood and fenders. Shared with the earlier road-sters were scooped-out door tops, a sharply sloped tail, and covered rear wheel openings. The windshield, which looked relatively high, was split and slightly vee'd. In all, the effect was virile and purposeful, and it is this styling that defines the 328 as the classic BMW for many enthusiasts today.

In road-ready form, the 328 weighed 1830 pounds, including oil, water, and its maximum 13 gallons of gas. It was built up on a ladder-type steel-tube frame with side members of 90mm (3.54-in.) diameter, to which three box-section crossmembers were electrically welded. The steering gear and front and rear suspension systems were lifted from the 319/1, and the hydrau-lic all-drum brakes came from the 326. The brakes were now self-adjusting, automatically tak-ing up any slack caused by lin-ing wear every time the car was backed up. The rear axle had a banjo-type pressed-steel casing, and a one-shot lubrication sys-tem was featured that delivered

*continued on page 65*

*The 1898 Wartburg: forerunner of all BMWs.*

*When Bayerische Motoren Werke bought the Dixi company of Eisenach, it became the German licensee for
production of the British-designed Austin Seven. Here, a sample of these early BMWs. Above: The Dixi-built
DA-1 touring car from 1928. The letters DA stood for* Deutsche Ausführung *(German version). An improved
model became the BMW 3/15 from 1929. Opposite page, bottom, the AM-4 sedan from 1934, an improved
extension of the AM-1 model introduced two years earlier. AM denoted* Automobil München *to further separate
this model from its Austin origins. Opposite page, top: The BMW DA-2 sedan from 1930 featured four-wheel brakes
and was a bit larger than the previous Dixi models. Total production for the year was 6702 units.*

*Opposite page, top: The BMW DA-1 with two-seat sports tourer body, one of the most popular styles. A total of 2012 were built through 1932. Bottom: BMW's first six-cylinder model was the Type 303, introduced in 1933. Shown is that year's four-seat sedan. A sunroof sedan, cabriolet, and two-seat sports model were also offered. Production totalled 3210 through 1934. This page: The AM-4 sedan from 1934. This was the final development of the basic Austin Seven design. A four-speed gearbox and larger 20-bhp four-cylinder engine were among the improvements.*

Opposite page, top: Succeeding the six-cylinder Type 303 was the Type 315, with a more powerful 1.5-liter engine and minor external changes. Shown is the four-window cabriolet, of which 2281 examples were built through the end of this series in 1937. Sedan and sunroof sedan were also offered, and about 980 chassis were fitted with various custom-built styles. This page and opposite page, bottom: A sports version, the 315/1, appeared in 1935 along with a larger-displacement 1.9-liter companion, the 319/1. Both were almost identical externally and lacked side curtains. Production totalled 242 and 102 units, respectively, through 1936.

*Opposite page, top: The Type 326, introduced in 1936, was BMW's most popular single model of the Thirties. Shown is an original two-door cabriolet with bodywork by Autenrieth. A four-door convertible and sedan were also offered, and series production totalled 6973 through 1941. Opposite page, bottom, and this page: A beautifully restored 1937 example of the romantic Type 328 roadster, one of history's most successful competition cars. Production totalled just 461 units in 1936-40.*

Another look at the splendid Type 328 roadster. The car shown above stands in front of the BMW Museum, while the car pictured below and on the opposite page is a restored 1938 example owned by a U.S. collector. The 328 was powered by a 1971cc ohv six rated at 80-bhp and featuring triple Solex carbs and hemispherical cylinder head. With the standard four-speed gearbox, the 328 could reach over 90 mph. This engine would have a long production life, returning in the postwar Type 501 sedan and also modified for the British-built Bristol, both of which continued well into the Fifties. Today, the 328 is a highly sought-after collectible.

Top: BMW's first four-door sedan appeared with the 326 series in 1936. Above: The Type 335 was BMW's largest prewar model, but saw only limited production in 1939-41 owing to its untimely arrival on the eve of WWII. Just 40 of these convertible sedans were built. Opposite page: The curvaceous Type 327 coupe of 1937-41, essentially a sports version of the Type 326.

*Besides the handsome closed coupe shown here, the Type 327 was also offered in cabriolet form. Both were two-seaters powered by the Type 326 hemi-head six with slightly higher compression and 5 more horsepower, and rode a shorter 108.3-inch wheelbase. A hybrid version, the Type 327/28, was available in 1938-40 with the 80-bhp tri-carb power unit from the Type 328.*

Above: The 1937-41 Type 327 coupe with typical two-tone paint and rear fender skirts. Below: The sleek Type 328 with racing Mille Miglia bodywork as campaigned in 1940.

*Right: The distinctive face of the Type 328. Lower right: Cockpit looks dated now, but was quite modern for the late Thirties. Below: Besides triple carbs, the 328 engine differed from other BMW sixes in its specific cylinder head. Top speed for the 1830-pound roadster was around 90 mph.*

continued from page 48
motor oil, not grease, to 17 separate points. Since the 328 was intended strictly as a two-seater, Fiedler decided to use the 94.5-inch wheelbase of its 315/319 predecessors. The tail was slightly longer, housing the fuel tank behind the rear axle, a small trunk above, and the spare wheel, which was imbedded in the trunklid. Overall length was 153.5 inches, width 61 inches, and height (to the top of the windshield) a rakish 55.1 inches.

Under its hood, the 328 was the very model of high-efficiency engine design, being the first BMW to employ hemispherical combustion chambers. The block was shared with the 326, but instead of a cast-iron cylinder head the 328's was made of aluminum, and 7.5:1 compression was specified. Valves were not arranged in line but splayed so as to obtain the hemispherical configuration. Valve actuation from the single chain-driven camshaft low down in the side of the block was a tricky problem that Fied-ler solved in a very clever manner. The large intake valves were opened by rocker arms and pushrods from the camshaft, as in the 326 unit, while the smaller exhaust valves, mounted in light alloy guides, were opened by a system of short horizontal pushrods transversely interposed between two sets of rocker arms on opposing rocker shafts. In other words, the camshaft operated 12 rocker arms on a single shaft. Six of them opened the intake valves. The other six operated the horizontal pushrods running across to six rocker arms, mounted on a shaft on the opposite side of the head. These in turn opened the exhaust valves. Dual-coil valve springs were fitted, so the engine ran easily up to 5500 rpm. The rocker shafts had individual covers (removable for inspection and adjustment), which could mislead some to mistake this for a double-overhead-camshaft unit. Spark plugs were centrally mounted in the hemispherical combustion chambers. Short, vertical passages to the ports fed fresh mixture from triple Solex downdraft carburetors with 30mm throats, and the exhaust gas passages were nearly straight. In normal production trim, the 328 six delivered a maximum 80 bhp (DIN) at 5000 rpm, good for a brisk 93-mph top speed.

Two different four-speed gearboxes were found in the 328, one made by Hurth, the other by ZF. The Hurth unit was the same one used in the 319 but having a slightly lower (1.50:1) third gear ratio. The ZF transmission was a close-ratio box, with a 1.25 third, 1.82 second, and 3.07:1 first gear. Most of the cars built for competition had the ZF gearbox matched to a 3.70:1 final drive ratio; the Hurth-equipped cars had a 3.88:1 rear axle.

The 328 offered acceleration that was sparkling for its time and for an 80-bhp car of this size. But it was not the performer painted by the romantic picture stories found in certain car magazines. For example, *The Autocar* in England tested one in 1938 and reported standing-start acceleration times of 3.4 seconds to 30 mph and 6.9 seconds to 50 mph. Extrapolating from that curve, we see that a 328 would need 10.4 seconds to reach 60 mph, 12.2 seconds to hit 70 mph, and about 17 seconds to pass 80 mph, arriving at 90 mph only after about 25 seconds at full throttle. However, the 328's racing record hints that more power and quicker sprinting ability were available. Some believe that Von Falkenhausen was getting a good 100 bhp out of the engines used in the factory team cars and those of factory-supported privateers during the 1937 season.

Few cars were more impressive than the 328 in European road racing during 1936-40. And, to the delight of their owners, older BMW's were still winning, too. The same day Ernst Henne won the 2.0-liter class in the 1936 *Eifelrennen*, Ralph Roese won the 1.5-liter class with his 315/1. Later that same season, Ernst Heinle set the fastest time of the day for 1.5-liter sports cars with his 315 in the Freiburg-Schauinsland hillclimb, while Anton Neumaier beat all other 1100cc sports cars with his Type 303 roadster. At the close of the 1936 campaign, A. F. P. Fane led a team of 319/1s to a team prize and victory in the 2.0-liter class of the RAC Tourist Trophy rally at Belfast, Northern Ireland.

Then came 1937, and the 328 simply stole the show, racking up over 100 wins that year alone. The victories are too numerous to detail here, but a few highlights will serve to illustrate this BMW's utter command of the road courses. A factory car driven by Henne was the fastest sports car and winner of the 2.0-liter class in the *Grand Prix des Frontieres* at Chimay, Belgium. Fane set a new record for

2.0-liter sports cars at Shelsley Walsh in 1937, a feat repeated by Paul Heinemann with another 328 a year later. Heineman also won the 2.0-liter class in the 1937 La Turbie hillclimb, while Kurt Illmann emerged victorious in that category at Schauinsland. Prince Bira of Thailand drove a 328 in the 1937 Tourist Trophy as BMW again captured its class, and Henne won the Bucharest Grand Prix. And we shouldn't forget the consistent performance of Heinrich Graf von der Mühle-Eckart of Austria, who won the 2.0-liter class in the International Austrian Alpine Trials.

The 328 continued its dominance in 1938. Mühle-Eckart finished first in class at the French Alpine Rally that year, winning an Alpine Cup by completing the run without a single penalty point. Count Giovanni Lurani and Prince Max zu Schaumburg-Lippe shared a 328 in the Mille Miglia, partnered by

*Below: The fastest prewar 328 in sprints and hillclimbs was this special speedster raced by Ralph Roese. Opposite page: 328s were out in force for the 1938 German Grand Prix. Paul Greifzu won in car 10.*

Fane and William Grover in a sister car. They were first in class and took a team prize. There were other important victories witnessed by big crowds that season. Illmann's 328 proved the fastest sports car in the *Avusrennen,* Ralph Roese won at Chimay and Antwerp, Fane set best times for sports cars at Prescott and Shelsley Walsh, and Paul Greifzu took the 2.0-liter class in the German Grand Prix.

It was in 1938 that the Wendler coachworks of Reutlingen received an order from a Dr. Rostberg for a special streamlined body to be mounted on a Type 328 chassis. Created by Paul Jaray, a leading exponent of aerodynamic design, this car

was estimated to have a drag coefficient of 0.30 to 0.32, amazingly low for this era. The complete car was fairly light at 2006 pounds, and could reach a top speed of 112 mph. This experiment encouraged BMW itself to delve into the art of low-drag design. For the 24 Hours of Le Mans in 1939, the factory fielded a streamlined 328 coupe with bodywork by Carrozzeria Touring of Milan, plus two standard-bodied roadsters. All three went the distance without incident. The coupe, driven by Prince Schaumburg-Lippe and Hans Wencher, finished fifth overall and first in the 2.0-liter class, averaging 82.5 mph. The roadsters finished 7th and 9th overall.

For the rest of the 1939 season, however, it was the stock 328s that triumphed on the tracks as well as in rallies. Helmut Polensky's 328 was the fastest sports car and the class winner at the Grossglockner hillclimb, while Peter Cristea achieved the same distinction in the ADAC *Eifelrennen* at the Nürburgring. Wolfgang Denzel won a cup by taking the class victory in that year's French Alpine Rally. Then Alex von Falkenhausen, with his wife Kitty as co-driver, came home third overall in the Paris-Nice Rally, and won the 2.0-liter category to boot. In 1940, Von Falkenhausen's job in the car branch was considered done, and he was promoted to chief of motorcycle

testing. Three years later he was placed in charge of all motorcycle development, which continued even as BMW was enmeshed in Germany's war effort.

Hitler's attack on Poland in September 1939 effectively spelled the end of auto racing in Europe, which would have no place for it as World War II spread from nation to nation. Yet the Type 328 would have one last competition fling. It came at the so-called "fake" Mille Miglia of 1940, better remembered as the Brescia Grand Prix. BMW fielded five Touring-bodied streamliners. Four were open-cockpit roadsters, the fifth a fastback coupe designed by Dr. Wunibald Kamm. The engines, tuned to run on racing fuel, had 9.6:1 compression and maximum power output of about 120 bhp at 5500 rpm. BMW scored an outright victory, thanks to the efforts of Fritz Huschke von Hanstein, who became racing manager at Porsche in the Sixties, and his co-driver, Walter Baumer. Averaging 102 mph over 920 miles on a closed circuit, mainly Italian *autostrada,* they beat the fastest Alfa Romeo piloted by Farina/Membelli. A second car shared by Adolf Brudes and Ralph Roese finished third, and the two remaining BMWs occupied fifth and seventh. This race was strictly an Axis benefit, but it was nonetheless a convincing demonstration of the 328's prowess.

Looking back, the BMW 328 stands as something of a miracle. At 7400 marks it was far from overpriced, and the market for this charismatic dual-purpose sports car was undoubtedly much larger than suggested by the modest production total of 462 units through 1940. Several car companies must have agreed, but they entered the field with only pale imitations, stylish roadsters on everyday chassis without any real racing potential. Among these cars were the Wanderer 26 S, Audi 225 Sport, and Hansa 1700 Sport. Other firms like Daimler-

Benz, Opel, and Ford contented themselves with convertible versions of their prosaic family models. So the 328 was truly a one-of-a-kind automobile: sleek, fast if not sensationally quick, rugged, and capable of holding its own in any company on and off the track. BMW would produce nothing remotely like it until the timeless Type 507 of the Fifties.

For all the attention that has been lavished on the 328 over the years, it is the Type 327 that was perhaps the greater masterpiece. It went into production as a four-seat sports convertible in November 1937, joined by a companion four-seat coupe in October 1938. Making the most of his "modular" approach to new model development, Fritz Fiedler conceived the 327 as the short 326 chassis (as used on the 320) and its front suspension combined with the 328's rear suspension. That meant a platform frame with the low, transverse leaf spring in front and two semi-elliptic leaf springs in back. The 108.3-inch wheelbase was shared with the 320, but the new model's sports car aspirations demanded long-hood proportions, which forced the

cockpit to be positioned much further rearwards relative to overall length. The result was very close-coupled accommodations but excellent visual balance and a lovely profile. Predictably, the 327's rear seat space and comfort were inadequate for adults, and there was hardly any more trunk room than in a 328. Steering and brakes came from the 326, as did wheels and tires (5.50-16). The rear axle was borrowed from the 320, geared at 3.90:1 instead of 4.38 or 4.55:1. The standard gearbox was the four-speed Hurth unit with freewheeling as introduced on the 326, and a close-ratio ZF was also available. This was outwardly the same gearbox used in the racing 328s, but the number of gear teeth was altered so that the 327's ratios were 1.48 on third, 2.28 on second, and 3.75:1 on first.

The 327 inherited the 326's twin-carburetor 1971cc six with "high-compression" head (6.3:1), so maximum available power was only 55 bhp (DIN) at 4500 rpm. The chassis was clearly capable of handling a lot more power, so the 80-bhp Type 328 unit was also offered beginning in April 1938 to create the con-

Opposite page: "Schorsch" Meier rode this
500cc supercharged twincam flat-twin
bike to win the 1939 Tourist Trophy race.
This page, left: The lone Touring-bodied
coupe used at Brescia 1940. Below:
Though close to the Brescia roadsters in
appearance, this is a Touring prototype
for a possible successor to the 328.

at 7450. The 80-bhp powerplant bumped prices to 8130 and 8100 marks, respectively—not all that much of a premium in view of the extra performance. The 327 would have an "after life" in the postwar world, but examples of the genuine article are all too few, a sad consequence of the outbreak of war. Production of the base-engine models totaled 1396 through early 1941. The 327/28 is predictably rarer: only 569 were built through 1940.

The ultimate 3-series model of the Thirties was the Type 335, the culmination of BMW's work on a 3.5-liter six that had been started shortly after abolition of the car tax. The new design was first shown as a fully developed prototype in 1938, but production did not commence until 1939 due to materials shortages in the wake of the Nazi arms buildup. Only 462 cars were actually completed, including prototypes (some sources put the count at 410).

The 335 was basically the 326 with a larger engine and a longer 117.5-inch wheelbase. The power unit was, in fact, new throughout, though its architecture had all the hallmarks of the 2.0-liter six. Bore and stroke were 82 x 110mm (3.23 x 4.33 in.), which gave a stroke/bore ratio of 1.34:1. Fiedler was satisfied with a four-bearing crankshaft, but discarded chain drive for the camshaft in favor of spur gears. It was noisier perhaps, but valve timing was more accurate. With its sizeable 3485cc (212.6-cid) capacity, this was a low-stress powerplant, and Fiedler settled for a compression ratio of only 5.8:1 and a single 35mm Solex carburetor. Maximum rated output of the initial production version was 90 bhp (DIN) at 3500 rpm, though that

fusingly named Type 327/28. The standard powerplant could produce a top speed of 77.5 mph and, despite a fairly hefty 2425-pound curb weight, the 327's average fuel economy was a tolerable 19.6 mpg. The tri-carb engine improved maximum velocity to a more interesting 87 mph, though fuel consumption inevitably declined, to 16.2 mpg.

Although there was little really new in it, the Type 327 was one of the finest touring cars built anywhere in the years just before World War II. Think of it as the prewar ancestor of today's 633CSi: a more stylish—and therefore less practical—version of a BMW sedan built around the same thoroughly proven chassis and mechanical components. Prices were reasonable all things considered. With the 55-bhp engine the cabriolet listed at 7500 marks, the coupe

could easily be doubled without any fundamental alterations.

Despite the 335's high weight—2867 pounds for the standard four-door sedan—Fiedler was able to use the 3.90:1 rear axle from the Type 327, albeit adapted to a wider track, and its four-speed ZF gearbox, which now had intermediate ratios of 1.355 on third, 2.165 on second, and 3.89:1 on first. Top speed was a conservative 90 mph and, at 14.7 mpg, mileage was inferior to what Hudson, Ford, Studebaker, Pontiac, and Dodge were obtaining from their even weightier models with engines of similar power and displacement.

The stretched frame gave the 335 an overall length of 190.6 inches. Tire size was increased to 6.00-16, which made for slightly wider tracks at each end, but suspension components were shared with the 326. Most of the body was too, being nearly identical from the cowl back except for a modernized tail that provided more truck space. The front end was straight 326, but the extra wheelbase made the hood longer. With all this, the 335 did not require any major retooling at Ambi-Budd, which produced the sedan body, and the big BMW could be assembled right alongside the 326 at Eisenach. Autenrieth and Hermann Graber offered two- and four-seat convertible bodywork on this chassis, which numbered 118 and a mere 40, respectively. Sports cabriolet and coupe styles were also built experimentally, but no more than one of each was completed. There were also 17 finished but unbodied chassis.

The last new BMW to appear before World War II was the Type 321, issued at the beginning of 1939. It was yet another "cocktail" car, the successor to the Type 320 and bodily similar to it. The front suspension was essentially the 326 design, with the lower transverse leaf spring and upper lateral links instead of the previous 319-derived ar-

rangement. Other differences from the 320 included tires enlarged by one size and a rear end mildly restyled to resemble that of the big 335. Like the 320, two-door cabriolet and coupe/sedan body styles were the only ones offered, priced at 5650 and 4800 marks, respectively. Series production was low, only 3814 units. Again, materials shortages were responsible.

As a major aircraft engine producer, BMW was destined to play a vital role in Hitler's mad, tragic quest for world domination. Yet regardless of *Der Führer's* plans for the Forties, BMW could look back on the last half of the Thirties with a great deal of satisfaction. It had established not only a coherent model line but one that fully exploited the cost-effective "mix-and-match" formula for product development, an approach still followed today. If this method tended to produce some fairly

*Opposite page: The Type 327 coupe of 1937-41. This page, top: The third-place 1940 Brescia car of Adolf Brudes/Ralph Roese. Above: Many of the Brescia cars survived to take part in this postwar Alpine rally.*

ordinary cars, at least it could occasionally produce some brilliantly capable ones like the 328 and 327, the most romantic and desirable BMWs of the prewar era. And the fundamental building-block design, The Type 326, proved quite successful in its own right. It was the single best-selling BMW series of the period, with a total of 15,936 produced over five years.

It's ironic that, even as war approached, BMW continued to make great technical and commercial strides with the sort of speed that had been characteristic of the firm since the Dixi days. Undoubtedly it was on the verge of even greater success. Although we can only guess at what it might have achieved had not war intervened, there's no doubt that further progress was delayed many years by Germany's crushing defeat. Bayerische Motoren Werke was about to enter the most painful and dramatic period in its history.

# STARTING OVER: WAR WOUNDS AND AMPUTATION

**B**ayerische Motoren Werke dutifully went to war along with the rest of German industry in late 1939. The previous decade had seen great technical progress and accelerated reform at all three BMW divisions, and the firm stood as one of the Third Reich's greatest assets on the eve of World War II. Yet by 1945, this proud, strong, eminently capable company would be reduced to a helpless cripple, one so badly shattered by the war's momentous military and political consequences that it would not fully recover until some 15 years later. Though no one could know it as Hitler's storm troopers marched into Poland, BMW was about to undergo the most profound changes it would ever experience.

Signs of change had been evident even before war was formally declared. Foremost among these was an expansion of BMW's aircraft operations. In 1939 the firm took over control of the Brandenburger Motorenwerke, makers of Bramo aero engines. This company had been established as part of the giant Siemens electrical combine, and its Spandau plant outside Berlin had been making Siemens & Halske air-cooled radial engines since about 1911. Talks about mutual assistance had begun in 1935, when former Bramo executive Fritz Hille came to Munich as a member of the BMW management board, replacing Franz Klebe, who retired. The acquisition of Bramo instantly doubled the size of BMW's aircraft division, which acquired the new

name of BMW Flugmotorenbau GmbH.

Though their quality and reliability were unquestioned, BMW's aircraft engines were outmoded by the end of the Thirties, ill suited for the new generation of warplanes then being developed by the airframe industry. (A final triumph for the old guard came in 1938, when a Focke-Wulf Fw 200 Condor powered by four BMW Type 132 engines made the round-trip from Berlin to New York in a record time of 45 hours.) With assistance from the Nazi government's aviation research establishment, Bramo injected new technology into BMW's aircraft branch. In preparation for this, BMW erected a modern new factory at Allach outside Munich, and later in 1939 this facility began turning out the BMW 801. Designed by Professor Kurt Lohner, this 14-cylinder double-row air-cooled radial was rated at 2000 bhp (at sea level). By war's end it had been improved to deliver 2400 bhp for takeoff, and in turbocharged form put out 1800 bhp at an altitude of 37,000 feet. Some 1300 of these units were completed by 1945.

Significantly, BMW was a leader in the wartime rush to jet propulsion. The firm's first gas turbine had been laid out as early as 1938. Designated the 109-003, it was 125 inches long, had a diameter of about 27 inches, and weighed 1344 pounds. Its single toroidal combustor was fitted with no fewer than 16 fuel nozzles, and with a six-stage axial-flow compressor

and a single-stage axial-flow turbine it produced 1760 pounds of thrust at 9500 rpm. A later version with a seven-stage compressor delivered 1990 pounds thrust. The final version, with an eight-stage compressor and two-stage turbine, produced 2760 pounds thrust. Laboratory tests on this design began in the fall of 1941, and the first flight tests were made in early 1942 with a Messerschmitt Me 262 fighter and an Arado Ar 234 bomber. But the project was abandoned before an acceptable prototype had been developed. Instead, work went ahead on a much larger jet, the 109-018. It weighed 5080 pounds and was 167 inches long. The unique thing about it was that it was suitable for both turbojet and turboprop applications. The jet version had a maximum thrust of 7700 pounds, while the turboprop (with two counter-rotating propellers) generated a maximum 7000 shaft horsepower. Among its main features were a 12-stage compressor and a three-stage turbine with peak rotor speed of 6000 rpm. It was still under development when American troops marched into Munich. BMW also got involved with rocket propulsion. One such effort, Project 3307, was a low-cost, expendable rocket intended for launching large-caliber mis-

*Looking every bit like a cobbled-up BMW prototype, this is actually Job 1 for the production Bristol 400, a British-built postwar cousin to the Type 327. This car is part of the permanent Bristol collection at Filton.*

325 was notable for its all-independent suspension with dual coil springs at each wheel, plus four-wheel steering and a handbrake that worked on all wheels as well. It was a heavy rig, tipping the scales at close to 4000 pounds unladen, and it thus ate up a lot of fuel, returning only about 10 mpg. Altogether, BMW built 3225 of these small personnel carriers between 1937 and 1942.

BMW also developed air and oil-cooled stationary engines of 1975cc (120.5 cid) and 3475cc (220 cid), both based on its prewar car engines. These were produced beginning around the start of 1942 for both civilian and military applications.

The year 1942 witnessed a milestone in BMW history: the retirement in October of company founder Franz Josef Popp. Fritz Hille was elected president and a new management board was selected, composed of Kurt Donath (another executive recruited from Bramo), Fritz Fiedler (technical director), Erich Zipprich, Max Wrba, and Bruno Bruckmann. Popp withdrew completely from the affairs of the company he had created, and lived quietly until his death in 1954.

American tanks stood at the gates of the Milbertshofen plant on May 1, 1945. Hitler's plan to blow the factory sky-high if Germany were forced to capitulate had been rendered academic, but it didn't do BMW any good. U.S. authorities ordered the plant demolished after it had been stripped of all useable machinery, which would be shipped off and dispersed as reparations among the 40-odd countries that had been at war with the Third Reich. The dismantling was carried out in 1946-47 and cost BMW some 4000 modern machine tools, plans, patterns, and

siles, but it did not get beyond the experimental stage.

In the midst of all this, BMW's automotive division was turning out military vehicles. Despite the Eisenach plant's relatively small production capacity, the firm had been ordered to shift to wartime manufacturing at an early date for a very simple reason: the German auto industry as a whole lacked the capacity to satisfy the army's vast needs. The number of car manufacturers had shrunk from 51 in 1925 to 13 in 1936, and fully 87 percent of industry output in 1937 was accounted for by only five: Opel, Auto Union, Mercedes-Benz, Adler and Ford. Because any extra production was

vital, small BMW began turning out a lightweight, non-armored, four-passenger car with four-wheel-drive. Designed by the *Wehrmacht* ordinance staff in 1936, it was intended mainly for use by signals and communications units. This vehicle, called the *Kraftfahrzeug* 3, was also built by Stoewer and Hanomag, and each manufacturer used its own engines. BMW's version was designated the Type 325, and although the company stated it was not designed exclusively for military use, it did not bear the BMW badge nor was there any doubt about its true purpose. Powered by the 50-bhp (DIN) twin-carburetor 1971cc six from the Type 326 passenger cars, the

hardware of all kinds with an estimated combined value of 100 million marks. And this came on top of a 380-million-mark loss from the confiscation of five *more* BMW plants. The Allach facility was turned into a vehicle repair depot for the U.S. Army. The Eisenach plant ended up in Soviet-occupied territory. BMW thus entered the postwar world an amputee, its main carmaking facility soon to be concealed behind the Iron Curtain. Now, company managers in Munich faced the formidable and depressing task of picking up the pieces.

Though Eisenach was hopelessly lost to BMW, its commercial potential was certainly not lost on the Russians. The facility was quickly acquired by an Autovelo, a Soviet-controlled industrial combine. The Ambi-Budd stamping and welding plants were relocated from Berlin to Eisenach, and production based on prewar BMW designs resumed in late 1945. Output was initially at the rate of five units a day. At first, only a warmed-over version of the Type 321 was built, but in 1948 the 327 was revived as well. The cabriolet, now designated 327/2, and the companion 327/3 coupe were outwardly the same as the prewar versions except for front- instead of rear-hinged doors, a revamped hood that opened without taking the hood sides with it and, on the coupe, a one-piece instead of split rear window. Amazingly, production continued through 1955. Then came a new model, the 340, arriving in 1949 to replace the 321. It was essentially a 326 sedan, but substituting for the familiar twin-kidney grille was a pyramid-shaped affair composed of nine horizontal bars and topped by an emblem: BMW's own blue-and-white quartered circle.

BMW AG still existed as a corporate entity in the new nation of West Germany, but its situation was desperate. Under Allied terms it could not build cars, motorcycles, or aircraft engines, and its only assets, if you could call them that, were the shell of the Milbertshofen plant and a claim to ownership of the Allach factory. Kurt Donath now took charge, assisted by Kurt Deby. They started rehiring former workers, who began to make pots and pans with the most primitive of equipment, bought secondhand or salvaged from bomb-damaged plants. Other domestic hardware followed, including bicycles. But Donath and Deby were occupied with thoughts of new motorcycles. In 1945, Deby secretly rehired Alfred Böning, who was instructed to design an all-new motorcycle with a 250cc engine. This became the model R-24, which was ready by July 1947. It had a 12-bhp (DIN) single-cylinder ohv engine, the usual BMW shaft drive, and the telescopic front fork adopted in 1935 (though it lacked the refinement of telescopic rear suspension as introduced on the R-51 in 1938). It was a good machine, but BMW still had no means of producing it.

Before the end of 1947, Donath had obtained permission from U.S. authorities to resume motorcycle production. Next he had to convince bankers to lend money for new factory equipment. Slowly and painfully, BMW built its first postwar motorcycles in 1948, mostly from spare parts scraped together by dealers from their prewar inventories. However, this wasn't manufacturing in the true sense: it was assembly. Donath, now desperate for a way to finance the necessary tooling purchases, put the company in receivership. A Munich banker, Dr. Hans-Karl von Mangoldt-Reiboldt, assumed the presidency. Another local banker, Hanns Grewenig, became sales director. Soon, equipment began flowing in for installation at Milbertshofen, and R-24 production finally got underway. Böning had also prepared a less expensive bike powered by a 125cc single-cylinder two-stroke engine, and this

started coming from the revitalized plant in short order.

Donath, who continued as technical director and general manager at Milbertshofen, became increasingly annoyed with the East Germans, who had been using the BMW logo ever since they had revived operations at Eisenach. The first postwar cars built there were three Type 321s hand-assembled from leftover parts, which naturally included the badges. By Christmas 1945 an additional 68 cars had been completed. The following year, Autovelo began to reorganize all car and motorcycle facilities within the Eastern sector, partly with the intent of giving the impression that the old BMW was back in business. And in a way, it was: 2000 cars came off the line in 1947 and another 4600 through mid-1948. But these were not products of free enterprise, which must have rankled Donath as much as the actual trademark infringement. He consulted with his lawyers. Legal remedies can be complex, but the solution here was fairly simple. The Eisenach branch of BMW AG was dissolved effective September 28, 1949, and was legally severed from the firm as of October 11. With this action, the Munich-based company legally became the sole owner of the BMW trademark.

For BMW, this wasn't a question of semantics or pride: it was a hard-headed business move. At the time, Autovelo was exporting about half of Eisenach's output to western countries, so by dint of continued usage it could have won rights to the logo, which would be a setback for the Munich firm. Following Donath's legal action and without really modifying its cars, Autovelo simply renamed them EMW (for Eisenach Motoren Werke) and changed the blue sectors in the emblem to Bolshevik red. In the end, though, the dispute would be meaningless. In 1954, Autovelo handed over its auto plants to a new East German organization in charge of state-owned in-

dustries, the VEB. In 1955, tooling from the old DKW factory at Zschopau was transferred to Eisenach, which then turned out a completely different car, the IFA F-9, based on a 1939 DKW prototype. Interestingly enough, it was named Wartburg. This spelled the end of the EMW 340 and any further models based on prewar BMW designs. After the last EMW 327s had been built, no further links remained between the East and West German automakers.

The main reason BMW took this trademark issue so seriously was that Donath, Deby, and Böning were already making plans for a new postwar model. This program would, presumably, be financed by profits from the motorcycle business, which was beginning to look up. The firm turned out 9450 motorcycles in 1949, virtually all of them R-24s. The lower-priced bike was discontinued after a very short run, which brings up another historical footnote. In 1948, Dr. Richard Bruhm of Auto Union GmbH paid a visit to Munich to propose a merger. The prewar Auto Union AG, located in the plains of Saxony, had also been lost to Autovelo. But two of its former leaders, Bruhm and Carl Hahn (father of the current president of Volkswagen) had gone west and had begun making motorcycles under the DKW banner at a small shop in Düsseldorf. They wanted the merger for BMW's motorcycle designs and manufacturing capability, which they saw as a means for reviving the DKW car. Donath refused, but a deal was struck: BMW would not make two-stroke motorcycles and DKW would not make cars with four-stroke engines. Thus, market boundaries between the two firms were drawn for years to come. As we know now, DKW cars returned in the Fifties, and Auto Union eventually reintroduced its prewar Audi nameplate, too (but not Horch or Wanderer). This, in turn, led to the modern Audis built by a subsidiary of Volkswagen AG that are strong competitors for today's BMWs.

However much Donath, Deby, and Böning may have wanted it, the idea of a new BMW automobile seemed faintly ludicrous in the late Forties. True, the firm was making motorcycles again, but only with great difficulty. And though the market looked promising, BMW's motorcycle volume was not nearly high enough to provide the profits needed for designing and tooling a car. Raw materials were still in short supply, the Allied ban on BMW car production had yet to be lifted, and the firm's meager facilities were devoted almost totally to bikes. No question about it: any postwar revival of the BMW car in the West was going to be a Herculean task for anyone who attempted it.

Just before the war, the designers at Eisenach had built two prototypes of a new model conceived as a possible successor to the Type 326. Designated the Type 332, it used essentially the same chassis and running gear, but was clothed in fulsome new envelope bodywork. One of the two prototypes built showed up later in the showroom of a Paris car dealer. The other surfaced at Munich, heavily damaged. Deby had the car restored, and for a time it appeared that the 332 might become BMW's new postwar model. But nothing came of it, for the reasons already mentioned. It's probably just as well, as its styling would have been hopelessly passé in the Fifties.

As BMW managers wrestled with the problem of how to start building cars again, two former company employees were actually doing it—in spirit if not in fact. One was Alexander von Falkenhausen, who had been chief of the engineering design office at the end of the war. In 1946 he set up his own company in the town of Regensburg with the idea of building sports and racing machines. Carrying the name AFM—for Alexander v.

Falkenhausen München—these cars were built at Ingolstadt in the private garage of Richard Küchen, a designer of racing motorcycle engines who now had time to spare and was eager to try new things. The original AFM was a two-seater powered by an 1100cc (67-cid) MG engine. This was followed by a similar car using a highly tuned 1069cc (65.2-cid) Fiat unit. Von Falkenhausen devised a 1500cc six, based on the prewar Type 328 powerplant, for his next car, which he drove to victory in a

*This four-place touring convertible from 1951 was one of about 80 cars built by the short-lived Veritas concern under the aegis of Ernst Loof. All were powered by derivatives of the 2.0-liter BMW six.*

race at the Hockenheim circuit in 1947. He also conceived an 1100cc four with three valves per cylinder (one large intake and two small exhausts) and four carburetors. A small number of these engines were built and sold to enthusiasts building their own racers. In 1949, AFM

77

completed several cars powered by 1971cc BMW sixes that had miraculously been recovered after being squirreled away during the war. (Legend has it that the Munich factory itself unearthed a cache of raw block castings and managed to turn out a batch of brand-new engines pretty close to Type 328 specifications.)

Also in 1949, AFM presented a beautiful Formula 2 *monoposto* powered by a 2.0-liter V-8 designed from scratch by Küchen. This was a pure racing motor, with hemi-head construction, four overhead camshafts, and quad carburetors. The block was aluminum, and employed wet liners screwed into cast-silumin heads. The camshafts were driven by gear trains from the crankshaft, noisy but very efficient. This engine, which put out 160 bhp (DIN) at 8000 rpm, weighed a mere 220 pounds, and the complete car weighed only 1150 pounds. Chassis design, executed by Von Falkenhausen, consisted of a tubular steel frame, independent front suspension via coil springs and upper-and-lower control arms, and a de Dion rear axle with torsion bars and very short radius arms.

AFM entered its F2 car in several events during 1950-51, usually with Hans Stück at the wheel. It proved extremely fast, but it was equally unreliable. Lacking funds for further development, Von Falkenhausen abandoned the effort and, ultimately, the entire AFM enterprise. He continued to demonstrate his enthusiasm for BMWs however, hauling out his old 328 in 1952 to contest the French Alpine Rally. With his wife Kitty as navigator he took first place, besting a slew of more modern cars. Two years later, in 1954, he would return to BMW as chief of engine development.

The other attempt at a BMW revival concerned Ernst Loof. He had been team manager at the 1940 Brescia race, and had managed to stash away one of the streamlined cars that proved so successful there. Loof spent the war as a member of the *Luftwaffe* staff, and was lucky to have survived unscathed. The car was also undamaged, and in 1947 he entered it at Hockenheim with Karl Kling doing the honors. It beat all other sports cars and won the 2.0-liter class. Sometime before this, Loof had come up with a scheme to produce a sports car based on Touring's 1940 Mille Miglia design but updated with a few re-finements. Operating under the Veritas name, he enlisted the services of Lorenz Dietrich and Georg Meier. Dietrich, a former sales executive, had spent the war years in occupied France as manager of the Gnome-Rhone engine plant. "Schorsch" Meier had been on the factory motorcycle racing team before the war, gaining notoriety by winning the 500cc class in the 1939 Tourist Trophy on the Isle of Man with his 56-bhp supercharged BMW. Like Ernst Henne, who also returned to the motorcycle business after the war, he was a BMW dealer.

The body for the proposed Veritas was penned by Loof himself. Other ex-BMW engineers did the rest, with Erich Zipprich responsible for the engine and Wilhelm Dorls doing the chassis. The first cars completed were equipped with secondhand BMW engines. Later examples had BMW-based engines with a new type of cylinder head. This featured hemispherical combustion chambers, obtained by using a centrally mounted overhead camshaft with the pushrods and rocker arms in a symmetrical arrangement for both inlet and exhaust valves. The camshaft was driven by a two-stage chain. The Veritas engine structure

*Opposite page: T. A. D. Tony Crook drives a Frazer Nash Le Mans Replica at England's Goodwood circuit in 1952. Left: A 1951 AFM single-seat racing chassis with a modified prewar BMW 328 powerplant.*

was new, with an aluminum block and wet liners, so Zipprich had full freedom to shorten the stroke of the original 2.0-liter six and chose "square" dimensions of 75 x 75mm (2.95 in.). Compression ratios varied from car to car.

Loof had hoped to sell his cars under the Veritas-BMW label, but the powers in Munich wouldn't permit it. A variety of different body styles was envisioned, but all the cars actually completed—fewer than 80—had virtually custom-built bodies owing to the firm's tiny size and its desire to accommodate the tastes of individual buyers. As a result, there was considerable variation from one car to the next, and it's doubtful that bodies other than open types were fitted. Planned models included a five-seat sedan and convertible with 7.2:1 compression and 100 bhp (DIN) at 5000 rpm, a three-seat coupe and convertible with a 110-bhp engine and 8:1 compression, and a roadster with compression raised to 8.5:1 and 120 bhp. Finally, there was a Formula 2 racing machine with a lofty 12.5:1 compression ratio and a claimed output of 150 bhp at 7000 rpm. All Veritas bodies were modern slab-sided affairs in the then-current idiom, with

BMW/Touring heritage most evident in the roadster. The coupe, sedan and convertibles showed the influence of Allard and Healey in Britain as well as the style of prominent French coachbuilders such as Figoni & Falaschi, Henri Chapron, and Saoutchik.

Veritas chassis design was a considerable advance over prewar BMW practice. The front suspension was of the parallelogram type, with upper and lower control arms for location and torsion bars as the springing medium, all much like Otto Winkelmann's later design for Chrysler Corporation's 1957 models. At the rear was a de Dion setup, again with torsion bars, not unlike the system used on the Auto Union 3.0-liter V-12 GP racing car of 1938.

The first Veritas cars were built with the most outrageous secrecy in a corner of the Allach plant. American forces were using this as a motor vehicle repair depot, remember, and Dietrich, who managed a section of the plant, took a considerable risk by inviting some of the Yanks over for a look. He may have thought that if they saw what his team was doing they would want to buy the cars, but if so he was unduly optimistic.

The Veritas group was summarily thrown out.

Moving into the French zone in 1948, Veritas set up a small shop at Messkirch (later called Rastatt) in the state of Baden. Whoever had the idea first, Loof or Dietrich, we shall never know, but it occurred to one of them that the firm might be granted subsidies by the French authorities if it built a French car under license. Both men were genuinely impressed with the Dyna Panhard, a small front-drive sedan powered by a 610cc (37.2-cid) flat twin not unlike a BMW motorcycle engine. Loof hurriedly drew up sports bodywork, called the car Dyna-Veritas, and made his pitch. The plan worked: the French agreed to provide the desired financial and industrial support. Late in 1949, the newly named Veritas Badische Automobilwerke GmbH took over a plant in Oberndorf am Neckar, and began producing its six-cylinder cars alongside the little two-cylinder models. But the auto business was not as profitable as Loof and Dietrich had calculated. When Dyna-Veritas sales proved below stipulations, the French withdrew their support and the venture was liquidated in 1951.

Loof made a fresh start in 1952 with new capital and rented premises in the paddock at the Nürburgring circuit. This operation was called Veritas Automobilwerk, Ernst Loof GmbH. Cash reserves proved inadequate for even this modest enterprise, and BMW took over the whole works the following year. Loof was rehired to work in BMW styling and body engineering, but became ill shortly afterwards and died of a brain tumor in March 1956.

The British also attempted to preserve BMW tradition in the

early postwar years, and their efforts proved far more successful than either Veritas or AFM. As mentioned in a previous chapter, BMW had signed with a British licensee before the war, A. F. N. Limited of Isleworth in Middlesex, makers of the Frazer Nash. This company was headed by a partnership of three brothers: H. J. "Aldy" Aldington, W. H. "Bill" Aldington, and D. A. Aldington. In the summer of 1945, "Aldy" was contacted by George White, managing director of the Bristol Aeroplane Company and grandson of its founder. Bristol was in a situation quite similar to that of BMW AG back in 1919. As a major producer of aircraft engines and military planes, Bristol needed to get into new product areas more appropriate for a peacetime economy. George White and his father, Sir Stanley, were car enthusiasts and quickly seized on the idea of becoming auto producers. The notion was a logical one in that Bristol already had a subsidiary that turned out buses.

Throughout that summer, expert teams of British government officials and industry representatives combed the factories and headquarters of the various German carmakers and their suppliers in search of technical advances they could borrow. It was natural, therefore, for George White to wonder about developments at BMW. And the first man to ask, he thought, was H. J. Aldington.

"Aldy" saw this as a great opportunity for A. F. N. Limited as well as for British industry in general, and his brothers agreed. Now it so happened that D. A. Aldington was with the Ministry of Supply at the time, and could thus make the wheels of officialdom turn. It wasn't long before he and "Aldy" flew to Munich to meet with Kurt Donath, who was eager to explore any potential source of revenue for his struggling company. The Englishmen got a very friendly reception, and their license

agreement from 1935 was not only renewed but expanded. They returned to London loaded with blueprints for BMW's 2.0-liter engine and the 327 body and chassis, plus tooling and production specifications.

George White was in a hurry, so events now moved swiftly. The Aldington brothers turned over their BMW license to Bristol in exchange for a seat on its board of directors, occupied by "Aldy." Then a new Car & Light Engineering Division was established at Bristol with G. H. Abell as general manager. John Bertram Perrett, newly appointed chief designer at A. F. N., was assigned to head engineering for the new car project. Then 34 years old, he had been a draftsman with Thompson & Taylor under Reid A. Railton, had worked for MG and Vauxhall, and had spent the war years at the Fighting Vehicle Research Establishment on the payroll of Vickers-Armstrong. Meantime, "Aldy" and D. A. won permission for Fritz Fiedler to leave Germany in order to supervise engine development. Body design and engineering were entrusted to 44-year-old Dudley Hobbs, a career aircraft designer who had joined Bristol in 1928. His assistant was Denis Sevier, another young engineer who had joined the company as an apprentice and stayed on after getting his engineering degree.

BMW's 1938-model 327 coupe became the pattern for the new Bristol, which was called the 400, a number chosen to provide continuity with established nomenclature (number "00" in the 4th series). Not surprisingly, the British car's box-section platform frame was adapted from the 327 design, retaining its torsion-bar rear suspension and the low-mount transverse-leaf-spring ifs. Wheelbase was stretched nearly six inches, however, to 114 inches, and overall length went up to 183 inches. Despite the use of aluminum for hood, doors and trunklid of the Bristol-built body,

the 400 was heavier than its German parent, having a dry weight of 2537 pounds versus 2425 for the 327. No major design changes were made to the engine, though it looked quite different from the BMW original due to the adoption of British accessories that included SU carburetors and Lucas electrical equipment. On a compression ratio of 7.5:1, maximum output was 80 bhp at 4200 rpm. The standard four-speed gearbox, rack-and-pinion steering gear, even the piston-type shock absorbers were all made by Bristol.

The production 400 was first displayed at the Geneva Salon in March 1947, but it wasn't until 1948 that the British weekly *The Motor* was able to put one through its paces. Its test car completed the 0-60 mph dash in 14.7 seconds, ran the standing-start quarter-mile in 19.7 seconds, and topped out at exactly 95.7 mph. Though the performance was hardly sparkling, the testers found fuel economy outstanding: 27.5 miles per Imperial gallon at a constant 60 mph, roughly 33 mpg U.S.

It wasn't long before owners began probing the Bristol's competition potential. A 400 finished third overall in the 1949 Monte Carlo rally, and in April of that year Count Lurani drove with H. J. Aldington to place third overall in the Mille Miglia. Bristols also acquitted themselves well in the French Alpine Rally and even in some minor hillclimb runs in Switzerland and Italy.

Fritz Fiedler reminded George White that BMW's prewar racing streamliners had been built in Italy by Carrozzeria Touring, a company whose lightweight Superleggera coachwork for Ferrari, Alfa Romeo, and Lancia was much admired. Bristol shipped one of its chassis to Milan, where designer Felice Bianchi Anderloni created a more modern body for it. White didn't like the front end, however, and the fender treatment

*A rare photograph of the "EMW 321," a postwar continuation of the original BMW 321 built briefly in East Germany by the Autovelo combine.*

was too close to that of contemporary Alfa Romeos to be acceptable. So, Bristol's own Dudley Hobbs reworked the design into a new and original shape that was not only prettier but also quite slippery (or aerodynamically efficient, as we now say).

The result was the new Type 401, basically Hobb's slicker body mounted on the existing 327-derived chassis. Taking full advantage of the change, Bristol acquired the rights to Touring's patented construction. This employed a cage-like network of fine steel tubes that provided a "skeleton" for the bodyshell, which was made up of aluminum sheets folded around the tubes but not rigidly attached to them. The engine was basically the same as before except for the adoption of triple Solex carburetors that boosted maximum output slightly to 85 bhp at 4500 rpm. The 401 made its public debut at Earls Court in October 1949, with production commencing at about the same time. Bristol continued the 400 through the spring of 1950, then

halted production after some 700 examples. The 401 would see 650 copies through 1953.

Before we look further into developments at Bristol, let's go back a bit to the Aldington brothers and Frazer Nash. Once Fiedler had completed his part of the Bristol project, H. J. Aldington brought him to Isleworth to create a brand-new Frazer Nash. It was to be closely based on the design of a 1943 BMW prototype that had been derived from the 1940 Brescia cars and was, at one time, intended as a postwar replacement for the 328. Now as the blueprints "Aldy" had brought back from Germany were too few and incomplete, he wanted Fiedler to fill in the blank spots. A. F. N. Limited just happened to have one of the Brescia cars on hand, which may have made the job easier. In any case, Fiedler finished it in just 30 days during the spring of 1947, and the new postwar Frazer Nash was a hit at that year's Earls Court motor show.

Fiedler's reconstituted design employed the 328 chassis and its high-leaf-spring front suspension along with the 326 rear suspension. But there were differences. The frame had similar steel-tube side members, but

instead of box-section crossmembers it had three steel tubes. Three models were listed: the Fast Roadster, with a streamlined open-cockpit body; the Competition, a stark two-seat racer; and the Cabriolet, a civilized four-place convertible. The latter had the 108-inch 327/328 wheelbase; the others were built on a 96-inch chassis. Engines came from Bristol, not surprisingly, with compression, camming, and carburetion supplied to A. F. N. specifications. The Frazer Nash models thus had power ranging from 80 to 125 bhp, with the more potent engines reserved for the racing-oriented roadsters.

After an inauspicious start, the Aldingtons' new cars did indeed prove to be worthy competitors. Dorino Serafini, better known for his rides on Gilera motorcycles before the war, got one of the first Frazer Nash prototypes and entered it in the 1948 Mille Miglia. He was in the lead when he crashed into an impertinent wall. The Competition model shown at Earls Court was purchased by Norman Culpan, who drove it in the Le Mans 24-hour race in 1949. "Aldy" went along as co-driver, and the duo came in third overall—remarkably, on the same set of tires they started with! Average fuel consumption was over 15 mpg and average speed was a creditable 78.4 mph. In honor of the feat, the Aldingtons offered a new Frazer Nash called the Le Mans Replica, which was guaranteed to be identical with Culpan's car in performance. A total of 60 was sold over a five-year period, and most of them led an active racing life. Franco Cortese drove one to win the 1951 Targa Florio in Sicily. For 1950 a Mille Miglia model was introduced to replace the Fast Roadster, followed by a Targa Florio variant for 1952.

Among the many enthusiasts taking note of the Frazer Nash successes were John Cooper and his father Charles N. Cooper, specialist builders of single-seat

racing cars in Surbiton, Surrey. In the fall of 1951 they approached Bristol about buying engines for their racers. From this came the Cooper-Bristol Formula 2 single-seater of 1952, the car that rocketed driver Mike Hawthorn to fame. The Cooper powerplant started off as a normal-compression 122-bhp engine, but it ended the 1952 season with a high-compression head and about 130 bhp. At the start of the 1953 campaign, compression ratio was upped to 10.0:1 and power climbed to 140 bhp. It would reach 150 bhp a few months later.

Cooper's experience encouraged Bristol to go racing under its own name, and the

firm fielded a three-car squad for Le Mans 1953. Identified as the Type 450, these cars had a chassis designed by David Hodkin of ERA, with coil-spring front suspension and a de Dion rear axle. They were competitive, but the effort failed when engine breakdowns put all three cars out of contention before the halfway point. Bristol returned in 1954 with a team of revised 450s, and this time the results were better: the Wilson/Mayers car with 145 bhp finished seventh overall and won the 2.0-liter class. A year later, Bristol was pulling 155 reliable horses from the basic 2.0-liter engine it had borrowed from BMW, and its three-car Le Mans team swept home 1-2-3 in class and 7-8-9 overall.

For Bristol's engine designers, these exploits were a welcome confirmation of the strength of the basic BMW engineering.

They now cheerfully set about readying a more powerful version for production. The main alterations included a cylinder head with bigger ports and valves, plus hotter camshaft profiles. The four main bearings were widened to handle the additional stress loads, and counterweighting was revised. With no change in compression ratio, this work raised output to an even 100 bhp at 5250 rpm. These and a few other modifications, such as Alfin brake drums and telescopic shock absorbers, turned the 401 into the Type 403, released in June 1953. Production was precisely 300 units through 1955. (There was also a 402, a convertible version of the 401, but it was not exactly a series production model. Only 24 were built from 1949 to '51.)

Bristol's next entry was the 404, a short-wheelbase (96-inch) coupe introduced in October

1953. Though it was devoid of any BMW hallmarks outside, its heart was pure German. Packing 105 bhp, it was fairly quick, with a top speed of 109 mph and accelerative reserves capable of 0-100 km/h (62 mph) in 16 seconds. The 404 was another scarce commodity, a mere 40 examples being completed through 1956.

Though they were few in number, Bristols began attracting attention on the other side of the Atlantic. One particularly interested party was S. H. "Wacky" Arnolt, a Chicago industrialist who had built his fortune as a supplier of marine engines during the war. Arnolt liked cars and operated one of the largest import dealerships in the Midwest. While visiting the 1952 Turin auto show, he spied a nice-looking body design from the house of Bertone and decided to order 100 copies for sale at his Windy City showroom. He went to MG for the mechanicals, and called the final product the Arnolt-MG. Though it looked nice, "Wacky's" car was predictably expensive ($3195), and with the anemic MG four it went nowhere fast. To Arnolt's disappointment, only 65 of these cars were completed.

Then he found out about the BMW-based 2.0-liter Bristol six. It seemed to be the answer to his first car's lack of poke, and he wasted little time in again contacting Bertone for suitable bodywork. The result was the Arnolt-Bristol, one of the most stunning cars of the period. The styling was the work of Franco Scaglione, a young artist with a scientific turn of mind, who managed to overcome quite successfully the aesthetic problems posed by the tall BMW/Bristol engine. The chassis came from England, being the short-wheelbase 404 platform. There were three distinct models. The Bolide, originally priced at $3995 (later $4250), was a topless roadster for sunny-days motoring or race work. The Deluxe, first $4765 and later

$4995, had a top, but didn't look quite as nice. There was also a closed coupe, with roll-up windows and a more civilized interior, offered at $5995.

With its stout engine having to move only about 2100 pounds, the Arnolt-Bristol ran like the wind. Typical performance figures were 8.7 seconds for the 0-60 mph dash, a standing-start quarter-mile of 17 seconds at 82 mph, and a top speed of 110 mph. The cars seemed born to race, and race they did. Arnolt himself entered three cars at the Sebring 12 Hours of Endurance in 1955 and again in '56, and they finished 1-2-4 in the 2.0-liter production category in both years. Interestingly, they ran in unmodified form, proving how close the Arnolt-Bristol was to the dual-purpose sports car ideal. "Wacky" made another bid in the 1957 event but, alas, it proved one race too many. One driver, blinded by the setting sun, rolled his A-B and was killed instantly. Arnolt blamed himself, and never raced his cars again.

The Arnolt-Bristols, like their British relatives, were quite rare. Only 142 were built altogether, and 12 were unfortunately lost in a warehouse fire. Of the 130 actually sold, only three were coupes. The rarest of the roadsters were those with aluminum bodies and large fuel tanks, modifications aimed at long-haul racing.

Back in Britain, Bristol was spinning off model variants with almost the same ease BMW had shown before the war. Appearing in 1954 was the Type 405, Bristol's first sedan. It was essentially a 404 coupe with an elongated 114-inch wheelbase and two extra doors. Power was supplied by the 105-bhp engine found in the 404 and the Arnolt-Bristol. Production totalled 340 units through 1958, plus an additional 43 chassis fitted with custom convertible bodywork by Abbott.

The last hurrah for BMW's 2.0-liter engine came with the

last of the six-cylinder Bristols. This was the Type 406, which arrived in 1958 as a square-cut four-seat coupe. It was continued through 1961 and production of 300 units. That year, Bristol Aeroplane Company sold its car division to T. A. D. "Tony" Crook and got out of the auto engine business completely. Crook would continue Bristol cars but not their BMW power, switching instead to the Chrysler-built V-8s that have been used in all subsequent models right up to the present.

While it was left to Bristol and Frazer Nash to preserve the great heritage of BMW's prewar engineering, the point needs to be made that the original 2.0-liter six was really good enough to last some 25 years. Despite the complexity of its unusual valve-train, this smooth, efficient motor with its hemispherical-head design seemed almost as advanced in the postwar world as it had been in the prewar era, surely a fitting tribute to the genius of its creators.

And that genius is something BMW never really lost. Even as the amputee struggled to survive in the aftermath of the war that had injured it, many of the talents that had brought BMW to greatness in the prewar years were still around, still with much to contribute. Indeed, the firm would have to have the likes of Fiedler, Von Falkenhausen, Loof and others if it was ever to recover from its near-fatal wounds. Equally important would be the new, younger generation of designers, engineers, and managers then entering the business world, for without a doubt the company's long-term future would depend on them.

BMW had survived. Now it was time for starting over. It was an entirely different company that began building cars in the early Fifties, one with little more than a vision plus a relative handful of creative, determined people. But, as history would prove, that would be quite enough.

# POSTWAR PANACHE: BAROQUE ANGELS, TIMELESS SPORTS' CARS

As the Forties drew to a close, one thing was uppermost in the minds of BMW's leaders: a return to car production. No one, including company president Kurt Donath, underestimated the difficulties, however, for BMW faced a situation symbolic of postwar Germany itself. It was now a company divided, its former automotive facilities irrevocably inaccessible within the borders of what was now East Germany (Deutsche Demokratische Republik). What facilities remained in the new state of West Germany (Deutsche Bundesrepublik) were in ruins, the result of the Allied bombing raids that ended forever Hitler's dream of a thousand-year Reich. BMW's prewar body supplier, Ambi-Budd of Berlin, was lost as well. As everywhere else in the land, rebuilding efforts were difficult and painfully halting. Worse, under Allied Control Commission edict the firm was barred from building aircraft engines, once the very foundation of its business. And, as noted in the previous chapter, it took considerable effort just to resume motorcycle production. With the future clouded by the political and economic uncertainties inherent in the new order, BMW's return to automaking was not so much a question of when but if.

Donath surveyed the situation with a pragmatic, if sometimes ambivalent, attitude. For him, it was essential to build up BMW's manufacturing capacity as the

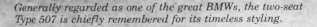

*Generally regarded as one of the great BMWs, the two-seat Type 507 is chiefly remembered for its timeless styling.*

85

literal first order of business, which meant turning out any sort of product for which there was a demand. That included motorcycles, of course, as well as utility vehicles, which were in very short supply at the time. It was the only way BMW could begin its long journey back.

As ever, Donath was looking for a shortcut. In 1948 he went to Ford Motor Company in Dearborn, where he proposed building Ford trucks, with a certain number of American-made components, at BMW's Milbertshofen plant. Ford officials considered the idea, but it conflicted with their plans for truck production at the company's own subsidiary in Neuss near Cologne. Donath was undeterred. Next, he went to Paris for a meeting with Henri-Theodore Pigozzi, chief of the *Societe Industrielle de Mecanique et Carrosserie Automobile* in Nanterre, which built cars under license from Fiat with the Simca name (an acronym of the full company title). At the time, the French had a mildly modified version of the Fiat 508C "Balilla," the Simca 8. Donath knew the firm was preparing an all-new model, the Aronde, to replace it, and offered to buy not only the production rights to the old car but also the press stamping tools for its body panels. Pigozzi countered that he would gladly sell the design but not the tooling. That effectively constituted a refusal for, without means for building the body, BMW had little use for the Simca 8. Donath returned to Munich, the problem now weighing on him more than ever.

While the boss was out looking for foreign models to build under license, BMW's engineering staff under Alfred Böning was studying an alternative: a car powered by a motorcycle engine that the firm was already producing. The feasibility of using this 750cc air-cooled flat twin for powering a four-wheeler had already been explored to some extent in Italy, where Berardo Taraschi, a motorcycle racer

with a workshop in Teramo, had built just such a car in 1947. He obtained the engines, complete with motorcycle gearboxes, from war-surplus auctions. Called the Urania, this machine was built up on a modern tubular steel frame and had lightweight sports roadster bodywork with aluminum panels. Its independent front suspension and rear axle were Fiat parts, purchased from junkyards.

But Böning had something else in mind: a small economy car. A prototype was duly constructed under the Type 331 designation, and it looked promising. It was powered by the

600cc engine from the R-51 motorcycle, hooked to a four-speed gearbox, and used a simple live-axle rear suspension. Peter Schimanowski designed a lovely coupe body for the prototype that was reminiscent of the 327 but shrunk to Fiat Topolino proportions. There is no doubt that the 331 would have found a ready market in the fuel-short Europe of the early postwar era. More importantly, it was within BMW's production capabilities. The body could be farmed out to one of the surviving coachwork firms, and an assembly line could easily be rigged up at Milbertshofen. But

*Opposite page, top: The prototype for the aborted Type 331 minicar from 1950. Bottom: Pinin Farina's proposal for the new 501. This page, above: The production Type 501 sedan of 1951. Left: 501 pre-production styling mockup.*

it was not to be. The project was killed by Hanns Grewenig, the banker turned sales director, who told the management board that it would be a mistake for BMW to return to the economy-car segment.

Grewenig had been installed as sales director by the bankers acting on behalf of BMW's receivers, but he was not without auto industry experience. He had been a plant manager for Opel in 1936, and became a member of that firm's board of directors three years later. Opel, of course, was part of General Motors by then and therefore a high-volume producer, so Grewenig's

experience there had little to do with his insistence that BMW concentrate on prestige models. Rather, it reflected his personal view of what BMW's cars ought to be, a view not unlike that of Franz Josef Popp. Grewenig definitely wanted high-class BMWs—powerful, well-built, superbly engineered machines that, by definition, would be restricted to a fortunate few.

Accordingly, Böning and his staff embarked on a new luxury model that ultimately became the first postwar production BMW, the Type 501. This large four-door sedan was powered by what was effectively an update of the prewar Type 326 engine, but was wrapped up in full envelope bodywork created by Schimanowski. The bulging, florid lines were reminiscent of the 326 and 335 "without exactly picking up where [they] left off," as Halwart Schrader described it. The main styling elements were a sweeping front fenderline that arced down through the

center-opening doors to terminate at the rear fenders, a rounded rear deck, a prewar-style vee'd hood, the familiar twin-kidney nose, headlamps nestled in vestigial "catwalks" between hood and front fenders, a one-piece windshield, and a rounded greenhouse with three windows per side. Grewenig apparently didn't like the styling, because he suggested that Donath ought to seek the services of Italy's Pinin Farina. A chassis was sent to the famous Turin coachbuilder, and returned to Munich with what amounted to only a facelifted version of the basic bodyshell already drawn up for the Alfa Romeo 1900 sedan. Rather than offer a "me too" car, BMW decided to stick with the Schimanowski design that, ironically enough, Farina himself later praised. Though the 501 was certainly distinctive and its curvy lines graceful, it was something of a throwback aesthetically, which may be why it soon acquired the nickname "Baroque Angel."

Appropriately for a "fresh start" product, the 501 was almost completely new from road to roof. Its chassis was a new perimeter type created by Böning, with box-section side members and four large-diameter tubular crossmembers. A narrow cradle for the engine and transmission extended from the mid-wheelbase crossmember to the front crossmember ahead of the front wheels. A steel floorpan was welded to the frame. The front suspension consisted of A-frame upper and lower control arms with a narrow base, assembled from straight, separate rods and anchored in rubber bushings at both ends. The lower control arm pivot shaft took the form of a longitudinal torsion bar, while the upper control arm was linked to a vane-type hydraulic shock absorber. The steering gear was absolutely unique, with a pinion on the lower end of the shaft meshing with half a crown wheel. You could describe this as segment-and-pinion or a rack-and-pinion setup with a semi-circular rack. The crown wheel segment was mounted on a vertical shaft that swung the Pitman arms, which were mounted on splines, from its lower end. The linkage included an idler arm, anchored in the frame. One Pitman arm was directly connected to the left wheel steering arm, while the other pulled or pushed a transverse tie bar linked to the right wheel steering arm. The rear suspension comprised a live axle with radius rods, laid out in a triangle extending from a bracket on the differential casing, and long longitudinal torsion bars that extended forward to the second crossmember just aft of the front wheel arches. Telescopic shock absorbers were mounted vertically, close to the wheel hubs. Ate (Alfred Teves GmbH) supplied the brakes, which had twin leading shoes in front and a total lining area of 147 square inches. Tire size was 5.50-16.

With its 111.6-inch wheelbase, the 501 chassis had the length to support the spacious sedan body. Nowadays the car looks a little high and chubby (overall width was 70 inches), but the proportions were certainly up to date for 1951. Though the frame was heavy, it had great rigidity, but the all-steel body exceeded Schimanowski's calculated weight by a considerable margin. As a result, the 501 carried a dry weight of 3153 pounds, which was a bit much for the 2.0-liter 65-bhp (DIN) six. The power-to-weight ratio worked out to a plainly dull 48.5 lbs/bhp, and it's obvious the 501 could have used more muscle. But BMW still had all the drawings for the 2.0-liter engine and it needed no development for production, so its application here was obviously another Donath shortcut.

Nevertheless, BMW managed several new refinements for its trusty six. The combustion chamber shape was reworked to permit knock-free operation on the low-octane gasoline then common in Europe (6.8:1 compression) and there was a new Solex carburetor with a two-position starting device. A new inlet manifold included an exhaust-heated hot spot with thermostatic control, and an oil/water heat exchanger was mounted on the right side of the block to speed oil warmup on cold days and to stabilize oil temperature during high-speed driving. Also, a reinforced crankshaft with bigger bearing journals was adopted and fitted with modern tri-metal bearing shells.

The 501 gearbox was a four-speed all-synchromesh ZF unit (S4.17). Unusually, it was mounted separately from the engine, under the front seat between the second and third crossmembers. A one-piece open propshaft took power to the rear axle, which had a final drive ratio of 4.225:1. Gearbox ratios were direct drive (1.00:1) on top, 1.45 on third, 2.35 on second, and 4.24 on first. In keeping with the fashion of the day, the gearlever was mounted on the steering column.

As you might expect, the 501's performance was sedate at best.

88

Top speed was only 84 mph, and the car needed a lengthy 27 seconds for the 0-100 km/h (62 mph) acceleration run. By contrast, the contemporary Mercedes-Benz 220, the closest German rival to the 501 in size, capacity and price, could reach 87.5 mph and hit 100 km/h from standstill in a more acceptable

21 seconds. Yet despite its sluggish off-the-line acceleration, the 501 did surprisingly well in competition. Though it lacked raw horsepower it did have a very capable chassis, which enabled the big sedans to maintain impressively high average speeds. As proof, Ernst Loof drove one in a 1953 production-

car race at the demanding Nürburgring to win the 2.0-liter class outright. He also posted the quickest lap times for all sedans in the contest, most of which had far larger and more potent powerplants. That same year, he drove a 501 in the *Tour de Belgique,* running against a field of 162 entries over a 764-mile road course. He finished an easy first in class.

Publicly unveiled at the Frankfurt auto show in April 1951, the 501 didn't start reaching customers until well over a year later. The main problem was body production. Donath and general manager Kurt Deby had decided BMW should have its own stamping, welding, and body assembly plant. Bodies on the initial 2045 cars were made by Karosseriewerk Baur, which at least enabled production to begin on a small scale while the new body facility was being equipped. Thanks to an infusion of Marshall Plan funds, BMW was able to purchase two big new Clearing presses, capable of stamping the roof as a single piece. Other tools and dies were ordered from Weingarten, but there were long delivery delays and the 1000th car wouldn't be

*Opposite page, top: The 501's torsion-bar live-axle rear suspension was new to BMW. Bottom: A 501 hardtop from 1953 with body by Autenrieth. It saw very limited production. This page, left: The 2.0-liter Type 501 six ready for installation. It was basically a carryover of the prewar engine. Below: Autenrieth's 501 coupe prototype had close-coupled two-passenger seating and fixed B-pillars. Note flat-top wheel arches.*

built until September 1, 1953. To keep manufacturing costs and complexity as low as possible, only a single paint color was available: black. Henry Ford would have surely approved.

Holding the line on costs was critical for BMW in these years. Quite simply, the firm was shaky, with too few sales and too little money. In May 1951 its capital stock had been written down, with three new shares being issued for every 10 old ones. Motorcycle sales had reached a plateau, and the Type 501, despite its generally favorable reception, had yet to turn a significant profit. Production delays were one reason, but the car's deliberately low volume and high price—fully 15,000 of the new deutsche marks—were probably more important factors. Competition was heating up, too: Daimler-Benz, Opel, Ford, DKW, and Borgward had all returned to the market by this time with attractive new postwar models. Finally, along with most everyone else, BMW was socked with sudden price increases for basic raw materials, including steel. As the decade wore on, it became increasingly clear that the road back to full fiscal health was going to be a rocky one indeed.

But there was one bright spot: the return of Fritz Fiedler. As noted in the previous chapter, he had been given a leave of absence to work with Bristol and Frazer Nash in England. Once he had finished these projects, he returned to Germany and ended up at Opel for a short time. But his loyalties remained with BMW, where there seemed to be more creative opportunities than anywhere else. There was certainly much to do in Munich, and BMW needed Fiedler's considerable skills in the worst way. By 1952 he had rejoined the company as chief of automotive research, engineering, and development. Böning continued as head of the drawing office.

Even before the first prototype had turned a wheel, Böning

knew from his calculations that the 501 would be underpowered. He also knew that customers in the high-end market where BMW was attempting to reestablish itself wouldn't put up with this for long. With approval from sales boss Grewenig, he started work on a new engine with greater performance potential than the venerable 2.0-liter six and intended, eventually, to slot in under the 501's hood. Unusually enough, it was a V-8. At the time, the only other European cars with V-8 power were the French Ford Vedette and the little-known Tatra, made in Czechoslovakia. The Vedette had originated in Dearborn's "Light Car," a project begun during the war that would have produced a new compact Ford on a 106-inch wheelbase for 1949. The program progressed all the way to a fully developed production prototype, only to be shelved at the last minute. Maurice Dollfus, president of Ford France, saw it as a way to get his operations going again, however. Eventually he convinced the parent company to ship all blueprints and the prototype to his factory at Poissy, where the Vedette started coming off the lines in late 1948. Predictably, it used a metric derivative of the smaller Ford flathead engine familiar since the Thirties, the V-8/60. Though this gave the Vedette a certain distinction, the car was

*Above: A 502-chassis Autenrieth cabriolet from 1954, styled by the firm's chief designer, Franz Trüby. Only a few of these were built. Right: Painted 501 bodies on the way to the Milbertshofen assembly line, 1954. Lower right: A 1955 example of Baur cabriolet coachwork on the Type 502 chassis.*

not a sales hit. High fuel consumption and dumpy looks were the main problems. The Tatra, created by noted Czech engineer Hans Ledwinka, was something else: a large four-door fastback sedan with an air-cooled V-8 mounted at the rear, very much like the ill-starred American-made Tucker in concept. But it was built only in tiny numbers, mainly for government officials, and as an Eastern bloc commodity it had little impact in the West.

On his return to BMW, Fiedler took charge of finalizing Böning's V-8, which in its basic layout was surprisingly close to Oldsmobile's 303-cid Rocket V-8, introduced in 1949. The cylinder banks were disposed at a 90-degree angle, with a five-bearing crankshaft driving a single camshaft positioned directly above it by duplex chain. The crossflow cylinder heads had overhead valves operated by pushrods and rocker arms. The valves were tilted at 12 degrees relative to the cylinder axes, creating wedge-shape combustion chambers, with the spark plugs at the "roomy" ends. The cylinder

banks were offset slightly to one another, with the bore centers about 20mm (0.78 in.) apart so as to line up the connecting rods correctly for side-by-side mounting as a pair on the same crankpin. The most obvious difference from the Olds unit was in the BMW's materials: a light-alloy block with cast-iron wet liners.

Heads were also light-alloy castings. The block was split on the crankshaft centerline, and main bearing caps were cast iron. Each cylinder liner had a deep flange at the upper end to locate it securely in the block, protruding above the deck so as to provide a firm fire seal between the head gasket and the head it-

self. At the bottom end the liner was a tight press fit, scaled by two rubber O-rings. The two-plane crankshaft was a high-tensile steel forging, machined throughout and boasting six counterweights. Connecting rods were stamped and coined steel forgings, split on the horizontal centerline, with caps attached by two bolts and castellated nuts.

Because of prevailing fuel prices and vehicle taxes, BMW's V-8 was much smaller than the Olds unit. Slightly undersquare bore and stroke dimensions of 74mm (2.91 in.) by 75mm (2.95 in.) were selected, giving swept volume of 2580cc (157.4 cid). On 7.0:1 compression and fitted with a two-barrel downdraft Solex carburetor, the result was a rated 100 bhp (DIN) at 4800 rpm, a useful 35-bhp gain over the Type 501 six. Unfortunately, production problems and BMW's continuing cash shortage forced repeated postponements, and it

wasn't until the Geneva show in March 1954 that the new engine was formally announced.

Not surprisingly, it showed up in a better-equipped Baroque Angel designated the Type 502, a number originally intended for a factory-built V-8 coupe that never materialized. Aside from its engine, the 502 was identical with its six-cylinder linemate except for a "V-8" emblem on the trunklid, longitudinal chrome moldings just below the beltline, and foglamps mounted in the forward portions of the front fenders. List price was 17,800 marks, quite a lofty figure at the time despite a steadily improving national economy, and only 190 units were sold the first year.

Alongside the 502, BMW presented two variations of the 501 in an attempt to boost sales. Designated the 501A and 501B, they were powered by an improved version of the 1971cc six with an additional seven DIN horsepower, bringing the total to 72 bhp at 4400 rpm. Though

basically the same as the first-series 501 in trim and equipment, the A boasted a lower price, now 14,180 marks, while the B was a simplified offering tagged at 12,680 marks. Partly on the strength of these more attractive prices, BMW car production more than doubled in 1954, reaching 3600 units.

Further variations of the Baroque Angel were not long in coming as BMW returned to its prewar practice of offering several different powerplants and/or engine tuning variations in a single basic body/chassis platform. In the spring of 1955 a detuned version of the 2.6-liter engine became available in what was named the 501 V-8. At the same time, the trusty six was enlarged to 2077cc (127 cid) via a 2mm bore increase to 68mm (2.68 in.), and also got tighter 7.0:1 compression. Though power output was unaffected, peak torque improved from 88 to 94 lbs/ft, both developed at 2500 rpm. The 2.0-liter six was continued in this form through 1958

for the 501/3, also called the 501 *Sechszylinder*. After this model, all the Angels would have the V-8.

Limited resources didn't allow BMW itself to build any body styles other than sedans. However, two of the firm's long-time body suppliers, Autenrieth of Darmstadt and Baur of Stuttgart, were back in business by the mid-Fifties, and began turning out a number of Angels in two-door coupe and convertible form to special order. In the main, these were all four-passenger cars with shorter greenhouses and consequently more closely coupled seating. Styling was generally the same as for the sedans below the beltline, although the Autenrieth bodies were a bit more modern in detail, boasting contemporary touches like squared wheel arches, lower hoods, slightly raked grilles, and even modestly wrapped windshields.

The next step in the Baroque Angel's evolution arrived at the 1955 Frankfurt show in the form

*Opposite page: Front foglamps nestled in the fenders marked the V-8-engine Type 502. This is a 1955 four-seat cabriolet, probably by Baur. This page: A 1956 convertible by Baur shows a neater folded top than the "bustled" car on the facing page.*

of a larger V-8. Bore was increased again, this time by 8mm to 82mm (3.23 in.), which boosted capacity to 3168cc (193.2 cid). Power went up as well, to 120 bhp (DIN) at 4800 rpm, thanks´to a higher 7.2:1 compression ratio and a switch to a Zenith carburetor with larger 32mm (1.26-in.) throat diameter, versus the 30mm (1.18-in.) venturi of the 2.6-liter engine's Solex instrument. This new version of the big sedan was simply called the BMW 3.2, and it was predictably quicker. The torquier (141 lbs/ft) V-8 shaved a full 2.5 seconds off the 0-100 km/h time, which was now 15 seconds flat, and allowed a longer-striding 3.89:1 final drive ratio that partially cancelled out the expected mileage penalty of the larger displacement. Average fuel consumption was around 15.6 mpg, versus 16.2 for the 2.6-liter model. An even more powerful version, the 3.2 Super, arrived in 1957, offering 140 bhp (DIN) at 4800 rpm and a 5-mph gain in top speed, to 110 mph. Both

these models and their smaller-displacement sibling, called the BMW 2.6 from 1958 on, continued through 1961 with few alterations. Two notable exceptions were the arrival of optional power steering in late 1959, followed by front disc brakes in 1960 (standard on the Super beginning in October 1959).

Through all these permutations, BMW remained faithful to column-shift control for the standard four-speed manual transmission despite the complex linkage required by the gearbox's remote mounting. The V-8 cars had a shorter first gear ratio (3.78:1) for better snap off the line. Their steering was also geared up a bit to keep steering effort about the same as with the lighter six. Turns lock-to-lock were 3.5 instead of 3.0, though that was still pretty quick for a big sedan. The steering itself was quite pleasant, so there were few demands for power assist, which explains why it appeared so late in the Angel's life. The early manual brakes on the

other hand (or should we say foot?) required a hefty shove, leading many buyers to complain. BMW responded, and stole a march on the rest of the German industry by being the first company to combine power assist (vacuum boost) with discs.

By the start of the Sixties, the Angels seemed more Rococco than Baroque, at least in appearance. A few years earlier, the firm had entered the economy-car field with the tiny Isetta "rolling egg" and the more conventional 700 (see next chapter), both of which were far more important than the Angels in keeping the company afloat. Though BMW still had no entry in the all-important mid-price market, the big four-doors continued to fill a definite if increasingly costly need at the upper end of the spectrum. The final versions, renamed the 2600 and 3200, appeared in 1961. There were two trim levels for each, standard and L (Luxus) with the smaller V-8, L and S (Super) with the larger. Styling had changed little since 1951, though the body had acquired a larger rear window and more chrome trim along the way. The standard 2600 offered 100 bhp (DIN) and a top speed of slightly better than the magic "ton"; the L boasted 10 more horses and a top end of around 103 mph; the 3200L had 140 bhp and could see 109 mph. All three of these had single-carburetor engines. The 3200S, reputed to be Germany's fastest production sedan at the time, employed twin Zenith carbs, which boosted power output to 160 bhp (DIN) at 5600 rpm, good for a top speed of close to 120 mph. Despite the addition of more standard features over the years, plus inflationary pressures from Germany's now-healthy economy, prices were remarkably little different from what they'd been in 1955, ranging from 16,240 marks for the base 2600 to 21,240 for the 3200S.

The final Baroque Angels were produced in 1963, thus closing a special chapter in

*Above: Shortly after their debut at the 1955 Frankfurt show, the sporty 507 and 503 were the stars of the BMW stand at the Turin Salon in the spring of 1956. Right and opposite page top and center: The two-seat 507 remains a good-looker from any angle. Opposite bottom: The four-seat 503 seems plain by comparison.*

BMW history. Despite their unfashionably voluptuous bodywork, they were significant as a bridge between BMW's pre- and postwar design practice. The early six-cylinder versions may have been short on straightline performance but were quite capable over the road, and the later 3.2-liter V-8 cars were decently quick. All were solid and well-built in the German manner, genuine *grand luxe* tourers able to transport five people in splendid comfort on long journeys. They reaffirmed BMW's eminence in the prestige market, and they sold tolerably well, though not well enough to overcome the firm's many handicaps in these years. Some 8900 of the six-cylinder models were built through 1958. The V-8s sold even better, with nearly 13,000 completed in 1954-63. The rarest of the breed have the 3.2-liter Super V-8: just 1328 were so equipped. Nowadays, BMW fanciers don't look on the Angels with much affection, but they were good cars and served the company well. They deserve to be remembered.

With the restoration of both car and motorcycle production, a return to the aircraft engine business was all that remained to complete BMW's prewar manufacturing triumvirate. In 1955, the Allies lifted their ban on aviation activity in Germany, and this paved the way for BMW to begin organizing the postwar equivalent of its former Flugmotorenbau division. This duly appeared as BMW Triebwerkbau, which was headquartered in the Allach plant that the firm had recently retrieved from U.S. authorities. Steps were also taken to recover

ager Hanns Grewenig, who wanted a broader, more varied product line for his dealers. That included a sports car based on the 502 chassis. But though he brought up the idea several times, it was repeatedly vetoed by the sober and realistic Kurt Donath, who sensed that things weren't going quite as well as Grewenig liked to think. Yet the notion seemed almost irresistible. With its lightweight V-8 engine and capable chassis, the 502 did indeed appear to have all the essentials for a modern, high-performance machine in the great tradition of the prewar 327 and 328. Grewenig instinctively knew the way, if only Donath had the will.

Oddly enough, it was BMW's perennial rival in Swabia that may have tipped the scales in favor of Grewenig's proposal. Daimler-Benz had campaigned a team of sleek coupes in international endurance events during 1952, reaping immeasurable benefits in free publicity and enhanced corporate prestige. Now it was about to launch a road-going derivative, a superbly designed supercar for the super rich, with unusual "gullwing" doors and a lusty 3.0-liter ohc six. When it was displayed in prototype form at the 1954 New York Auto Show, the new 300SL caused a quiet riot, and its impact was certainly not lost on BMW management. Here, conceivably was an example the Munich company might profitably emulate, on its own scale and in its own idiom.

The 300SL was one of the first European cars built with an eye to the U.S. market, and the decision to produce it was undoubtedly influenced heavily by Max Hoffman. A Rolls-Royce and Bentley dealer during the Thirties in his native Austria, Hoffman had emigrated to America, where he set up a plastics factory in 1941. The business prospered during the war and Hoffman became very rich. When peace returned, he decided to get back into the import-car busi-

de facto ownership of the former Bramo plant at Spandau, to which BMW still held title. This facility would be given over to motorcycle parts, and eventually all of BMW's motorcycle operations would be transferred there. Allach resumed production with the General Electric J-79 turbojet engine, built under license for the Lockheed F-104G Super Starfighter aircraft. Be-

fore long, BMW added a line of Lycoming industrial gas turbines, and also developed small gas turbines of its own design under the direction of a young engineer named Hans Hagen. BMW was beginning to look like an industrial powerhouse again.

Despite the slow buildup of car production, some members of the management board were feeling euphoric. One was sales man-

Top: A contemporary BMW publicity photo shows the handsome 507 posed in a fake concours d'elegance setting. The lady is not identified. Above: Like the 507, the companion 503 was styled by talented industrial designer Albrecht Goertz. He later did several designs for Nissan, including the original 240-Z of 1969-70.

ness, and from his fashionable showroom in New York City he quickly built an empire that stretched from coast to coast. In its heyday it owned the distribution rights for, or had some hand in selling, virtually every major foreign make that ever landed in the U.S. Needless to say, the size of his business gave Hoffman considerable clout, which he used as the instigator of new models like the 300SL and the later 190SL, D-B's sports car for the "masses."

Significantly, Hoffman was an astute market analyst who just happened to love BMWs. He had raced BMW motorcycles in his younger days, and had come to respect the firm for its engineering ability and high-quality craftsmanship. Looking at the two-seat sporting cars then available in America, he spotted a gap that BMW might be able to fill. Basically, it was the big hole between the 300SL, which he considered too "rich" and rare for middle-class Yankees, and lower-priced British roadsters like the MG TD and Triumph TR2, which he thought too anemic and crude. As for the several Detroit sports cars then on the market, especially Chevrolet's Corvette, he dismissed them all as pretenders, deficient in performance, handling, styling, and quality. What he thought buyers would really go for was a true sports car combining svelte looks

with Teutonic solidity, plus the one feature any American could relate to: a V-8. Of course, he knew BMW already had such a car, cleverly disguised as the 502 sedan. All it needed was an appropriately beautiful body—the same formula, incidentally, that would lead to the 190SL.

Back in Munich, Grewenig ultimately carried the day, and in early 1954 he got the BMW management board to approve his sports car idea in principle—shrewdly, while Donath was laid up in the hospital. When the president returned and learned what had happened, he expressed his displeasure but made no move to halt the project. Overall design responsibility was handed to Fritz Fiedler, who was instructed to use existing components as much as possible without compromising looks or roadability. But now he had to come up with two cars, not one: a four-seat coupe/convertible, designated Type 503, and a companion two-seater, the Type 507.

Fiedler began logically with the chassis. He designed a new, lightweight structure with box-section side members spaced to the fullest practical width. These were connected via three large-diameter tubular crossmembers: one below the radiator, one at mid-wheelbase, and one just ahead of the rear axle. The 503 would use the 111.6-inch wheelbase of the 501/502 sedans, as well as their separately mounted transmission and front subframe under the engine. For the 507, wheelbase was shortened to 97.6 inches and the gearbox was moved up to the clutch bellhousing. While the 503 inherited the sedans' column shift linkage, the 507 was given a new floor-shift selector. Both models were fitted with 16-inch wheels, which increased tire rolling radius compared to the sedans. This amounted to numerically lower overall gearing, so final drive ratios were adjusted to compensate. The 503 had a standard 3.90:1 gearset, and a
*continued on page 113*

Had WWII not intervened, this Touring-bodied roadster might have been BMW's next Mille Miglia competitor. Style is similar to that of the actual 1940 competition cars based on the 328.

BMW returned to automaking in the postwar era with a series of luxury sedans that earned the nickname of "Baroque Angels" due to their flowing body contours. Above: The V-8 Type 502 was produced from 1954 to '61. Shown is a rare cabriolet variant with coachwork by Bauer. Near right: A 1955 example of the standard Type 502 sedan. Power was supplied by a 2.6-liter all-aluminum V-8 with 100 bhp (DIN). Production of this model was 5955. Far right: Another special body on the 502 chassis, this time a coupe by the Autenrieth works of Darmstadt. The first of the "Angels" was the Type 501, which appeared in 1952 and continued through 1955, powered by what was essentially BMW's prewar hemi-head 2.0-liter six.

A curiosity of BMW's postwar history was the Isetta bubblecar, built under license from ISO in Italy. Several variations on this basic design were offered from 1955, all with the unique "front door" that lifted the steering wheel/column up and forward for entry/exit. The red example is the initial 1955-57 version with triangular side windows. The blue car illustrates the facelifted design introduced in late 1956. All the two-passenger models were powered by single-cylinder engines of either 250cc or 300cc. An export version with a single rear wheel was also built.

A pristine example of the lovely Type 507 two-seater, photographed in Colorado Springs in 1983. Built on a shortened 501/502 sedan chassis, the 507 employed a tuned version of BMW's 3.2-liter all-aluminum V-8 with 150 bhp (DIN). Created partly at the behest of U.S. importer Max Hoffman, it was styled by Count Albrecht Goertz, with lines that remain arresting even after nearly three decades. Only some 250 cars were completed, all prime collectibles today.

Originally slated to sell for around $5000, the 507 came to the U.S. in 1956 with a $9000 price tag. This, plus delivery delays and BMW's limited production capacity, stunted the high sales potential of this masterful machine. Besides its styling, the 507 remains surprisingly modern in its cockpit design, general roadability, and performance.

An outgrowth of BMW's experience with the Isetta was the rear-engine Type 700, which debuted in late 1959. Shown here a 1960 example of the short-roof Coupe model. A more conventional two-door sedan was also offered. A true economy car, the 700 was powered by a 700cc air-cooled flat twin. Styling was the work of Michelotti in Italy, and its clean simplicity was matched by the basic interior furnishings. Production was 79,599 units through 1964. With 30-32 bhp (DIN), top speed was in the region of 75 mph.

Replacing the Type 700 sedan in 1962 was the 700LS, mainly a more luxurious version of this minicar design with a 6.3-inch longer wheelbase. More than 93,000 were built through 1965. A Coupe version with a twin-carb 40-bhp engine was also available on the longer chassis, but only 1730 of these were built. The extra wheelbase length in these models was given over mainly to extra rear seat space. As with the earlier 700s, the air-cooled flat twin was a four-stroke design, not a two-stroke as on rival DKWs of these years.

Another member of the Type 700 family was the 40-bhp Sport, appearing in Coupe form only in 1960. An open version with bodywork by Bauer arrived later. Shown here is the 1963 model, which was renamed CS that year. Though the hotter flat twin later found its way into the 700LS models, the Sport/CS was unique in having a rear anti-roll bar for more balanced handling. Like all 700s, suspension was by means of front leading arms and rear semi-trailing arms plus coil springs all-round. Production ended in 1964.

111

*Above: The 1966 BMW Glas 3000 coupe with ohc V-8 and styling by Frua of Italy. Below: The 1963 edition of the important 1500 "New Class" sedan.*

continued from page 96

3.42:1 axle was optional. The 507 was geared at 3.70:1 in standard form, but both 503 ratios were offered optionally. Gearbox ratios followed a similar pattern. A close-ratio set was adopted for the 507, with a 1.36 third, 2.07 second, and 3.39:1 first. The direct-drive top gear gave 2900 rpm at 100 km/h (62 mph). Standard gearing on the 503 was 1.39 on third, 2.35 on second, and 3.78:1 on first. An optional "sports" setup offered a faster first and a closer second and third.

The front suspension on both the new sports cars was a modified version of the 501/502 layout. Rear geometry on the 503 was also lifted from the sedans, but the 507 had a different arrangement. This comprised a ball mount on the rear axle attached to both leading and trailing arms, giving more precise fore/aft axle location and better absorption of torque reactions, plus a Panhard rod for lateral location. Longitudinal torsion bars were retained with a modified linkage, and adjustable Koni shock absorbers were fitted front and rear. The steering gear on both models was taken straight from the 502. The two-seater boasted the luxury of a telescoping steering column, which enabled the driver to adjust reach independently of the relationship between seat and pedals. Brakes were also similar to those of the 502, initially the all-drum system adopted with the 3.2 V-8 in 1955, plus vacuum assist. Front discs from the contemporary BMW 3.2 Super were specified for the two-seater beginning in 1958 but, curiously, were not extended to the 503.

There was no question about the powerplant. It would be the 3.2-liter enlargement of BMW's alloy V-8. The new sports cars got two carbs instead of one, however, still Zenith 32 NDIX. Because of their greater power and consequent need for greater oil flow, engines in both had a conventional oil pump driven by

a roller chain from the crankshaft, but there were differences in other specifications. The 503 ran on 7.5:1 compression, good for 140 bhp (DIN) at 4800 rpm. The 507 unit had a high-lift camshaft, polished combustion chamber surfaces, a different spark advance curve, and 7.8:1 compression, all of which yielded 150 bhp at 5000 rpm. The first 507s were equipped with welded-up aluminum fuel tanks holding 29 gallons. This left no space for luggage when the spare wheel was carried in the trunk, so a smaller 17.5-gallon tank was soon adopted. This was shaped to fit around the spare, thus freeing up extra space.

The new sports cars went from concept to finished reality in the unusually short time of just 18 months, bowing at the Frankfurt auto show alongside BMW's uprated 3.2-liter sedans in September 1955. This rapid completion was due in part to young Count Albrecht "Graf" Goertz, a German-born industrial designer who won the styling assignment for both models. Goertz had worked almost all his adult life, showing little aptitude for academic studies in his school-age years. After emigrating to America in 1936, he got a job as an assembly line worker at the

*Contemporary "phantom" view of the Type 502 shows the separately mounted gearbox (under the front seat) and sturdy chassis common to all "Baroque Angels." Note the forward engine mounting.*

Menasco aircraft engine factory. In 1940 he moved to California, where he opened an auto repair shop and began designing a small number of custom bodies. He soon became a naturalized American citizen, and served in the U.S. Army Air Corps during World War II. He returned from a tour of duty in the South Pacific with a portfolio of sketches, and in 1948 landed a job with Raymond Loewy Associates, then under contract to Studebaker. There he worked on new Studebaker models, including the project that produced the lovely 1953-54 Starliner/Starlight coupes. He left in 1951 to open his own studio in New York City, where he lives and works today.

The influential Max Hoffman played a key role in BMW's decision to hire Goertz. The designer recently related that Hoffman attended the 1954 New York auto show, where he saw some preliminary sketches for BMW's new sports car. Though it's not clear whether these related to the 503 or the 507, it is clear that he didn't like what he saw.

*Above: The 1961-63 3200S was the ultimate Baroque Angel. Right: The 502's underhood layout. Note toolkit. Opposite page: A 1957 Autenrieth 502 cabriolet.*

Hoffman happened to remember a custom-built coupe Goertz had conceived in Los Angeles back in 1938, and urged him to submit some new ideas. Goertz followed Maxie's advice, and had the contract by November.

This must have rankled some people in Munich, especially Ernst Loof, who submitted the initial 507 body proposal in early 1954. It wasn't bad for the period, being low to the ground and curvy. But it looked heavy, and some of its details were clumsy, such as the half-moon front fender vents and a pouting horizontal-bar grille. This design progressed as far as a running mockup, built by Baur, and Loof himself gave it an unauthorized showing at a concours held in Bad Neuenahr in September. But it would never be seen again. Hanns Grewenig thought it looked too much like certain Veritas styles, though he never explained what was wrong with that, as BMW had recently taken over the remains of Loof's business.

Fortunately, however, BMW chose the Goertz designs in anticipation of a large order from Hoffman, who had used similar leverage at D-B with the production 300SL. We say "fortunately,"

because what emerged were two of the handsomest sporting cars ever created. The 507, in particular, has long been recognized as a landmark: graceful, perfectly proportioned, and nearly timeless in its appeal. The 503 seemed rather ordinary by comparison, suffering from its longer wheelbase, plainer bodysides, and a more awkward nose treatment—but then many other cars of the mid-Fifties looked far worse. Interestingly, no less an authority than Pinin Farina praised the 503, preferring it over the 507, though it was the two-seater that won the widest critical acclaim on both sides of the Atlantic. As a matter of fact, it still does.

BMW's new sportsters went into production shortly after their public debut, the 503 commencing in May 1956, the 507 following in November. We have no way of measuring their effect as showroom traffic builders, but it's certain they added a much-needed dose of panache to coun-

ter BMW's rather stodgy image, even though neither would have the aura of competition success like the all-conquering 328. Prices were high. The 503 originally listed at 29,500 marks; the 507 cost 26,500. Predictably, sales were extremely modest. Only 413 of the four-seaters and a mere 252 of the two-seaters were completed before both types were discontinued in March 1959.

Hoffman was very excited about the new cars, especially the 507. In his view, the two-seater's commercial success in America hinged on a selling price of around $5000 and annual production of at least 5000 units. He probably could have sold at least that many at that price. Production began very slowly, however, and the first 507s didn't reach his showroom for a full two years after announcement. By then the price had escalated to $9000, far too high compared to the 507's natural American rivals, the V-8

Chevy Corvette and Ford's Thunderbird. In later years Hoffman admitted that, at the time, he thought things might work out this way. In all, it was too bad BMW couldn't have delivered more 507s at a more competitive price.

Undeniable charisma combined with low production make both these BMWs eminently collectible automobiles today. And despite the march of progress in the years since, they remain surprisingly modern and pleasant cars to drive, particularly the 507. In a contemporary test of the two-seater for *Motor Revue* magazine, Uli Wieselmann reported 11.1 seconds for the 0-100 km/h (62 mph) run and 28.2 seconds from rest to 100 mph. With the normal 3.70:1 final drive, the 507 had a top speed of 122 mph according to his results, though some sources state that nearly 130 mph was available. As writer Eric Dahlquist noted in the premier issue of *Collectible Automobile* magazine in March 1984: "Even modified Corvettes of the period were pressed for numbers like these, let alone being able to sail along at 24 mpg at a steady 60 mph."

Wieselmann praised the 507's full instrumentation, precise shift linkage, clutch and brakes, but had some reservations about the steering and various body and hardware details. Dahlquist described the engine as having "a different character compared to the typical cast-iron Detroit mill, broadcasting a unique, far-away kind of 'alloy sound' that gives the impression of light metal parts whirring away with great purpose." As for ride and handling, Dahlquist noted that "with its near equal 50/50 weight distribution, the 507 has great oversteering ability, just like a race car. You can hang the tail out a mile with only the slightest variations in pressure on the sensitive throttle. By contrast, the ride seems almost 'trucky,' though it's not harsh. The tubular chassis confers high torsional rigidity...and there is virtually no cowl shake or rattling even on rippled roads."

*The rare cabriolet version of the Type 503, styled by Albrecht Goertz, like the two-seat 507. Only 412 examples of the 503 were built altogether between 1956 and early 1959.*

The point needs to be made that, even with their light-alloy bodywork, the 503 and 507 were rather heavy, not much lighter than the big sedans. The four-seater's dry weight was around 3300 pounds, compared to 2900 pounds for the two-seater. The larger, roomier 503 wouldn't match a 507 in acceleration, needing 13 seconds to reach 100 km/h from rest. And, due to different gearing, it was down on top speed, which was around 115 mph. Still, this level of performance wasn't bad for a solidly built and luxuriously outfitted 2+2. In fact, it's more accurate to describe both these cars as high-speed tourers rather than dual-purpose race-and-ride machines—more T-Bird than MG, if you will. One significant running change was made to the 503 in September 1957. The gearbox was moved up and bolted directly to the engine, as in the 507, and a more precise, easier-to-use floor-mounted shifter was adopted.

The 503 and 507 were low-volume products even for a firm of BMW's small size, built slowly, one at a time. Because of this, it's safe to say that no two examples of either were exactly alike. By the time production was underway, Alex von Falkenhausen had returned to

BMW. After developing the R-280 motorcycle/sidecar combination, he spent 2½ years as head of 507 engine and chassis development. When the sports cars were phased out, he was promoted to chief of engine development for the entire automotive division.

As the most exciting BMWs of the Fifties, the 503 and 507 were a fitting close to the decade in which the firm had made its dramatic comeback. They were also a convincing demonstration of the talent and capabilities that had made it all possible. But high-priced sports cars and luxury sedans weren't enough. BMW still needed a mass-market car, one that could be produced easily and cheaply, and sold in high volume at competitive prices. Only then could the firm begin building the kind of solid financial foundation that would ensure its future as an automaker. One possible solution appeared in the mid-Fifties, a curious little economy model that was a complete contrast to the Baroque Angels and the timeless sports cars that were doing so much to enhance the marque's reputation. The Isetta would be something completely different for BMW, and the story of this odd but fascinating car is the subject of the next chapter.

# ECONOMY MEASURES: THE ISETTA SOLUTION

*A look at the architecture of the BMW 600, the big "Isetta." Space utilization was remarkably good for the 114.2-inch overall length. Note tiny engine, unusual frame shape.*

**V**isitors to the Frankfurt *Automobil-Ausstellung* in 1955 had every reason to be impressed by the BMW stand. For a company that had been reduced almost to rubble only a decade before, the number and variety of cars on display was nearly unbelievable. Alongside the new 3.2-liter version of the posh Type 502 sedan were BMW's two exciting sports

models, making their world premiere. The lovely Type 503 and the even lovelier Type 507 attracted a great deal of attention, and left little doubt that BMW had come a remarkably long way in a short time.

Also on view at Frankfurt was a prototype that served as a perfect symbol of the company's startling resurgence. Designated the Type 505, it was a large

four-door limousine intended to challenge no less than the Mercedes-Benz 300 as the car favored by politicians, dignitaries, and status-seekers all over the Continent. It was powered by the newly enlarged light-alloy V-8 in its basic 120-bhp (DIN) form, hooked to the four-speed gearbox from the 502 and driving the 3.90:1 rear axle of the 503. Styling was the work of

Giovanni Michelotti of Italy, executed by the Ghia-Aigle coachworks of Lugano, Switzerland. The lines were appropriately formal, and even flattered the Mercedes by imitating its tall greenhouse and resolute rear fender contours. The front end carried the now-customary twin-kidney grille, and there was a concession to contemporary fashion in the modestly wrapped windshield. Dimensions also mimicked the 300, with a 120.8-inch wheelbase, an overall length of 201 inches, and a dry weight of 3583 pounds.

The 505 would have been a grand addition to the line, a genuine *Grosser* BMW, but it never materialized. One possible explanation, related by author Halwart Schrader, concerns then West German chancellor Konrad Adenauer, who "climbed into the 505's rear seat before a tense group of BMW officials [and] knocked his hat off, thereby wiping out any chance BMW had of becoming a politicians' carriage. Just how apocryphal this story is cannot be confirmed today; suffice it to say only two 505s

were built...one was sold, one kept by the factory and used for the occasional state visit to Bavaria...A similar car was put together in 1963 by BMW in Munich."

There was another car on the BMW stand at Frankfurt 1955,

and it was something else altogether. Called the Isetta, it was a tiny egg-shaped economy runabout barely half the size and weight of a Volkswagen Beetle. What was it doing here among *luxus* sports cars and the limousine-like Baroque Angels?

To answer that question, it's necessary to go back a few years.

As explained earlier, BMW had decided to reenter the auto market with a high-priced, low-volume luxury sedan rather than a mass-production model. This came mainly at the urging of sales manager Hanns Grewenig, who wanted to reestablish the marque's prewar prestige in the postwar world, but the strategy also made economic sense. The firm's resources were extremely limited at the time, and a low-production product was more feasible because it involved less capital investment for tooling and materials. From the beginning, it was assumed that revenue from motorcycle sales would be the prime source of cash for the new car, and for a time it appeared this alone would be sufficient. Unfortunately, motorcycle sales began to sag in the mid-Fifties as vehicles with four wheels came to have greater status than two-wheelers among a growing number of increasingly affluent Germans. Soon, BMW was forced to bolster financing for car production by securing sizeable bank loans. But even this wasn't enough, and in April 1955 it took the somewhat drastic step of selling its Allach engine plant for 25 million marks to MAN (Maschinenfabrik Augsburg-Nürnberg), the diesel engine, heavy truck, and engineering equipment maker.

BMW had made a fast return to the motorcycle field, and issued a stream of new and improved models in the early Fifties. The original single-cylinder R-24 of 1948 was succeeded by the R-25/2 in 1951-53, which in turn was replaced by the R-25/3, built through 1955. The great flat-twin bike had been out of the picture since the demise of the 750cc R-71 in 1944, but it returned in 1950 with the R-51/2, a development of the original R-51 of 1938 and powered by a 500cc ohv twin delivering 24 bhp (DIN) at 5800 rpm. This design continued in 1951-54 as the R-51/3, which gave way to the all-new and very modern R-50 of 1955. In 1952 a 600cc flat twin arrived for the model R-68, packing 35 bhp at 7000 rpm and capable of 100 mph flat out. This evolved into the R-69 three years later. The 600cc twin also powered the R-67/2 and R-67/3 sidecar combinations of this period, but had different camming and carburetion giving 28 bhp at 5600 rpm, plus meatier low-end torque. BMW also returned to all-out racing machines with a new limited-edition 500cc RS (Rennsport) cycle in 1953.

With all these new models, BMW motorcycle production reached nearly 30,000 units in 1954, up dramatically from the 9400-plus of 1949 and the 1950 total of slightly more than 17,000. But the following year, 1955, sales dipped to 23,000 units, and proceeded to slide precipitously to a mere 5400 by 1957. Equally worrisome was the decline in car sales that began about the same time. After peaking at 4567 units in 1955, deliveries sagged to around 3400 the next year, and by 1957 the total stood at a disheartening 1700. The handwriting was on the wall: unless something was done—and quickly—BMW faced the grim prospect of losing not only its car business but its motorcycle business, too.

It was in this climate that the firm joined forces with the makers of the Isetta. Eberhard Wolff, chief of BMW automotive development at the time, first encountered this cartoonish little vehicle at the Geneva salon in 1954. It really was unusual: very small and built strictly for two, with a single bench seat that you reached from the front of the car, which opened like a door and took the steering wheel, steering column, and windshield with it. The front wheels were spaced relatively far apart while the rear ones were close together, made possible by the sharply tapered body, and carried on an axle with no differential. The engine was a 9-bhp 326cc (20-cid) two-stroke twin mounted just ahead of the axle, offset to the right. Drive was taken to the axle by an enclosed chain from a four-speed motorcycle-type gearbox.

An Italian creation, the Isetta had been produced since mid-1953 at Bresso, near Milan, by a company known as Iso (Isetta is the diminutive form of this name). Its founder and president, Count Renzo Rivolta, had started by making refrigerators in a suburb of Genoa in 1938, moving to Bresso in 1942. When Piaggio introduced its Vespa motor scooter and Lambretta followed with one of its own, Rivolta decided to give them some competition. His Iso scooter was soon joined by a line of light motorcycles and three-wheel utility vehicles. But the Isetta

was a departure, a product of original, if slightly offbeat thinking and a fearlessness even Henry Ford would have admired. The Italians embraced it lovingly, so much so that it was given its own class in the famed Mille Miglia endurance contest from Brescia to Rome and back again. It was hardly a race car, of course. In standard trim it could only run up to about 45 mph tops, and it needed 20 seconds just to reach 25 mph. Its real charm was exceptional fuel economy, and at 50 mpg it's easy to see why the Isetta was so popular in a nation where owning a car was a luxury few could afford at the time.

It occurred to Wolff that the Isetta might be just the product BMW was looking for. It was small and inexpensive to build, so it could be priced to sell for not much more than a motorcycle, yet it was more civilized. Here, presumably, was an easy way for BMW to get into the mass market—and, in the process, pep up its anemic cash flow. Wolff suggested all this to engineer Fritz Fiedler, who passed on the recommendation to president Kurt Donath. Pragmatic as always, Donath was ready to go ahead, but he knew he could never get the idea past

Grewenig if the sales director decided to oppose it. But Grewenig was less of an obstacle now, having been chastened by the experience of favoring prestige cars that were proving ever more difficult to sell. He had a lot to make up for, and wanted to support any project that would make money so as to get his name associated with a genuine success. Accordingly, he came out in favor of building the Isetta under license.

With all that settled, BMW began talking with Count Rivolta in mid-1954. Iso's boss received them eagerly, for he had indeed been searching for a German licensee. The reason: de-

spite its initial success, the
Isetta was beginning to slip in
popularity at home. This was
mainly due to renewed competition from Fiat, which was
ready to make war against anything that dared to step into its
primary market. The bubblecar
had to face the Fiat 500C head
on, and the outlook was not
good. The upshot was that Rivolta smilingly sold BMW not just
a license but complete Isetta
body tooling as well. That was a
big plus, because it enabled German production to be started
that much sooner. The first
BMW-Isetta came off the line in
April 1955, and the 10,000th example was turned out less than
eight months later. List price in
Germany was 2580 marks, or
just over one-fifth the cost of the
least expensive six-cylinder 501.
Among the several changes
made for the German version
was substitution of the single-
cylinder 247cc (14.9-cid) R-25
motorcycle engine in place of the
noisy, dirty Italian two-stroke.
As tuned for the Isetta, it delivered 12 bhp (DIN) at 5800
rpm, with peak torque of 9.6 lbs/
ft at 4500 rpm. The all-indirect
four-speed gearbox had a 1.17:1
reduction on top gear in combination with a 2.31:1 final
drive ratio. The fuel tank held
only 13 liters, or a bit less than
3.5 gallons.

The Isetta proved to be as
popular in Germany as it had
been in Italy, at least at first. In
its first full year of production,
BMW delivered nearly 13,000
copies of what came to be affec-
tionately known as *das rollende
Ei,* the rolling egg. "Rolling," as
opposed to "running," was certainly the right word. Even under the most favorable conditions, the Isetta's top speed was
a mere 53 mph, and it needed a
lengthy 40 seconds to hit 50 mph

from a standstill. Average fuel consumption was given as 42.7 mpg. Buyers loved the thriftiness but they desperately wanted more power, so in December 1955 the original Isetta 250 was supplemented with a new 300 model with all of one extra horsepower. The engine, still an ohv single-cylinder unit, was borrowed from the R-27 motorcycle, and delivered 13 bhp at 5200 rpm and peak torque of 12.4 lbs/ft at 4600 rpm from its 297cc (18.1 cid). There were no changes in gearing or tire size, so any measurable difference in performance was, predictably, negligible.

A bit later, in October 1956, a second Isetta body type appeared. The original Iso styling had triangular side windows and a wraparound rear window. The new version was longer overall (92.7 versus 90.0 inches), and had sliding side windows running almost the full length of the car. Retained were the hoodless "front door" and the flanking round headlamps mounted in individual teardrop-shaped pods. In both Isettas, the tiny spare tire and wheel (4.80-10/10x13) were carried ahead of the engine behind the small bench seat, and the gas tank was perched out back behind and slightly above the little motor.

Count Rivolta didn't stop with licensing the Isetta to BMW. He worked a similar deal with a French firm, Velam of Fourchambault, and with a company in Brazil that sold the bubblecar as the Romi-Isetta. BMW exported a three-wheel version of its Isetta to Britain through its old friend A. F. N. Limited. This model was intended to capitalize on the lower tax rates accorded three-wheelers in the U.K. and, for a time, the Aldington brothers were selling 500 a week. In 1956, though, they sold their distribution rights to Dunsfold Tools of Brighton, which formed a subsidiary, Isetta, Ltd., to build its own version, but the bubblecar craze died before operations got underway. Microcars

were popular elsewhere in Europe during the Fifties, and the Isetta spawned several imitators in Germany. These included the Heinkel Kabinenroller (also built under license by Trojan in England), the Fuldamobil, the "which way is it going" Zündapp Janus (designed by Dornier) and the Goggomobil.

BMW continued its basic two-passenger Isetta right up to 1962, but sales slowed down drastically after 1957. All told, the firm built 161,728 of the little "econo-eggs," which made a contribution to its fiscal health out of all proportion to their size. Yet despite its initial popularity, the Isetta failed to bring in the kind of revenues needed to put BMW solidly in the black. Aggravating the profit/loss picture was Kurt Donath's policy of never allowing fluctuations in turnover to interfere with capital investment, even if it meant going deeper into debt. As an example, BMW plowed some 63 million marks back into its operations from 1948 to 1956 —14.5 million for plant and 44.6 million for machinery.

To bolster sagging Isetta sales,

it was decided to field a larger companion model around the same basic theme, more of a proper car. Designed by Willy Black, it looked much like the two-passenger "egg" but had a second seat to give four-passenger accommodation, plus a longer body with a conventional-opening curbside door on the right for rear seat access. Called the BMW 600, it arrived in August 1957. Wheelbase was stretched from the 59.1 inches of the 250/300 models to 66.9 inches, overall length increased to 114.2 inches, and tire size went up to 5.20-10. The original A-shape tubular chassis gave way to a more car-like perimeter affair with box-section side members and straight-tube crossmembers. The front end was much the same as before, with leading-arm and coil-spring front suspension and the front door *cum* steering column. The rear wheels were placed further

*Opposite page, top: This BMW body design augmented the Isetta 250/300 lines in late 1956. Below: The BMW 600, the grown-up Isetta. Opposite bottom: A racing 600 in the Eisenstadt hillclimb, 1959.*

apart for a 45.7-inch track (versus the 48.0-inch front track), and were suspended by coil springs working with an entirely new suspension. The 600 was, in fact, the first BMW to employ the *Schräglenker-Hinterachse* or semi-trailing-arm independent geometry that would be a feature of every subsequent production BMW right up to the present, except for the mid-engine M1 of the late Seventies. It was a good compromise between the traditional solid rear axle so beloved in Detroit and the quirky swing-arm irs favored by makes like Mercedes-Benz, Porsche, and Volkswagen. It would be widely copied, ironic in view of

its beginnings in this humble little car.

Because of its greater size and weight—1213 pounds versus 794 pounds for the smaller Isettas—the 600 was powered by a larger engine. It was still a motorcycle unit, borrowed from the sidecar-equipped R-67 model, and was still rear-mounted. But it boasted twice as many cylinders, being an air-cooled flat twin. Here it was installed VW-fashion, i.e., behind the gearbox and differential and with the cylinders lying transversely. To make room for it, the fuel tank was relocated and the spare tire moved up to the front door. Maximum output was still modest, however: 19.5 bhp (DIN) produced at 4500 rpm, and 25.8 lbs/ft torque. The all-indirect four-speed transmission had a 0.846:1 overdrive top gear ratio and a 1.27:1 third. Final drive was 5.43:1, giving the 600 a top speed of 64 mph. That may not sound like much of an improvement, but the engine was smooth, willing, and revvy. And, like the Beetle, the 600 could cruise all day near its maximum speed, in this case about 62 mph. Average fuel consumption was listed at 39.2 mpg, indicating that, with intelligent gearing, a larger engine can be about as economical as a smaller one in a car of similar size and weight.

Though it was a big advance on the Isetta for practicality and refinement, the 600 was not the car that would turn BMW's fortunes around. The problem was that it had to compete against a number of even more practical and more refined models in the 1.0-1.5-liter class selling for not much more than its base price of slightly under 4000 marks. These included the increasingly popular VW Beetle as well as more up-to-date designs from Opel and Ford Germany. In all, the "big Isetta" proved a big disappointment to BMW, which managed to sell only about 35,000 before giving up on the venture in 1959.

With the large Baroque Angels at the top, the little cars on the bottom, and nothing in between, there was clearly a gaping hole in BMW's model lineup. And filling it was becoming increasingly difficult with every passing year. As it had been several times before, the main problem was money: banks were simply unwilling to underwrite development costs for the all-important mid-market model, a sum then estimated at around 40 million marks. In early 1957, financial executive Heinrich Richter-Brohm stepped in as president on Kurt Donath's retirement. At the same time, sales manager Grewenig also retired, succeeded by Ernst Kämper. Both men quickly realized that the 600 was a stopgap at best, with insufficient sales potential to offset fully the huge losses caused by dwindling demand for the high-priced BMWs. The new president ordered a crash program to get the all-important new middle-class car to market as soon as possible, and work on a new four-cylinder engine proceeded during 1958 with this in mind. But BMW was in a "Catch-22" predicament: as long as it remained an iffy credit risk, the firm had almost no hope of obtaining the necessary level of financing.

Then salvation. First, the influential Deutsche Bank agreed to advance 2 million marks. It was hardly enough to design and tool the all-new gap-filler, but it would enable BMW to update the 600 into something with broader market appeal. The firm's Austrian distributor, Wolfgang Denzel, took it upon himself to contact Giovanni Michelotti, who had trained at Stabilimenti Farina and now headed up his own studio that had designed complete bodies for coachbuilders like Allemano, Ghia, Bertone, and Vignale. Working with a lengthened 600 chassis and retaining its rear-engine layout, Michelotti penned a slant-roof two-door coupe with tidy if innocuous lines. The Ger-

mans liked it but wanted more passenger room, so it was decided to produce two body styles, the coupe and a longer-roofed sedan. Meantime, Hermann Krages, a wealthy lumberman from Bremen, had been quietly buying up large blocks of BMW stock. This injected some 15 million marks into the firm's depleted coffers, but it also precipitated a series of boardroom dramas involving various refinancing schemes and calls for Richter-Brohm's resignation. Rumors of a merger or outright takeover started circulating. In the end, Richter-Brohm was forced out at a stormy stockholders meeting in December 1959. Ironically, he resigned just as the 600's replacement was starting to catch on.

Indeed, the new BMW 700 met with surprisingly favorable buyer response early on. Like the 600, it was engineered primarily by Willy Black, so the two were similar in suspension design and use of the rear-engine layout. But no parts were interchangeable, and the 700 was a much more serious proposition in its size and styling. It was still on the small side, with an overall length of 140 inches, wheelbase of 83.5 inches, and a dry weight of just 1411 pounds. Yet it did offer genuine four-place seating and, with Michelotti's conventional body lines, looked more like a real car instead of a "toy" like the 600.

As planned, there were two body styles. The coupe arrived first, in August 1959, followed by the boxier sedan four months later. Sheetmetal on both was virtually the same below the beltline, but the difference in greenhouse height and length showed up in the sedan's more generous rear headroom and less confined driving position. As in most other rear-engine cars, the trunk was up front, under the "hood," and there was a small amount of additional luggage space behind the rear seat. A departure for BMW was the use of unit body/chassis construction,

with the bodyshell welded up from sheet stampings and reinforced to withstand stress loads. The suspension employed 600-style geometry, with front leading arms and rear semi-trailing arms, plus coil springs all-round. The old spindle steering mechanism on the 600 gave way to a proper rack-and-pinion system, and drum brakes were fitted at each wheel.

The 700 engine was basically an enlargement of the 600's ohv air-cooled flat twin. Bore was increased from 74mm (2.91 in.) to 78mm (3.07 in.), and the crankshaft, derived from that of the Isetta 300, had throws giving a 73mm (2.87-in.) stroke. Swept volume thus worked out to precisely 697cc (42.5 cid). Initially a single Solex 34PCI carburetor and 7.5:1 compression were specified, yielding 30 bhp (DIN) at 5000 rpm and peak torque of 33.7 lbs/ft at 3400 rpm. The gearbox and final drive were also inherited from the 600, but the 700's 12-inch-diameter wheels and tires effectively raised overall gearing. Top speed for the sedan was a creditable 74.5 mph. The coupe, with its lower roof, could reach 77.5 mph. Mileage for either model averaged 33.6 mpg, giving the 700 a comfortable margin over the contemporary VW Beetle.

The 700 sold well, and by April 1960 the factory was building 155 units a day. That wasn't prodigious production, but it was an improvement over Isetta 600 levels. Not surprisingly, BMW wasted little time spinning off new models. The first appeared in August 1960, the 700 Sport. Offered only in coupe form, it featured a higher 9.0:1 compression ratio and twin Solex carbs, which boosted output to 40 bhp (DIN) and top speed to 83 mph. A rear anti-roll was added for improved cornering. A natty cabriolet built by Baur arrived shortly after the coupe. In 1963 the name was changed to CS, though specifications stayed the same. Not many of the little convertibles were built, just 2592

Above: More like a real car than the 600 or Isettas, the BMW 700 appeared in 1959. This is the original coupe. Left: "X-ray" view of the rare 1964 700LS "long-wheelbase" coupe. Only 1730 were built.

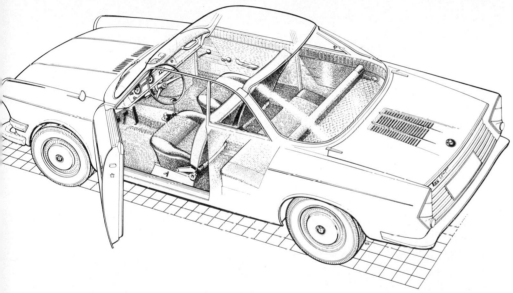

through 1964. Coupe production totalled 11,139. Another variation was the 700 Luxus, a replacement for the original sedan and basically the same except for a six-inch longer wheelbase. Introduced in 1962, it was intended to make the little BMW more competitive in rear seat passenger room against slightly larger cars like the DKW Junior. Arriving in 1963 was the 700LS, the same car with simplified equipment and a slightly lower price. There was also a "long-wheelbase" coupe with the 40-bhp engine available briefly in 1964. Only 1730 were built.

For its size and performance, the 700 was a bit expensive. The sedan's original list price was 4760 marks at a time when the simplest VW Beetle cost 3790. The coupe was even more pricey: 5300 marks. Yet these cars did accomplish their mission. The 700 was the best-selling postwar BMW to date, and when production ended in November 1965 the tally read some 188,000 over five years. Compare that to the big six-cylinder and V-8 cars, which numbered only 23,000 over a time span nearly twice as long.

The 700 marked the last time BMW would build a car powered by one of its motorcycle engines. The reason, quite simply, is that by this time it no longer needed to do that. BMW had introduced a significant new automotive design earlier in the Sixties. Usually referred to as the "New Class," it would be the template for the great sports sedans and sports coupes that returned BMW to profitability and raised the marque's reputation to new heights later in the decade. We detail the birth of this important model and its exciting evolutions in the next chapter. Before we leave this one, however, it's appropriate to take a brief look at what happened to BMW motorcycles in later years, a subject not without interest to fans of BMW cars.

Let's begin with 1955. The R-50 and R-69 models appearing that year boasted articulated frames, an innovation that resulted in a superior ride. In 1960 a hydraulic steering damper was added to the R-69 and maximum output of its engine was raised to 42 hp (DIN). The articulated frame ultimately spread to BMW's single-cylinder machines beginning with the R-27 of 1960, which also marked the first use of rubber engine mounts for a motorcycle.

An entirely new family arrived in September 1969. The main distinction of this group, called the 5-series, was that the heavy cast-iron flat twins of yore were discarded in favor of aluminum-block engines with Perlit liners. Also featured were a new cylinder head with a more compact and efficient combustion chamber, and a new crankshaft, a one-piece steel forging with three steel-backed tri-metal bearings inspired by the crank design of BMW's 2.8-liter six-cylinder car engine introduced the year before. These machines, which replaced all the earlier models, comprised the 32-bhp R-50/5, the 40-bhp R-60/5, and the 50-bhp R-75/5 They were called 5-series because they represented the fifth-generation design since 1948.

Then came a sixth generation in 1973, the R-60/6, the R-75/6, and the 60-bhp R-90/6. At the same time, a 67-bhp R-90S was added to the line as a super-performance machine. All had a five-speed three-shaft gearbox with ratchet-type shift. The R-75/6 and R-90/6 were fitted with front disc brakes, and the R-90S employed a dual disc brake at the front. These bikes were simply electrifying. The R-75/6 could accelerate from rest to 100 km/h (62 mph) in 6.3 seconds and reach 93 mph in 14.5 seconds. Figures for the R-90S were less than five seconds and 125 mph from rest in 35 seconds, respectively.

In January 1976, BMW Motorrad GmbH was established

as a separate company, with capital stock of 12 million marks and headquarters in both Berlin and Munich. The Spandau works then employed 1500-1600 workers, and had an annual turnover of some 170 million marks. Hans Koch, then 46 and a member of the BMW management board since 1971, was named president of the new firm. He left in November 1976, succeeded by Rudolf Graf von Schulenburg, who was given a brand-new product line, the 7-series. This comprised the R-60/7, R-75/7, R-100/7, R-100S, and R-100RS. Despite these excellent machines and the efforts of sales director Horst Spintler, BMW sales suffered over the next few years. From 9071 units in 1976, production slipped to 7896 in 1977, then to 5059 the following year. In the summer of 1978, the R-60/7 was replaced by the R-65 and the R-75/7 evolved into the R-80. Two new entries at the low end of the lineup were the R-45N, a 27-bhp low-compression model, and the R-45 with 9.2:1 compression and 35 bhp. In December 1978 a new management team took charge, with Dr. Eberhardt C. Sarfert as president, Karl Gerlinger as sales director, and Richard Heydenreich as chief engineer for product development.

BMW planned to invest 200 million marks in its motorcycle subsidiary in 1979. Most of this would go to modernization and expansion of the Spandau plant. Simultaneously, Heydenreich and his staff got busy on the product front. They had determined that BMW had become an "old man's" bike in the eyes of keen riders because the physically wide flat twin restricted the safe lean angle on curves. Meanwhile, the highly competitive Japanese manufacturers

were fielding more manageable motorcycles of equal or better performance, often boasting advanced features like four-cylinder engines, fuel injection, turbocharging, and water cooling. BMW's motorcycle engineering, despite all the progress it had seen in power-plant design, frames, suspension, and brakes, remained firmly anchored to the principles laid down by Max Friz back in the early Twenties.

What emerged from all this was a clean-sheet motorcycle designated the K-100. Unusually enough, it was conceived around

a car engine, the small all-aluminum four designed by Peugeot and introduced with its front-drive 104 economy model in the late Seventies. It was the right size, a little shy of 1.0 liter (945cc/58.2 cid) and the right weight. Here it was laid flat, with the crankshaft in the fore-and-aft plane on the right side of the frame. This positioning, made possible because the engine was designed for installation in the car at an angle of 72 degrees from vertical, was the brainchild of Josef Fritzenwenger, a young engine specialist and motorcycle enthusiast

*Opposite page, top and center: The 700LS sedan of 1963-64 shows off its tidy if bland Michelotti styling. Bottom: Baur built this natty 700 Sport cabriolet from 1961. This page, right: The 67-bhp R-90S motorcycle could hit 120 mph flat out.*

employed in the Munich design office. The layout was so unusual that BMW filed a patent application for the combined driveline and engine installation. Many Japanese four-cylinder bikes have vertical, transversely mounted engines, which means that the crankshaft turns at 90 degrees to propshaft rotation. Such an arrangement is better suited for chain drive, which is taboo at BMW and explains the Fritzenwenger concept. In the K-100, all rotation takes place in the same plane and in a direct line from the crankshaft via the gearbox to the propshaft.

Development criteria for the K-100 were laid down by R. P. Michel and K. V. Gevert. Powerplant design was assigned to the small-engine group on Karlheinz Lange's staff in Munich, and Martin Probst was placed in charge of engine testing and development. Probst had previously worked with Paul Rosche on the engine for BMW's Formula 2 racing car, and was particularly well qualified for this task. Naturally, BMW wanted to incorporate lessons from auto racing experience in the new motorcycle engine, but the K-100 emerged with a very different design and materials. The F 2 unit had a cast-iron block and four valves per cylinder, while the motorcycle engine appeared with a lightweight aluminum block and two valves per cylinder. It was designed as an inline four with 67mm (2.64-in.) bore and 70mm (2.76-in.) stroke, giving 987cc (60.2 cid). The aluminum cylinder head carried two camshafts driven by roller chain, with the cams working against bucket-type valve lifters. The valves were splayed at a narrow angle of only 19 degrees, permitting a very compact combustion chamber as well as nearly straight alignment of the ports with their headers. Intake valve head diameter was set at 34mm (1.34 in.), exhaust valves at 28mm (1.10 in.), sizes being restricted by the small bore.

As in BMW's recent passenger car engines, the K-100 unit makes extensive use of electronics. The ignition system has a breakerless electronic distributor with a frequency cut-out for protection against over-revving. The fuel injection system employs Bosch LE-Jetronic control, with a fuel shutoff on deceleration (down to 2000 rpm) to maximize fuel economy. On a compression ratio of 10.2:1, the K-100 engine delivers maximum output of 90

commenced in October 1983.

The K-100 is truly a formidable machine, the ultimate BMW bike. It weighs only 536 pounds with a full tank, so its performance is predictably devastating. From a standing start it hits the 100 km/h (62-mph) mark in 4.2 seconds, roars on to 100 mph in 11 seconds flat and —given a brave rider—blasts up to a top speed of 137 mph. Even a good many of today's high-performance exotic cars are hard pressed to go that quickly, let alone deliver an average of 34 miles per gallon of gas. Unfortunately, buying a K-100 will set you back about as much as a good mid-size European car, some 15,600 marks. That's equivalent to the current price of an Opel Ascona, the German version of the U.S. Chevrolet Cavalier, or the home-market edition of the American-made Renault Alliance. So the K-100 is clearly not something the faint-hearted should even consider. Like today's brilliant BMW automobiles, it is a machine for the connoisseur, engineered with eminent skill, crafted with painstaking care, and endowed with other-worldly capabilities.

Of course, the K-100 is only the crown for the BMW motorcycle line, and it was never the firm's intent to eliminate its beautiful flat-twin bikes. Current plans call for production to be split about evenly between the two model groups—23,000 of the twins and 22,000 of the fours. Those are high figures considering BMW's generally higher prices, but there's every sign that the firm can achieve those levels—and, in the process, return to its place of honor among the world's motorcycle makers.

bhp (DIN) at 8000 rpm and 63.3 lbs/ft of torque peaking at 6000 rpm. Interestingly, these figures corresponded exactly to Probst's original targets. BMW's customary three-shaft five-speed gearbox with dog engagement was adapted to the new engine, mounted adjacent to a counter-rotating clutch. Engine dynamometer testing was begun in February 1981, and prototype machines were on the road that fall. Production of the K-100

# FIRM FOUNDATIONS: THE NEW CLASS AND THE "02" SERIES

**O**nly a few short years after it returned to the auto business, BMW found itself on the brink of financial collapse. The explanation for this apparently sudden reversal was as plain as the huge gap in the model lineup. Quite simply, BMW had yet to produce a genuine money-maker by the end of the Fifties. Impressive though they were, the Baroque Angels

and the snazzy Type 503 and 507 sports cars were simply too expensive to have more than limited sales potential. And once actual sales started sliding, their high production costs made them increasingly—and enormously—unprofitable. The little Isetta and its larger 600 derivative provided only temporary relief and did not sell in sufficient volume to offset losses from the big

cars. Motorcycle sales were in a slump, too.

What BMW needed most was a four-cylinder family car sized and priced between these extremes. It would be aimed at the profitable middle market, expanding rapidly as the postwar German economic "miracle" took hold, and would need to be designed for high-volume production. Heinrich Richter-Brohm

said all this to BMW's management and supervisory boards shortly after he took over as president in 1957. But the new mid-range car wouldn't appear during his tenure. By the time it did, it was almost too late.

The origins of what would become the BMW 1500 date from 1955, when initial development work toward a new family model began under the Donath regime. The project envisioned a four-seat sedan powered by a 1.6-liter slant four, essentially half of the existing 3.2-liter V-8. While this approach had obvious cost and manufacturing advantages, it also had problems. The big-bore/short-stroke cylinder dimensions were fine for a V-8, but would have meant insufficient low-end torque in the four. And the V-8's beefy crankcase and crankshaft would have made for a needlessly heavy engine in view of the 2400-pound curb weight target. A full-size styling mockup completed in 1956 was uninspired—too large for a four-seater, heavy-looking, and bearing definite Detroit hallmarks, including a gimmicky reverse-slant rear window. Road tests of a four-cylinder prototype disguised as an Alfa Romeo were conducted the following year, but proved inconclusive. In 1958 the concept was redefined as a more ordinary car with four/five-passenger seating and a large trunk. It was more practical perhaps, but it was also more pedestrian, lacking the sporty, fun-to-drive character of previous small BMWs.

Meanwhile, Helmut Werner Bönsch joined the firm in 1958 to take charge of quality analysis, marketing and product planning. Bönsch was a competent, perhaps brilliant, all-around engineer who had designed and raced competition

motorcycles for a number of years. His career included positions with Siemens Electrical, Deutsche Shell, and Mannesmann Steel Products before he joined the board of Kronprinz Wheels. Part of his new job at BMW involved making comparisons with competitors' cars. One day in 1960 he discovered that the Pinin Farina body used for the Lancia Flaminia coupe would fit the BMW 3200L chassis with practically no modification. He went to management with the idea that a successor to the four-seat 503, which had been discontinued in 1959, could be created at low cost by simply putting a twin-kidney front on this body and mounting it on the sedan chassis. Management split on the proposal, and the "anti" faction won, led by technical affairs board member Dr. Robert Pertuss. Instead, Pertuss ordered Fritz Fiedler to contact Bertone about styling and production of a new body. An agreement was signed, and the 3200 CS bowed

at the Frankfurt auto show in September 1961.

The 3200 CS is an interesting car historically. It was the last production BMW to employ the light-alloy V-8 and, though no one knew it at the time, it served as the styling model for the next generation of grand touring BMW coupes that would appear in the mid-Sixties. Despite the bulky ladder-type frame familiar from the 503 and the big sedans, the new Bertone body was elegant and tasteful, with the possible exception of the front end. Notable design highlights included a thin-section roof, notched rear side windows, slim A- and C-pillars, and a low beltline. Power was supplied by the 160-bhp (DIN) engine from the 3200S, teamed with a four-speed manual gearbox. Despite its rather high 3310-pound curb weight, the 3200 CS could reach 125 mph maximum, about seven mph up on a 503. The virtually hand-built body and deliberately limited production made this quite

131

an expensive commodity—29,580 marks—and only 603 examples were completed between January 1962 and September 1965. Though an aging chassis and running gear rendered it obsolete almost from the day it appeared, the 3200 CS was a pleasant surprise coming from a company that had just been through an extremely troubled period.

The troubles had been going on for a long time, of course, and they came to a head in 1959. That year, BMW lost 15 million marks on an annual turnover of 150 million marks, and its financial position was precarious. Earlier, the company had managed to stave off two takeover bids. One came from none other than American Motors president George Romney, who hoped to strengthen his firm by linking up with a European producer known and respected for its engineering. The other came from Sir William Rootes, chief of the Rootes Group in England, which was then beginning to establish ties with Chrysler. Tariffs on British imports were high in these years before the Common Market, and it's likely that "Sir Willy" was interested in BMW mainly as a sales and distribution point on the Continent for his various Hillman, Humber, Singer, and Sunbeam models.

A merger or outright takeover involving a foreign company was out of the question for the prideful Bavarians, but what else could be done? On December 9, 1959, some 800 people filed into Munich's Congress Hall, where a general assembly (stockholders meeting) would decide BMW's fate. Dr. Hans Feith, chairman of the supervisory board, put forth a proposal on behalf of the firm's chief creditor, the Deutsche Bank. It amounted to a merger with Daimler-Benz. BMW's capital stock would be devalued from 30 to 15 million marks, followed by a new stock issue to raise net capital worth to 70 million marks. All the new

shares would be purchased by D-B, in which the bank held a 27 percent interest.

It seemed like a good way for the bankers to protect their money, but it met with howls of protest from the BMW dealers and minority shareholders in attendance. Both groups feared that what the money men described as "a strong partner" would be *too* strong, that D-B would eventually swallow up both the BMW company and its cars. Dealers feared their franchises would soon be worthless, while the small shareholders wanted something more than the cheap payoff the bank was offering, especially since the price of BMW stock had just hit rock bottom.

A cool-headed Frankfurt attorney, Dr. Friedrich Mathern, made a counterproposal: why not raise fresh funds from other, more diverse sources? His motion was sustained by 21 percent of the votes, enough to block the bank's plan, and the meeting adjourned. In protest, Deutsche Bank withdrew from the supervisory board. Though it probably held enough claims to call for bankruptcy proceedings, the bank didn't exercise this option. One likely reason is that some of those involved BMW suppliers, whose interests the bank also had to consider. Quick liquidation of the company's assets just to recover a portion of the outstanding debt obviously wasn't going to do anyone any good, least of all the 6900 workers then on BMW's payroll.

As noted earlier, Hermann Krages, the Bremen lumber baron, played a key role in BMW's fortunes in this period. He had begun buying company stock steadily but in small blocks in 1956. In two years he amassed 30-35 percent of the total shares, making him easily the largest single stockholder. The second largest held 13-18 percent and was identified as the Quandt Group. In May 1958, BMW raised an additional 15 million marks through a bond

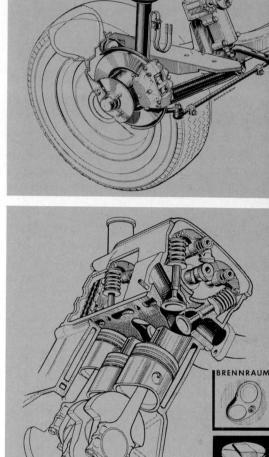

Top: The New Class pioneered MacPherson-strut front suspension at BMW. This detail shows the setup on the later 1800/2000. Above: Hemispherical combustion chamber shape was retained for the New Class four-cylinder engine, but valvegear was much simpler than on the old 2.0-liter six. Opposite page, lower right: The New Class semi-trailing-arm rear suspension. Top and lower left: New Class assembly at Milbertshofen 1963.

issue subscribed to in its entirety by the Quandt interests. The following year, Krages sold his holdings through a group of banks, and much of it ended up in Quandt hands. By mid-1960, these two brothers were in firm control and would thus chart the course of BMW and its products over the next few years.

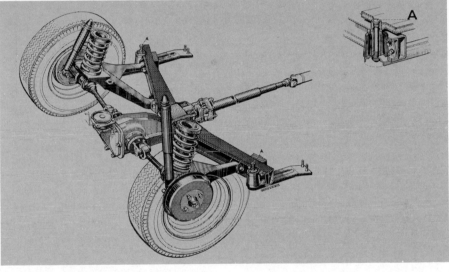

Harald and Herbert Quandt were certainly no strangers to wheeling and dealing. Actually, they were half-brothers, the sons of Günther Quandt, who got his start by investing in ailing industrial concerns in the troubled years after World War I. By 1923 he had become chairman of Accumulatoren-Fabrik AG of Hagen and Berlin, the corporate ancestor of Varta battery, and in 1927 he bought control of the Petrix Chemical Works in Hamburg. Through wit and wile he managed to sail a solvent ship through the Depression, and became even more prosperous during Hitler's reign. Though Günther never got involved with BMW, his sons somehow decided that they would one day have a say in its affairs. The reasons have never been explained.

Herbert was born in 1910 out of his father's first marriage. Harald was born 11 years later when Günther was married to Magda nee Ritschel, but that ended in divorce when Harald was eight. She remarried in 1931, becoming Mrs. Josef Goebbels, and Harald grew up as the stepson of Hitler's propaganda chief. During the war he fought in Sicily and was taken prisoner, which may have saved him from a premature death in the infamous Berlin bunker in 1945. Herbert, meantime, had been

*Above: Herbert Quandt, along with his half-brother Harald, rescued BMW in 1960. Below: the 1500 in pre-production auto show form, 1961. Right: Base New Class was upgraded to a 1600 in 1964. Opposite page, bottom right: The 1500's ohc four "exploded." Clockwise from top left: 1963 1800, 1969 1800, 1966 2000, 2000 TI-lux circa 1969, and 1971 1800, all variations on the successful New Class theme.*

raised by his father and learned every aspect of his business. Harald joined him after the war, and the two began speculating, each building up large individual investment empires. Though introverted and secretive, Herbert became known as a gambler, while Harald was very guarded with money despite being more open and gregarious.

Word that the Quandts were buying into BMW like players in a giant Monopoly game leaked out in May 1960. Harald stopped at 26 percent, but Herbert kept adding to his pile until he had 40 percent of the total shares. Stockholders were summoned to another meeting late that November. After four hours of wrangling it was decided to slice the number of outstanding shares by one-fourth while doubling capital value to 22.5 million marks through yet another stock issue. This block was offered at 40 percent above par, and Herbert was apparently the sole buyer. The brothers now held some two-thirds of BMW's stock between them, and soon

the only question in Munich was what they would do with the company now that they had it.

It didn't take long to find out. Neither took an active role in day-to-day operations at first, and neither assumed seats on either BMW board, delegating trusted representatives to key offices instead. In February

1960, Gerhard Wilcke, a staff lawyer for Herbert Quandt, took a seat on the supervisory panel. Heinrich Richter-Brohm resigned as president the very next month. He had known all along how to save BMW, but had been powerless to do anything about it.

Other personnel changes followed in rapid-fire succession.

Harald Quandt, who was more personally interested in cars than his brother, hired Dr. Robert Pertuss away from the Wilhelm Karmann coachworks in October to supervise technical staff and oversee manufacturing. On the product side, he picked up Wilhelm Gieschen from the remains of Borgward, which was about to leave the car business. Though primarily a manufacturing engineer, Gieschen was charged with product planning, design engineering, testing and development, and outranked both Fritz Fiedler and Helmut Bönsch. To revive flagging sales, Paul Georg Hahnemann, marketing manager at Auto Union in nearby Ingolstadt since 1957, was lured to Munich. Though the door to BMW's executive suite seemed to be a revolving one in these years, the president's chair sat empty until 1962, when Karl Heinz Sonne, chief of the Quandt-owned Concordia Electricity Corporation, was named to fill it.

BMW had been granted a reprieve. Now, bolstered by the Quandt fortunes, the firm put top priority on the flagging family car project. In 1960, all the earlier work was scrapped in favor of a much smaller, lighter package to be powered by a totally new engine that would come from Alex von Falkenhausen's drawing board. Fiedler assumed overall responsibility for this program, which proceeded not under the usual project code number but simply as the Neue Klasse, the "New Class." Peter Schimanowski had retired by this time and Alfred Böning was working elsewhere as chief engineer for special projects, so Eberhard Wolff was named head of chassis engineering for the Neue Klasse and Wilhelm Hofmeister handled styling and body engineering.

At one point, Gieschen suggested that the 1100cc (87-cid) water-cooled flat four from the now-discontinued Hansa and Goliath cars, complete with all production tooling, could be acquired at very low cost now that Borgward was on the ropes. He may have been somewhat biased, having worked for Hansa-Lloyd in the Thirties and at Borgward beginning in 1949. The idea was considered but rejected. BMW wanted at least 80 bhp (DIN) and ample low-end torque for the New Class, and the Borgward engine was simply too small. Even with twin carbs it didn't put out more than about 55 bhp and, due to tight cylinder spacing and the dimensional constraints of its crankcase design, it could not be stretched beyond 1.3 liters (79 cid).

Von Falkenhausen was instructed to come up with a clean-sheet inline four of about 1500cc (91 cid), with provision for future expansion up to 1.8 liters (110 cid). As it turned out, he didn't have to start from scratch. Back in 1958 he had drawn up a 1.0-liter (61-cid) sohc four intended for possible use in the little rear-engine 700 then being developed. It was dyna-

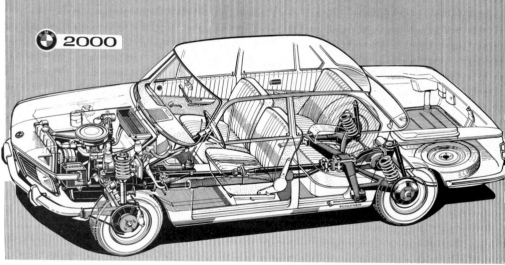

mometer tested in 1959 but, apparently, was never actually tried in a car. Now it was taken off the shelf to become the basis for the new family car powerplant.

The New Class was first shown in prototype form at the Frankfurt auto show in September 1961. Simply labelled "1500," it was a masterpiece, a genuine breakthrough. Like the 328 and 327 before it, the New Class was ahead of its time in many ways, and its styling and engineering would be widely copied not just in Germany but in Britain, France, Italy, and

Sweden. It was so good, in fact, that it would become the blueprint for virtually every production BMW over the next two decades. Most importantly, it was the commercial success BMW so desperately needed—the firm foundation on which the company could build a secure future. As Halwart Schrader put it, the New Class was "destined to be a new beginning."

The 1500 owed absolutely nothing to the previous big V-8 cars, but the influence of Willy Black was evident in its unit body/chassis construction and semi-trailing-arm rear sus-

pension, both pioneered at BMW with the little 700. In size, the New Class was closer to the Baroque Angels, but actually it was what we would call a compact. Wheelbase was 100.5 inches on an overall length of 177 inches. Track dimensions were fairly generous for the 65-inch overall width, being 54 inches at the rear and 52 inches front. Nowadays, the 1500 looks unfashionably tall, a function of its 56-inch unladen height, but Hofmeister's clean, functional lines have stood the test of time remarkably well. The New Class, of course, established the BMW look now so closely associated with the marque, distinguished by a low beltline and tall greenhouse, slim pillars all-round, a flat hood and rear deck, plus gently rounded corners and straight-through fenderlines. Though undeniably boxy, this shape offered excellent space utilization even without the packaging advantages of front-wheel drive, and the simple body

contours were amenable to the most modern manufacturing processes of the day. In fact, the 1500's basic architecture was probably the most advanced of any European sedan then on the market.

The suspension was equally up to date. The New Class was one of the first production cars to employ the simple MacPherson-strut front suspension arrangement that has become near universal in the years since. In Wolff's configuration the bottom end of the struts, with their concentrically mounted coil springs, were linked to the outer ends of lower control arms consisting of simple transverse beams. The inboard ends of the arms were joined to drag struts hinged at a point farther forward on the main structure. All suspension elements were isolated in rubber. Spring rates were fairly stiff by today's standards and contributed to roll stiffness (roll center height was a scant 4.33 inches above ground), but a separate stabilizer bar was fitted. Wheel travel was 3.36 inches in both jounce and rebound. Without the stabilizer, body roll would have caused the outside front wheel to assume positive camber in a tight turn while the inside one would tend toward high negative camber. With the bar, camber varied essentially

within a narrow range on the negative side. The static camber setting was 0.5 degrees negative.

The rear suspension consisted of two pressed-steel semi-trailing arms acting on vertical coil springs and telescopic shock absorbers, mounted behind the springs with pronounced "sea-legs" splaying. The arms were angled at 20 degrees to the transverse plane in order to minimize this geometry's inherent camber changes on deflection. The arms' inner and outer mounting points, however, were at the same height. Under 0.5g lateral acceleration both the front and rear outside wheels assumed about 1.5 degrees positive camber, with roughly similar negative camber angles on the inside wheels. The rear roll center was 5.15 inches above ground, giving an almost horizontal roll axis, which promoted good handling balance.

The New Class had a relatively high polar moment of inertia, with the engine mounted far forward in the chassis and the fuel tank and spare in the extreme rear, so the car was quite stable directionally. Like all trailing-link rear suspensions, this BMW design also had the advantage of contributing some anti-dive effect on braking. Because of its forward location, the driveline's center of gravity coincided with the vertical line from the front wheel axis, yet weight distribution was only moderately nose-heavy at 53.5/46.5 percent front/rear. Predictably enough, the 1500 was a basic understeerer, but it had fine road-holding, the long-travel suspension keeping all four tires on the road even under high roll conditions, and the car was capable of posting impressively high average speeds. Brakes comprised solid discs, made by Dunlop, at the front, with ample 10.5-inch-diameter rotors, and 10-inch drums at the rear. Steering was a Gemmer-type worm-and-roller mechanism supplied by ZF and geared to provide 3⅓ turns lock-to-lock for a fairly compact turning radius.

The New Class arrived with the first four-cylinder engine BMW had built since the old side-valve Austin-based unit of the Thirties. Here, the choice was dictated by the need for a physically short powerplant that could be positioned above or ahead of the front crossmember so as to keep the transmission as far ahead of the passenger compartment as possible in the interest of interior space. As installed, it was canted 30 degrees from vertical, which had three advantages: a lower hoodline, a lower center of gravity, and improved accessibility.

Von Falkenhausen remained faithful to hemispherical combustion chambers for this new four but, since it was all-new, he could abandon the complicated valvegear of the old 2.0-liter six. In its place were a single overhead camshaft driven by duplex chain from the crankshaft, plus overhead valves, staggered and splayed at a 55-degree angle, opened by simple rocker arms and closed by single coil springs. An easily adjustable chain tensioner was mounted high up in the block. A separate chain drove the oil pump, while the ignition distributor shaft was turned by skew gears from the rear end of the camshaft. The

linerless cylinder block was made of cast iron, extended well below the crankshaft centerline, and had deep, wide water jackets. The head was made of die-cast aluminum, with copper-alloy valve guides and valve seat inserts. The cam cover was also an aluminum-alloy casting, while the sump was made of stamped steel. The forged-steel crank ran in five main bearings and had four counterweights. Bore and stroke dimensions were 82 x 71mm (3.23 x 2.80 in.) for 1499cc (91-cid) swept volume. A Solex 34 PICB carburetor and 8.8:1 compression were specified, resulting in a maximum 80 bhp (DIN) at 5700 rpm and a peak

87 lbs/ft of torque at 3200 rpm. The 0.866 stroke/bore ratio ensured good cylinder filling and low mean piston speeds, which in turn meant ample low-range torque and reduced wear. Despite the highish peak torque speed, the torque curve was almost flat from 1750 to 4850 rpm.

The 1500's standard gearbox was a four-speed manual unit with Porsche-type synchronization on all forward speeds, operated by a rather spindly remote-control lever located centrally on the floor. It was a very pleasant gearbox, the only possible complaint being the exaggerated spacing between second and

*Opposite page and above: First of the 2.0-liter New Class models was the 2000 C/CS coupes of 1965-69. Except for odd nose, styling owed much to the earlier 3200 CS designed by Bertone. Right and below: Longer nose and new six produced the 2800 CS for 1968 ('71 shown).*

third gears. The jump from the 3.82:1 first to the 2.17:1 second wasn't too bad, but third was 1.36:1, and a ratio of around 1.80:1 would have been much better for driving in hilly country. Top, of course, was direct drive. The gearbox had a long extension, and a torque tube was bolted to the final drive unit, making the propshaft quite short. This was done partly to get a low floor and partly to reduce driveline noise and vibration.

In typical German fashion, the 1500's final drive gearing was a bit too low (high numerically) for truly relaxed high-speed cruising. The 4.38:1 differential yielded 16.2 mph/1000 rpm in top with the standard 6.00-14 tires, so the top speed was around 92 mph. With a curb weight of 2337 pounds, the power-to-weight ratio worked out at an unexciting 29 lbs/bhp. But performance was respectable, and 0-100 km/h (62-mph) acceleration of 15 seconds flat was possible given a determined driver. Average fuel consumption was quite good at 21.4 mpg.

The New Class was an unmitigated success in spite of its rather high price. In Germany

the base figure was held to 9485 marks, which put the 1500 directly even with the Mercedes-Benz 190 but 100 marks above the six-cylinder Opel Rekord and 2000 marks above Ford's front-drive Taunus 17M. In America, import-car wizard Max Hoffman sold it at $3550 East Coast port-of-entry. Commented a colleague at the time, "You can get a Pontiac Catalina for less!" Maybe so, but nowhere else could you get sophisticated engineering and German craftsmanship in a practical four-door that was also fun to drive. The New Class was in a class by itself, and it wasn't long before motoring writers began describing it quite ac-

curately as a "sports sedan," which it undeniably was.

The 1500 did not last long in its original form—only through December 1964 and a bit less than 24,000 units. The reason was that BMW had something better: a complete lineup based on the New Class body and chassis. Cooked up by Helmut Bönsch and Paul Hahnemann, the plan was to give BMW broader market coverage with minimal investment. It wasn't really a new idea, of course, as anyone who recalled the transformation of the six-cylinder Type 303 into the four-cylinder 309 in the Thirties could attest. Here, the program envisioned an

upgraded 1500 with a choice of 1.8- or 2.0-liter versions of the new four. Meantime, a smaller and lighter model based on the New Class chassis design would be readied for the 1.5-1.6-liter price bracket. It seemed like a good plan, especially as sales were now going great guns (they tripled in 1964). Now in the pink

of financial health, BMW eagerly spent 130 million marks on new model development and plant improvements, and expanded the Milbertshofen work force to 10,000.

The first of the new "cocktail" variations was the 1800, launched in September 1963 as an alternative to the original

1500. The new four was treated to a bore and stroke job, which brought dimensions to 80mm (3.15 in.) by 84mm (3.31 in.) and capacity up to 1773cc (108 cid). With 8.6:1 compression and a two-barrel Solex 36-40 PDSI carburetor, output climbed to 90 bhp (DIN) at 5250 rpm and maximum torque improved to 96 lbs/

A scaled-down two-door derivative of the New Class, the "02" series was BMW's high-volume line in the late Sixties and early Seventies. Opposite page, center left and right: The initial 1600-2 model, circa 1969. Top left and right: The 1.8-liter Type 1802 was added in 1971, when the 1600-2 was renamed 1602. Bottom and right: The 2002 arrived in 1968.

ft at 3000 rpm. Other changes included revised first and second gear ratios, adoption of ZF power steering and Ate vacuum-assisted brakes as standard, and first-time availability of automatic, the three-speed 3HP 22 transmission from ZF. Styling was virtually unaltered apart from chrome rocker panel moldings and the appropriate badges. The 1800 would be continued all the way through 1968, and production totalled a satisfying 102,090 units.

Following the 1800 by a few months was a more interesting variation, the 1800 TI (*Turismo Internationale*). Compression was bumped to 9.5:1, and twin two-barrel Solex carbs were fitted. Maximum power rose to 110 bhp (DIN) at 5800 rpm and peak torque improved to 100 lbs/ft at 4000 rpm. Production totalled 18,417, again through 1968.

BMW was clearly beginning to exploit the sporting capabilities inherent in the New Class, and it went a step further with yet a third version of the 1800 in 1964. Called the TI/SA (SA denoting *Sportsausführung*, sports version), it boasted 10.5:1 compression and larger-throat Weber carbs, which raised maximum power output to 130 bhp (DIN) at 6100 rpm. Torque was up only fractionally, to 106 lbs/ft, but it now peaked at 5250 rpm, indicating this model was clearly aimed at competition. And indeed it was. BMW sold exactly 200 of these cars, and they all went only to licensed racing drivers. To help make up for the low-end torque deficit, a five-speed Getrag gearbox was standard. Buyers could opt for final drive ratios of 4.11, 4.22, 4.75 or 5.86:1, and a limited-slip differential was offered at extra cost.

The basic New Class chassis was capable of handling the extra power, but the TI/SA got stiffer springs, a reinforced front stabilizer bar and a new rear bar just for good measure. The steering was geared up to reduce turns lock-to-lock to 3.0, and the front disc brakes acquired larger-diameter rotors. Wheel and tire sizes were unchanged from the normal TI, but BMW approved radial tires as original equipment for the first time, sized at 165HR-14. As a "homologation special," the TI/SA was predictably short-lived, offered only in 1964-65.

At the opposite end of the spectrum was the 1600, arriving in 1964 to replace the 1500. The basic chassis and four-door body were retained, as was the list price. The principal difference was a bigger-bore engine (84mm/3.31 in.) with 1573cc (96 cid), 83 bhp (DIN) at 5500 rpm and 83 lbs/ft torque at 3000 rpm. The gearbox from the base 1800 was adopted, and final drive gearing was changed to a longer striding 4.275:1. Another interim variation, the 1600 was phased out in early 1966 after 10,278 examples.

Next on the menu was the promised 2.0-liter engine, created by combining the crank from the 1.8-liter unit and an extended 89mm (3.50-in.) bore. Output from the resulting 1990cc (121.4 cid) was 100 bhp (DIN) at 5500 rpm with single

Solex 40 PDSI carb or 120 bhp at the same engine speed with twin Solex 40 PHH two-barrel instruments. The newly enlarged four debuted in 1965 for two new coupe models built on the 100.5-inch-wheelbase sedan chassis, another example of cost-minded planning by Bönsch and Hahnemann. The single-carburetor version, called 2000 C, was offered with either four-speed manual or three-speed automatic transmission, while the twin-carb 2000 CS came with manual only. The main interest in the coupes centered on their new body. Built by Karmann of Osnabrück, it was quite similar to the Bertone-styled 3200 CS in overall appearance, but bore a blunt, unattractive front end. *Road & Track,* which tested a 2000 CS in 1966, observed that the coupes were about three inches lower compared to the sedans, with "a shorter greenhouse for the proper sporting look. And here is the distinguishing mark of the car; while it looks, feels, and is sporty, it also happens to have fairly generous seating for four—and occasionally five—people. The term 2+2, as generally used today, wouldn't be fair to the coupe at all. There are simply no other comparable cars within $500 of the price."

*R&T's* performance figures for the 2000 CS are illuminating. The magazine's four-speed car with a 3000-pound test weight and 3.90:1 final drive managed the 0-60 mph sprint in a brisk 11.3 seconds and ran the quarter-mile in 18.2 seconds at 76 mph. "It suffers," said the editors, "from the safe deficiency that most other European cars do, namely not enough performance for adequate, effortless performance considering the price," which was a lofty $5185 as tested. But the chassis earned high praise: "To say simply that the suspension is effective would be an understatement...On the worst surfaces, with potholes, dips, and bumps, it's downright uncanny, for there doesn't seem to be an irregularity that can trip it up, even at twice the speed we'd dare go in a domestic sedan...Combined with the impressive ride is equally impressive roadholding...It's difficult to break loose a tire anywhere either in cornering or in acceleration, though the inside rear wheel lifts finally...Put the ride, handling and steering characteristics together and you have the impression of a rather heavy, substantial vehicle, though not oppressively so." Summing up, R&T described the 2000 CS as a car "for the person

who values finish, detailing, finesse and integrity over pretense, excesses and sure obsolescence...It may not have as much performance as we like, but...the rewards are worth the sacrifice."

BMW would eventually attend to the coupe's lack of outright go, but the 2000 C/CS sold respectably well all the same. Through

their phaseout in mid-1969, production totalled 11,720.

It was only a matter of time before the 2.0-liter four found its way into the New Class sedan, and it did in January 1966 with the 2000 and 2000 TI. The former employed the 100-bhp "C" engine, the latter the 120-bhp "CS" unit. Gearbox ratios were shuffled once again, and ZF au-

tomatic was offered as an option for the base model only. Final drive ratio with either gearbox was 4.11:1 as in the C coupe, while the TI had the 3.90:1 CS gearset. A minor styling update brought purpose-designed rectangular headlights to replace the previous round lamps, and the former vertical taillights gave way to a mildly reworked back panel with horizontal clusters incorporating the backup lights. With a curb weight of 2536 pounds, the TI had a top speed of 112 mph and could scamper from 0 to 100 km/h (62 mph) in 12 seconds. Fuel economy suffered, but not much, the average working out to 17.4 mpg. There was also a plusher model called the TI-lux, a name later contracted to "tilux." Selling at around $4300 in the U.S., it was mechanically identical with the normal TI but had higher-grade interior trim and ammenities.

BMW production topped 60,000 for the first time during 1966, and three out of every four cars built had the 2.0-liter engine. They were fine machines but expensive, selling directly against larger and/or more prestigious models from Alfa Romeo, Mercedes-Benz, Citroën, Rover, and Volvo. Price would be an increasingly sensitive point with BMW in the years ahead. But though some debated whether the cars were worth what the factory charged, no one doubted their capabilities.

A key factor in BMW's growing success in the mid-Sixties was the character of its cars, a combination of practicality and verve found nowhere else. This reflected the thinking of sales boss Paul Hahnemann, who

*Opposite page, above: The injected 2002ti bowed with the 100-bhp base version, had 20 extra horses. Below: Baur's natty 02-based cabriolet was offered beginning in late 1967. This page, left: The later targa-roof model, a 1970 2002. Below left: The 130-bhp (DIN) 2002tii engine. Below: Driving lights were standard on Touring 2000tii.*

143

*Touring hatchback derivative of the "02" bodyshell appeared in 1971. Unhappily, it was never brought to the States. Shown is the 2000tii model. The hatchback was also offered in 1.6- and 2.0-liter standard form. All were phased out in 1974.*

early on had evolved a theory about market "slots" where BMWs could be positioned without any direct competition. It was left to Helmut Bönsch to define the actual model specifications that would fit the slots Hahnemann picked out. These were years of high enthusiasm that pervaded all departments at BMW. The company was finally prospering, and its cars were adding new lustre to the marque. For the second time since the war, BMW had made a spectacular recovery.

An important technical change updated the 1800 sedans in 1968. Combining the 1600 crankshaft with the 2000 block produced a revvy short-stroke powerplant. As installed in a second-series 1800, this 1766cc (107.7-cid) unit had 89mm (3.50-in.) by 71mm (2.80-in.) dimensions for a stroke/bore ratio of 0.798. Power output with a single Solex downdraft carb and 8.6:1 compression was 90 bhp (DIN) at 5250 rpm. Customers must have appreciated the engine's improved smoothness and quietness, because sales of the 1800s shot up by 30 percent in 1969. That same year, BMW introduced its first fuel-injected model, the 2000 tii. It differed from the carbureted 2000 TI/tilux in using Kugelfischer mechanical injection instead of twin carbs, which pushed power to 130 bhp (DIN) at 5800 rpm and yielded a four-mph gain in top speed, now 115 mph. Built through 1972, the tii was a rare bird: only 1952 examples.

BMW took a significant step towards balancing its model line in March 1966 with the 1600-2. The "-2" designation did not indicate a second-generation New Class but a completely different series with two doors instead of

*continued on page 161*

*A handsomely restored example of the twin-carb 2000CS coupe from 1967 based on the New Class sedan.*

Opposite page, bottom: Introduced in 1962, the 3200CS was the last production BMW styled by Nuccio Bertone, who acted as a consultant on the 1500 New Class sedan project. Total production of this 3.2-liter V-8 2+2 was a mere 603 units. This page and center spread: Based on the New Class chassis, the 2000C and CS (shown) coupes had lines reminiscent of the 3200CS, but were styled in-house by Wilhelm Hofmeister. Production of these four-cylinder models ran through 1969 and some 11,720 units.

One of the most successful BMW model groups in recent years was the "02" series of two-door sedans with engineering very close to that of the New Class four-doors. This basic design was sold with a variety of engine/equipment permutations through 1975, when it began to be phased out in favor of the 3-series. Shown above and on the opposite page is the 2002 ti variant of 1968-71. Like other "02s," it was powered by an sohc four, here with twin carbs and tuned to deliver 120 bhp (DIN). Right: BMW considered bolting two fours together to create this 3.6-liter V-8 in 1969, but abandoned the idea as too costly.

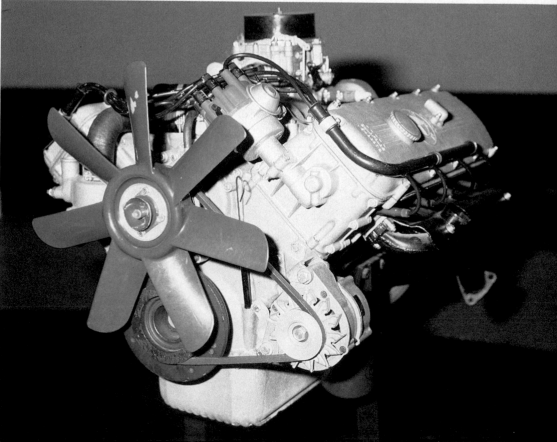

149

*Two variations on the "02" small sedans. This page: The Bauer cabriolet conversion of the standard 1602 model, offered in 1971-75. Opposite page: Bowing in early 1971, the Touring hatchback body type was not officially imported to the U.S. Shown is a 1972 example equipped to 2000 model specifications.*

Top and above: The handsome six-cylinder 2800CS was announced in 1968 to succeed the four-cylinder 2000C/CS coupes. Bodywork was again supplied by Karmann of Osnabrück, and differed mainly in the longer nose needed to accommodate the "big-block" BMW six. 2800CS production totalled precisely 9399 units through 1971. Opposite page: Wings, fins, and lightweight body panels marked the 3.0 CSL, a limited-production version of the 3.0 CS/CSi coupes intended mainly for competition. Shown is a 1973 example. CSL output was 1039 units from 1971 through 1975.

*This page and opposite page, top: The mid-engine BMW Turbo was first shown in 1972 to announce the Munich Summer Olympics and BMW's new headquarters building. It was built on a modified 20002 chassis and featured gullwing styling by then chief designer Paul Bracq. Production was never seriously contemplated. Opposite page, bottom: The mid-engine M1 arrived in 1978 as a joint effort of BMW and Lamborghini. It's shown here in racing trim. All M1s use a 16-valve injected version of BMW's ohc six.*

Another variation on the "02" sedan series, here the Bauer cabriolet version of the mid-range 1802 sold from 1971 to '75. The main difference between this series and the 2000/2002 models was, as the numbers imply, in engine displacement. For the 1802 it was 1766cc, good for 90 bhp (DIN), compared to 1990cc for the 2002 variants. Note the fixed central pillars and cloth rear roof area of this Bauer design.

An unusual glimpse at the artistry of former BMW design chief Paul Bracq. Above: Some styling ideas obviously related to the Turbo show car as sketched in the early phases of the E-26/M1 project. Right: Three variations on the theme eventually adopted for the production 6-series coupes. Opposite page, top: An advance sports car study circa 1975, with a 1938 Oldsmobile pictured for emphasis. Bottom: Two versions of the V-12 coupe proposed in 1972-73, plus a classic 328 roadster and a modified Turbo for comparison. The V-12 project was aborted because of the first energy crisis.

BMW Coupé 1973

More design ideas from Paul Bracq. Above (from top of illustration): A study based on the original 5-series sedans of 1972, a Type 327 coupe from the late Thirties, and another sketch for the stillborn V-12 coupe, all circa 1975. Left: The influence of the mid-engine Turbo show car is again seen in this proposal for the V-12 coupe, with a Type 327 once more used for contrast.

*continued from page 144*

four. The new bodyshell, still built in unit with the chassis, was smaller and lighter, though styling was clearly in the New Class mold. Wheelbase was trimmed by about two inches to 98.4 inches. Main chassis components were borrowed from the 1800 four-doors, but the "02" had a narrower 52.4-inch rear track, exactly matching the front. The 1600-2 took over for the four-door 1600, and its lighter 2073-pound curb weight gave it superior performance. With slightly more power on tap—85 bhp (DIN) at 5700 rpm—it could run up to 101 mph and reach 100 km/h from rest in 13.2 seconds while returning 20.4 miles for every gallon of gas.

The 1600-2 was the least expensive BMW in a long time, and it caused a lot of excitement when it was announced in the U.S. at a suggested $2557 East Coast P.O.E. Said *Road & Track:* "It's still a BMW... and it isn't

offered as a stripped-down price-leader model to get you into the store... The interior... is completely and satisfactorily finished off. It isn't as rich in all details as the costlier BMWs, but the materials are of good quality, in good taste, and put together well; there's almost no resemblance to the almost naked appearance of most economy models." Once again, *R&T* praised the roadability of a new BMW, describing the 1600-2 as "no less than excellent. There is some body lean, but it isn't unsettling [and] the steering takes the car where it is pointed and with good bite at both ends; there is dead-neutral steering at any speed you're likely to use. The steering feels as if there is a lot of caster and the straightline stability is without fault." The editors undoubtedly spoke for a lot of buyers in concluding that the 1600-2 "is a great automobile for the price. It retains all the good things that have made

BMWs one of our favorite cars and does it at a price that puts any number of other manufacturers to shame."

Model variations on the new "02" platform were inevitable, and they didn't take long to appear. The first was the 1600 TI, introduced in September 1967. Engine specs were revised to include twin Solex carbs and higher 9.5:1 compression, which boosted output to 105 bhp at 6000 rpm and top speed to 109 mph. But it didn't last because of what came next: the thrilling 2002. The 2.0-liter four in the lightweight two-door was a combination tailor-made for the U.S. (the 1600 TI wouldn't have cleared federal emissions limits),

*Still more "02" variants (clockwise from top right): The American 2002 of 1975-76, Baur's 1802 cabriolet from 1974, the European base-model 1602 (also from '74), and the plain-Jane 1502, a price-leader holdover model offered in 1975-77.*

*Other drivers saw this end of the rapid 170-bhp 2002 Turbo most often. Note rear spoiler, flared wheelarches. This model was a victim of the energy crisis, and only 1672 were built in 1973-74.*

and it proved a solid hit. Introduced along with the single-carb 100-bhp standard version in 1968 was the even hotter twin-carb 2002 ti, with 120 bhp (DIN), a 115-mph top end, and 10-second standing-start acceleration to 100 km/h. In February 1971, the ti moved over for the 2002 tii, a 130-bhp stormer with near 120-mph top speed and vivid off-the-line go.

It wasn't long before the 2002 replaced the 1600 as BMW's volume seller in the U.S. It enjoyed great success in the early Seventies, and probably won more converts to the marque than any single model since the glamorous 507. Unhappily, safety and emissions standards wreaked increasing havoc each year. By 1974, the 2002 was saddled with ugly "rubber baby buggy bumpers" and the tii was in its final season. Through it all, however, the 2002 remained an entertaining little car and good value, and BMW even managed to maintain much of its original sparkle by fitting a revised cylinder head and a more efficient two-barrel

carburetor beginning with the 1973 models.

Meanwhile, the "02" series was evolving in Europe. The same month the 1600 TI arrived, a handsome full convertible was announced with the normal-tune 1.6-liter engine and bodywork by Baur. A 2002 variant replaced it in 1971. Also that year, the 1600-2 was renamed 1602, and a 1.8-liter model, the 1802, was added. At the same time, a companion three-door hatchback body style called the Touring came on stream in 1600, 1800, and 2000 form. The Baur convertibles saw only limited U.S. imports and the Touring hatchbacks regrettably were never officially sold here. The 1600 Touring was struck after only one season, but the other versions continued through 1974. BMW also built a limited number—about 5800—of the three-doors with the potent tii injected engine.

The hottest of the "baby Bimmers" was undoubtedly the 2002 Turbo, unveiled at the 1973 Frankfurt show. It may have disappointed some, coming only a year after BMW had displayed its mouth-watering mid-engine Turbo prototype, but at least you could buy this boxy little bolide. And considering its great per-

formance, the 2002 Turbo was remarkably inexpensive, around $6600 in Germany. The 1990cc tii engine with Kugelfischer injection was treated to a BLD-type turbocharger from KKK and compression lowered to 6.9:1 in the interest of preventing harmful detonation under boost. The result was 170 bhp (DIN) at 5800 rpm, 130 mph flat out, and 0-100 km/h acceleration in a mere eight seconds flat. Looking every inch the factory hot rod it was, the Turbo sported a lowered suspension, prominent front air dam (with "2002 Turbo" in mirror-image lettering so drivers ahead would know what was about to pass them), a rear spoiler, and wide wheelarch extensions. It was plenty conspicuous in its brilliant white paint and never intended for the average buyer, but the 2002 Turbo debuted on the eve of the Arab oil embargo that touched off the first energy crisis, and that put a big damper on sales. The model was killed off in 1974, and only 1672 were built.

The final version of the "02" was a low-compression (8.0:1) plain-Jane offering, the 1502. Introduced in 1975, it was mainly a response to the oil shock, priced to sell at an attractive 11,390 marks and powered by the 1573cc engine. Sell it did—so much so that BMW continued it even after it phased out the other "02" models to make way for the modern 3-series cars that replaced them in 1975-76.

With the New Class and the "02" series, BMW reached new heights of prosperity and prestige. Both model lines were spectacular successes. Some 350,000 of the four-doors were sold through the end of this design in 1972, and nearly 864,000 of the two-doors found buyers during a 10-year production run. BMW had come off the ropes to become the undisputed world champion of sports sedans. Despite some pretty fair efforts from rival automakers, it's a title BMW has yet to relinquish—and likely never will.

With its move into the 1.8- and 2.0-liter displacement classes, BMW began competing openly against the lower end of the Mercedes-Benz line in price and performance. But something even more ambitious was in the works: a new six-cylinder engine in the 2.5-3.0-liter range. It was to form the basis for a wholly new group of luxury models from Munich—a direct challenge to the senior Mercedes.

The decision to proceed with the new six was taken in early 1965 after a considerable amount of market research and an in-depth report by Helmut Werner Bönsch. Sales director Paul Hahnemann endorsed the idea, as did representatives of the Quandt interests. Gerhard Wilcke, who had been on the supervisory board since 1960, became BMW's new president on April 1, 1965. Former president Karl Heinz Sonne had other fish to fry, but maintained his board membership until he left the Quandt group in 1970 to become president of Klöckner-Humboldt-Deutz of Cologne, a company three or four times the size of BMW.

The six-cylinder project was started without the guidance of Fritz Fiedler, who had retired by this time (he died in 1972). The firm had also been through a change of technical directors with the retirement of Dr. Robert Pertuss in late 1963. Wilhelm Gieschen took over the job. For Fiedler's replacement, BMW managers decided not to promote from within but instead hired Bernhard Osswald away from Ford. He was charged with all research and product development and had a seat on the management board, so his authority was even greater than Fiedler's. After Osswald's arrival, Gieschen assumed the title of director for production and quality control. Alfred Böning was still on the staff, though some-

# POWER POLITICS: THE BIRTH OF THE BIG SIX

*The frontal aspect of the 3.0 CS, which bowed in late 1971 as the larger-capacity successor to the 2800 CS.*

*This page, top: The 2500 in its original 1968 form. Above: Both big sedans used all-MacPherson suspension. Opposite page, top left: A later 2500 with blacked-out grille. Lower left: The appropriately badged 2800 from '68. Upper and lower right: Both models shared modern BMW dash and drop-down decklid toolkit.*

what on the sidelines, and he retired in 1970 after a career spanning more than 30 years.

It seemed almost incredible that a Ford man was now the head of engineering for BMW's future models, but Osswald was no ordinary auto executive. He had joined Ford in Cologne in 1951. After a few months in chassis and transmission engineering, he was given charge of engine design, and went on to create the firm's ubiquitous 1.5-liter (91-cid) V-4, then a 1.7-liter engine for the Taunus 17M. He was later promoted to chief of product development, and supervised activities involving all phases of car design except the body structure. Among his accomplishments were easier shifting for all German Ford models and improved handling on the FK-100 van. He also cured the worst problems in the front-wheel-drive Fords of the day, making them competitive in performance, fuel economy, and roadability. Interestingly, Osswald had been offered the job of technical director at Volkswagen in 1964, but that would have meant moving to Wolfsburg, which he wasn't prepared for. Then BMW invited

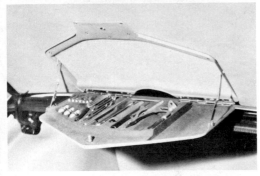

basic construction principles so thoroughly established by the New Class and continued in the smaller two-doors: unit body/ chassis, all-independent all-coil suspension with MacPherson struts in front and semi-trailing arms at the rear, and a slanted inline engine with single chain-driven overhead camshaft, cast-iron block and light-alloy head. Dimensions and packaging closely paralleled the "New Generation" Mercedes-Benz W114/W115 models introduced in January 1968. The big BMWs followed in September. Wheelbase was 106 inches, overall length 185 inches, width 69 inches, and height 56 inches. Dry weight was kept down to below 2900 pounds, which gave both versions very favorable power-to-weight ratios. Styling and body engineering were executed entirely within the BMW organization under Wilhelm Hofmeister, and New Class design themes were clearly evident here, too. BMW's customary glassy, square-cut lines trans-

him to Munich to discuss an appointment as board member for research and engineering. He didn't hesitate a second. His first assignment was to fix the adjustment problems of the 1800 TI engine. He also developed the 1800 TI/SA and the two-door "02" models before tackling the big one, the new six-cylinder model.

It would be tempting to think

of the 2500 and 2800 that emerged as simply stretched versions of the New Class design with two extra cylinders, but there was more to them than that. Their bodyshell was all-new, their chassis incorporated many innovations, and their new six-cylinder engine had certain basic differences from the four-cylinder units. What the new models did inherit were the

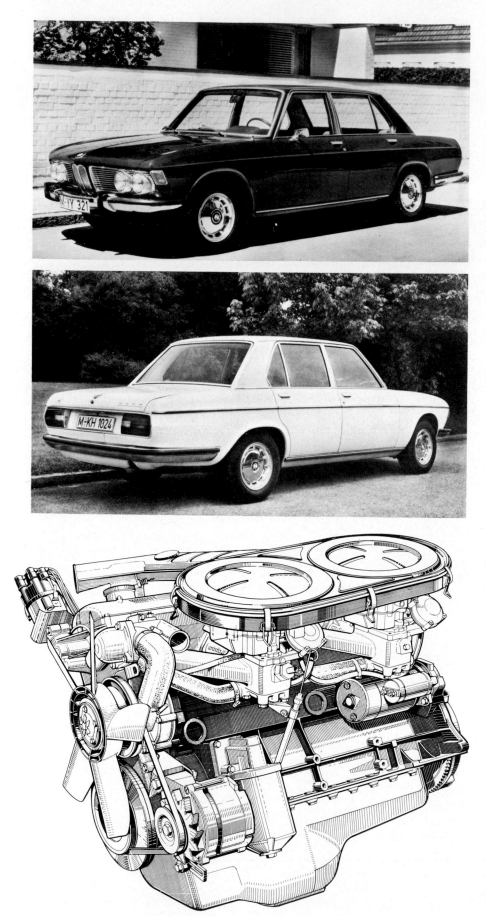

lated handsomely to the larger proportions, but subtle detail touches gave the 2500/2800 a look all their own—crisper yet somehow broad-shouldered.

Designated the M-52, the new six-cylinder powerplant did not correspond exactly in cylinder dimensions to any of the four-cylinder units then in production. The 2.5-liter version had a bore and stroke of 86 x 71.6mm (3.39 x 2.82 in.) for swept volume of precisely 2494cc (152 cid). The 2.8 had the same bore and a longer 80mm (3.15-in.) stroke for 2788cc (170 cid). Design alterations mainly involved combustion chamber shape and the cooling system. The fours employed pentroof chambers with two "pockets," one facing each valve, and the spark plugs squeezed as close to the center as possible. The new six had a three-pocket shape, with the area around the plugs opened up to form its own pocket. This was called a tri-spherical chamber, and BMW's U.S. advertising promoted it with the tongue-twisting German name *Der Drei-kugelwirbelwannenbrennraum.* In evolving this shape, Alex von Falkenhausen worked on a theory that made turbulence a secondary consideration in efficiency. What mattered was that the mixture be properly directed past the intake valve. The aim was to let the mixture flow accompany the flame front travel, from the spark plug to the most remote areas, so as to obtain complete combustion with a minimum of residual hydrocarbons.

Helmut Werner Bönsch pointed out other features of the new six at the 2500/2800 press introduction: "We were able to take back spark timing by seven degrees. That lowered the heat loss through the cylinder walls and reduced the hydrocarbon content

*Top and center: Apart from engine size, 2500 and 2800 differed only in standard equipment and price. The light car is a 2800. Left: A factory line drawing of the twin-carb 2.5-liter M-52 six, initially rated at 150 bhp (DIN).*

in the exhaust gas. The thermal value of the plugs was reduced from 230 for the *Autobahn* and 200 for ordinary driving to 175 for all conditions. Improvement of the intake ports helped us gain a few horsepower. The valve guides, which usually form unwanted turbulence in the intake ports, have been made more aerodynamic by means of a metal rib running through the port area to give it a uniform cross-section. We had learned from our racing engines how to avoid wobbling of the piston at high revs," he continued, "for even the best combustion is worthless if the gases blow past the rings. In these engines there is no wobble even at 8000 rpm. We mounted the crankshaft on seven main bearings, but that wasn't enough for us. We also added a counterweight to each crank web, 12 in all, to make sure our six-cylinder engine would be exquisitely balanced."

Accompanying the new engine was a cooling system remarkable in having one main circuit and two auxiliary circuits. One auxiliary line went to the heater element, the other to the intake manifold and carburetor base for preheating the charge. The main circuit was equipped with a double-sided thermostat that sensed coolant temperature not only at the "hot" engine outlet but also at the "cool" radiator outlet. By balancing one against the other, the thermostat could reroute a major proportion of coolant to the block rather than passing it on to the radiator, thus protecting the block under conditions when extremely cold water from the radiator could set up thermal shock in a warm engine. A viscous clutch was employed to slow the fan at high rpm and turn it off completely at high speeds when ram-effect action alone was sufficient for cooling. Another interesting detail was the oil pump, an Eaton gear-type design in which a roller with four blades ran eccentrically in a five-lobe casing. It was very quiet, and offered

extremely high capacity at high rpm.

In their initial form, both the new sixes ran on 9.0:1 compression and had dual two-barrel downdraft Zenith 35/40 INAT carburetors. The 2.5 unit's maximum output was 150 bhp (DIN) at 6000 rpm, which compares with 170 bhp at 6000 rpm for the 2.8. Peak torque was 156 and 174 lbs/ft, respectively, both at 3700 rpm. The new sedans shared a standard four-speed Getrag gearbox with a 3.85 first, 2.08 second, 1.375:1 third, and direct (1:1) top gear ratios. Optional at extra cost was the ZF 3HP 21 automatic with hydraulic torque converter and three-stage planetary gearing. Final drive ratios were 3.65:1 for the 2500 and 3.45:1 for the 2800, the latter with standard limited-slip differential.

In chassis and suspension layout the new big cars were a mixture of old and new. For example, ZF worm-and-roller steering was used as on the four-cylinder models, but the sixes had all-disc instead of disc/drum brakes, with solid rotors carrying four-piston calipers. The front suspension retained the smaller models' MacPherson-strut layout but with an important difference. Here the struts were inclined rearwards at 14.5 degrees from vertical and were not centered on the hub. The hub also sat more to the rear so that the effective inclination was only 9.5 degrees. This geometrical trickery was claimed to have several advantages, such as less castor action and lighter steering effort, greater horizontal compliance, and stronger resistance to nosedive in hard braking. The rear suspension differed in that the coil springs were not mounted directly on the semi-trailing arms as in the four-cylinder models but on a Mac-Pherson strut (Chapman strut) rising from the hub carrier with a slight inward inclination. The 2800 offered the additional refinement of Boge Nivomat self-levelling rear shock absorbers.

The revised rear suspension reduced bending strains on the wheel hubs as well as wheel bearing loads, and repositioning the springs left more free space around the tires for accommodating wider wheels and tires if needed.

The new top-line sedans were quite well received despite high prices. The 2500 listed initially at 14,485 marks, the 2800 at 17,250—figures that put the big Bimmers head to head with the Mercedes 250S and 250SE. Nevertheless, Paul Hahnemann's sales force managed to move 36,000 in 1969 alone, indicating just how much buyers liked these posh *Autobahn* flyers.

Both the new models came to America, and *Road & Track* magazine waxed almost ecstatic about the 2500 in its 1969 test. Enthused the editors: "The all-new six-cylinder engine is a jewel. At low speeds it combines a sporting exhaust note...with a modest amount of BMW cam-drive whine and practically no other underhood noise; as the revs climb toward its redline of 6200 rpm it takes on a snarl delightfully like that of a Porsche 911. At low speeds it belies its modest 2.5-liter displacement with surprisingly generous torque and flexibility, but out on the freeway it sounds much too busy in spite of the easygoing 3.54:1 final drive." *R&T* called the handling "exemplary," generally neutral "with slight power-off oversteer. Rough surfaces bring out the expected BMW suspension suppleness and utter lack of body flexing or rattling...Two problems typical of BMW semi-trailing rear suspension remain [namely] wheel patter on brutal clutch engagement and inside rear wheel lifting on hard cornering—neither of which is a serious problem."

Though the 2500 may have seemed underpowered, *R&T*'s performance numbers proved otherwise. The magazine's manual-shift test car needed only 10 seconds in the 0-60 mph

dash, and trotted through the quarter-mile in 17.3 seconds at a terminal speed of 81 mph. More impressive was its 20.9-mpg overall fuel mileage, excellent for a car of this bulk and swiftness. Here was the best of all worlds—except for the $5284 sticker price, which must have put off more than a few potential customers. "But that's the price you pay for top quality," summarized *R&T*, "and there is no doubt that its performance is faster, more sporting and longer-legged than that of its nearest competitor." Which meant the small Mercedes.

BMW observed a milestone in 1968 when daily production exceeded 500 cars for the first time in history. More than 100,000 came off the Munich assembly lines for the calendar year. The model line was now exceptionally strong, and almost every car in it was proving to be a sell-out year after year. In 1970 the firm passed another important benchmark with production of its one millionth postwar car.

Though it was still a small producer by, say, GM standards, BMW had become profitable enough that it could now afford to bring out new models much more quickly than it ever did before. The new six seemed like a natural for the Karmann-bodied coupes, which had been criticized for their tepid performance. Accordingly, a new six-cylinder model, the 2800 CS, was unveiled alongside the big sedans at the Frankfurt show in September 1968. Retaining the basic body structure of the now-superseded 2000 C/CS, designer Wilhelm Hofmeister extended wheelbase by three inches—to 103.3 inches—all of it ahead of the cowl, and grafted on a longer, more attractive front to accomodate the longer engine. The awkward old "pug" nose was replaced by a more integrated and pleasing ensemble bearing a definite family resemblance with the new sedans, and their front suspension was applied to the coupe as well. *Road and Track* opined in 1970 that the styling changes gave the 2800 CS "a crisp aggressive appearance. It looks *right.*"

And it performed beautifully: 0-60 mph was a 9.3-second trip, and the quarter-mile post flashed by in 17.4 seconds, at which point the 2800 CS would be doing 82 mph. It was no muscle car, of course: just a stunningly capable high-performance GT. *R&T* admitted that this svelte new BMW "awed and made covetous every member of the staff and everyone else who saw or rode in it. It impressed us as a car that simply conquered all road conditions with polished authority, a car as much for enthusiastic hard driving as for sedate, comfortable cruising. *But*—it costs over $8000 basic, over $8500 as equipped, and close to $9000 with tax and license. [This is in 1970 dollars, remember.] It was already unattainable by mere mortals, before the re-evaluation of the German Deutsch mark, at $7600...The answer to this, of course, is that the BMW is a far more stable, balanced, totally usable car than any other we can think of, and there is nothing remotely approaching the 2800 CS for significantly less...Anyone [with this kind of money] to spend must find the 2800 CS close to irresistible."

Franz Josef Popp and Hanns Grewenig would have been proud of this car. The 2800 CS was truly the kind of premium product they had labored so long for—available only for the fortunate—*very* fortunate—few. BMW turned out only 9400 of them through April 1971, and just 1167 were exported to the U.S.

The new six had been designed with possible displacement increases in mind, and the 3.0-liter version introduced in April 1971 formed the basis for an expanded fleet of luxury BMWs. This 2986cc (182-cid) unit, created by stretching the M-52 bore to 89mm (3.50 in.), was offered in twin-carb form with 9.0:1 compression and 180 bhp (DIN) at 6000 rpm, and with Bosch D-Jetronic fuel injection and slightly higher 9.5:1 compression, good for 200 bhp at 5500 rpm. Sedans so equipped were designated 3.0 S and 3.0 Si, respectively, and were additions to the lineup. The 2800 CS was phased out in favor of the

corresponding 3.0 CS and 3.0 CSi coupes.

Also appearing in 1971 was the Bavaria, a canny bit of marketing strategy intended to bolster U.S. sales of the big sedans, which had never lived up to company expectations. *Road & Track* described it as "simply a detrimmed 2800, and not very detrimmed at that." The Bavaria replaced both the 2500 and 2800, but was priced less than either of them. The East Coast port-of-entry figure was $4987, about $1200 under the former and a whopping $2000 below the latter. Though factory production totals don't break out the Bavaria separately from other models, the pricing tactic was apparently a success, and *R&T* was moved to rate this "one of the best buys among luxury sedans." In 1974 the Bavaria was joined by an American-market 3.0 S, which was supplanted the following year by the injected 3.0 Si. Both these were fully equipped cars with such standard amenities as leather interior and full power assists.

Back in Munich, Gustav Ed-

*Right and bottom: A longer nose and six-cylinder power completely transformed the 2.0-liter Karmann-built coupe. Shown is the initial 2800 CS from 1968. Above: The more economical 150-bhp 2500 CS bowed in 1974 as an "energy crisis" special. Only 844 were built. None were sold in the U.S. Opposite page: The later 170-bhp 3.0 CS in 1974 American guise.*

erer had been named head of six-cylinder engine development in 1972, and he decided the big BMWs could use still more power. The result was a 3295cc (201-cid) six, created by lengthening stroke to 88.4mm (3.48 in.). It appeared in March 1974 for a new model, the 3.3 L. As BMW's first direct contender in the limousine market since the aborted Type 505 of the Fifties, it was essentially a 2500/2800 on a four-inch longer wheelbase (110 inches) and boasted full-house luxury equipment. That included automatic transmission, of course, but four-speed manual was available to special order—presumably for enthusiastic chauffeurs. With twin Zenith carburetors and 190 bhp (DIN) at 5500 rpm, the 3.3 L had a top speed of 127 mph plus remarkable acceleration, capable of reaching 100 km/h (62 mph) from rest in 9.0 seconds flat.

In late 1976, this engine was revised with Bosch L-Jetronic fuel injection for a replacement model, the 3.3 Li. Stroke was slightly reduced, to 86mm (3.34

in.) for 3205cc (105.5 cid), and a new combustion chamber was incorporated, designed by Dr. Georg Vorberger. Maximum output climbed to 197 bhp (DIN) at 5500 rpm, but performance and fuel economy (around 13.5 mpg) were practically unaffected. Priced identically with the increasingly popular Mercedes-Benz 450SE, the 3.3 Li sold somewhat above expectations, but only 3030 of the 3.3-liter limos were built altogether. Incidentally, there were also 2.8- and 3.0-liter L (*lang*, long) sedans available from 1975 through the end of the big BMW four-doors in 1977.

While most cars of the early Seventies seemed to become more boring with each passing year, BMWs only seemed to become more exciting. For proof, look no further than the 3.0 CSL. Introduced along with the revised 3.0-liter CS/CSi coupes in early 1971, this was another "homologation special," produced only in sufficient volume to qualify for international endurance racing. The "L" in this designation stood for *leicht* (lightweight) not "long," and the CSL weighed in several hundred pounds under its production stablemates. Initially it was powered by the normal twin-carb 2985cc six. In early 1972 a miniscule quarter-millimeter bore increase was made to bring displacement up to 3003cc (183.2 cid), and Bosch D-Jetronic injection was substituted for the

carbs. Later that year, racing CSLs began appearing with a variety of aerodynamic addenda, including a chin spoiler, little longitudinal airfoils on the front fenders, a large rear spoiler suspended between two tall fins on the rear fenders, and yet another spoiler at the rear edge of the roof. For the final version, stroke was upped to 84mm (3.30 in.) to produce a 3153cc powerplant rated at 206 bhp (DIN) at 5600 rpm, which enabled the CSL to blaze through the 0-100 km/h run in a mere 7.0 seconds. Other features included racing-style bucket seats, small-diameter sports steering wheel, and larger wheels and tires. Theoretically you could buy one of these and use it on the road, but very few people did, and astounding prices (31,950 marks in 1971, rising to 42,260 by 1975) assured that only the well-heeled ever got the chance. Only 1096 examples were built (some sources state 1039) through 1975. Most CSLs wound up on the track, where they did surprisingly well against the lighter, more powerful Porsche 911s in GT-class enduros. The 3.0 CSL was truly BMW's "ultimate driving machine" in these years.

Harald Quandt, whose faith and fortune had pulled BMW back from the brink of near-certain disaster in 1960, ironically did not live to see the success of the new six-cylinder models. He perished along with a small group of friends when his private plane crashed en route to Italy in September 1967. His half-brother Herbert took over his BMW holdings as part of the estate settlement. Harald's lieutenant, a young man named Eberhard von Kuenheim, joined Herbert's office with the special assignment of keeping an eye on BMW. Born to a family of the Prussian aristocracy, Von Kuenheim served with an anti-aircraft gun crew in World War II at the age of only 15. After the war he found him-

self orphaned and poor and fled to the west, where he found a job as an assembly line worker with Bosch in 1946. Bosch recognized his talents and arranged a scholarship at the Stuttgart Technical University. He returned with an engineering diploma, but left Bosch soon afterwards to try his luck as an export market salesman for a small machine-tool manufacturer. He was hired by Harald Quandt to work on his private staff in the Bad Homburg office.

The sudden death of Harald Quandt had major repercussions for the business world and BMW in particular, for the company's survival as an independent concern was once again in doubt. Rumors of a merger with Daimler-Benz began cropping up in 1971, based on the fact that the Quandt family owned about 15 percent of D-B. Rumors also surfaced about a link between BMW and Volkswagen following the Audi/NSU merger in 1969 that soon became a VW subsidiary. In response, Herbert Quandt declared that if he were ever forced to dispose of his BMW interests he would sell only to Daimler-Benz. In light of this, some of BMW's 18,000 small shareholders began to fear that

Quandt might work a stock exchange deal with Daimler-Benz, which might then give D-B enough of a voice in BMW to block any action contemplated by the other stockholders. But it never came to pass, nor did any other tieup. Volkswagen president Kurt Lotz did offer up to 750 million marks for a controlling interest in BMW on two occasions in 1970, but Quandt turned him down. He was also approached by DAF of Eindhoven in the Netherlands in 1971. DAF needed to broaden its product base, and proposed that BMW shift some of its production to Eindhoven in exchange for free access to BMW dealers, who would sell DAF cars in the Netherlands and other markets. It came to nothing, and DAF was absorbed by Volvo five years later.

Meantime, BMW was in the throes of another management shake-up precipitated, at least partly, by Harald Quandt's death. It began in September

*Below: The European 3.0 CS, circa 1975. Bumpers were tidier than on U.S. models. Opposite page, top: The American 3.0 Si sedan of 1975-76. Bottom: A beautifully maintained example of a late (1973) 3.0 CSL. Note unusual roof-mounted spoiler.*

1969 when Gerhardt Wilcke resigned as president, due to ill health. Sales director Paul Hahnemann was appointed deputy president, and fully expected to be named chairman. Instead, it was Von Kuenheim, a man 18 years younger, who was installed, effective January 1, 1970. Hahnemann had acquired decision-making authority far beyond the usual domain of a sales director, but in the ensuing months he found his clout diminishing. He clashed openly several times with the new chairman, who resented Hahnemann's free-wheeling style and could not tolerate what he viewed as a direct challenge to his leadership. Matters came to a head in the fall of 1971, and Von Kuenheim issued an ultimatum to Quandt, threatening to leave unless Hahnemann were fired. The sales boss left on October 31, two days before his 59th birthday. He had been well liked by BMW workers, who staged a 24-hour strike to protest his ouster. Hahnemann had undeniably worked wonders for BMW. When he joined the company it was producing only 50 cars a day. When he left, it was turning out 750 cars a day. Filling his shoes would not be easy, but BMW made a good choice in his replacement, hiring Robert A. Lutz away from Opel, effective January 1, 1972. We'll have more to say abut Lutz in a later chapter.

Two other key personnel changes occurred in this period. One involved production and quality control chief Wilhelm Gieschen, who reached retirement in 1971. His successor was Hans Koch, a graduate of the Aachen Technical University who had worked for Ford Germany as well as the Kotz and Sons axle manufacturing concern and Boge, the shock absorber company. Under Koch, BMW production would reach new heights. The second change came in late 1975 with the retirement of Alex Von Falkenhausen as chief of engine development. Taking his place was Karlheinz Lange, a recruit from Porsche in Stuttgart.

In 1977 the curtain fell on the first generation of the modern BMW sixes. Production of the big sedans totalled 208,305 of all types, while the lovely Karmann-bodied coupes numbered 44,254. These are the cars that announced BMW's return to the luxury market in no uncertain terms: smooth and spirited, beautifully engineered, solidly built, and blessed with what can only be called "soul," unusual for machines of such elegance and refinement. And in the end, that's what makes these cars special, their artful compromise of seemingly incompatible qualities: high performance with good fuel economy, restrained style with surprising practicality, German sturdiness with Italian *brio*. You can't ask much more than that from any car—at any price.

173

# BMW GOES RACING: MOTORSPORT, ENGINES, ADVENTURES

A "special production class" racer based on the first-generation 3-series awaits testing in the Pininfarina wind tunnel.

It took about 20 years for BMW to get back to formal competition activities after World War II. Pause to ponder that a moment. Here was an outfit that had dominated much of the racing scene in the Thirties not only with its cars but with its motorcycles, a company that knew better than any other in Europe the truth of that old Detroit marketing maxim "race on Sunday, sell on Monday." Yet in the war's devastating aftermath, BMW couldn't even think about a return to racing before about 1965. To be sure, some individuals scored hard-fought victories in BMWs during the Forties and Fifties, but the factory itself had neither the money nor the manpower to indulge in something so frivolous: it was too busy fighting for its life. Then everything changed. The Quandt brothers' eleventh-hour financial rescue was followed by solid profits from the highly acclaimed New Class cars. By the time the two-door "02" series appeared in 1966, BMW could, at long last, literally afford the luxury of engaging in competition.

When the original 1600-2 was unveiled to the press, product chief Bernhard Osswald was asked whether the company had any plans for a sports racing version. Evidently he forgot about the 1800 TI/SA of just two years earlier, because he replied that such a car would be developed "over my dead body." But the truth was that a new BMW with racing aspirations was already on the way. It appeared the very next year, in fact: the 1600 TI. Drivers Dieter Quester and Hubert Hahne challenged Porsche for the European hillclimb championship in 1967, and renewed the attack in 1968 when the even more promising 2002 was announced. That season, factory-prepared 2002s began showing up in Group 5 for European Touring Car Championship events. Suddenly, it seemed BMW was back. If it wasn't, then at least independent speed shops such as Schnitzer,

*Engine tuning wizard Ludwig Apfelbeck shows off his radial-valve cylinder head for the BMW Formula 2 engine.*

Alpina, Koeppchen, and Heidegger were, because they made the 2002 into a formidable racing weapon, with or without factory help.

Racing 2002s packed about 190 bhp (DIN), compared with 100 bhp for the road cars. This output was achieved by going to a wilder camshaft, fuel injection, and "blueprinted" internal parts. Other modifications included fat eight-inch-wide wheels and tires, appropriately widened fenders, stiffer springs and, later, a special five-speed gearbox. These potent "Baby Bimmers" proved their mettle right away. Dieter Quester won Division III (over 1600cc) in the 1968 European Touring Car Championship with his 2002, and another car won the European mountain championship that year. The 2002 would go on to take the German rally championship for four consecutive seasons, 1969-72.

BMW knew that 190 bhp in a 2205-pound car wouldn't be enough for the 1969 season, not against the 225-bhp Porsche 911, which was then classified as a touring car. Rather than accept defeat, BMW engineers decided to exploit the latitude of the Group 5 rules and started experimenting with turbocharging. The result was the 2002ti Turbo with an Eberspächer blower that raised output to 275 bhp at 6500 rpm and top speed to 143 mph. Quester again won the Division III title in the touring car series. For the 1970 season this engine was spinning out a full 290 bhp, remarkable for a 2.0-liter four.

Privately entered 2002s soon appeared in other racing classes. The Schnitzer brothers, Josef and Hermann, got 190 bhp out of their Group 2 ti in 1969 and no less than 205 bhp in Group 5 tune. Bodies were stripped for lightness, so that the Group 2 car weighed 1962 pounds and the Group 5 car only 1918 pounds. Schnitzer's 2002ti rally engine that year was tweaked to produce 175 bhp at 7400 rpm, with 10.7:1 compression and dual two-barrel Solex 45mm sidedraft carburetors.

Another firm building unbeatable BMWs was Alpina, the creation of Burkhard Bovensiepen. His family ran a typewriter factory at Kaufbeuren, and that's where he first began transforming cars. Later he set up his own shop at nearby Buchloe. Paul Frère tested an Alpina-prepared Group 5 2002 in February 1969. Its engine had been wound up to 180 bhp (at 7000 rpm) via 11.0:1 compression, high-lift camshaft, polished connecting rods, lightened flywheel, and twin Weber 45 DCOE two-barrel carbs. A five-speed gearbox and limited-slip differential, borrowed from the production 2002 tii, were fitted, and the car had a lowered suspension and quick-ratio steering. It did 0-100 km/h (62 mph) in six seconds flat, and needed a scant 15.2 seconds to reach 100 mph (160 km/h) from rest. Moreover, Frère found the Alpina to be faster than a Lamborghini Miura V-12 or a Porsche 911S around the Vallelunga track near Rome.

The 2002 Turbo was ruled out of Group 5 for 1970, but it was allowed to compete in Group 7, reserved for two-seat racing cars. This was as good as a ticket to the nearest museum.

Simultaneously, the unblown 2002 was classified in Group 2 (modified touring cars), and Schnitzer, Alpina, and Koeppchen all worked on tuning for this version. They obtained about 220 bhp thanks to a four-valve head, 11.0:1 compression, and fuel injection. Schnitzer also developed a four-valve head for 1972, retaining the chain drive to the camshaft, which allowed him to use the entire bottom end, too. The firm claimed 225 bhp for its "rally" engine kit, while a "Formula 2" kit with carburetor was rated at 265 bhp and the same package with fuel injection delivered a claimed 270 bhp.

The 2002 was finally ousted as the dominant European racing sedan by the Cosworth-powered Ford Escort. The 1972 season was a poor one, but BMW decided to make a renewed offensive the next year. This involved a new four-valve head and 11.0:1 compression, good for 270 bhp, plus a five-speed gearbox, limited-slip differential, and gumball 245/14 tires at the front and 260/14s at the rear. The complete 1973 racer had an all-up weight of 2029 pounds. It had promise, but didn't live up to it. Still, BMW was not greatly up-

*Above and opposite page top and lower right: The 1972 mid-engine Turbo show car inspired the limited-production M1 that enjoyed minor competition success in the late Seventies. Near right: Apfelbeck's tall 16-valve racing head as installed on the production 2002 four. Opposite page, lower left: The 1977 version of the potent BMW Formula 2 power unit.*

set, since its racing emphasis had shifted by this time from sedans to Formula 2.

The prelude to BMW's emergence as a builder of Grand Prix engines went almost unnoticed. It all began in 1966, when Alex von Falkenhausen mounted a BMW four in a Brabham chassis and proceeded to set a number of unofficial world speed records. The following year, the company formally entered Formula 2 under its own banner with a new car built on a Lola chassis. Hubert Hahne and Jo Siffert were contracted as drivers, and Klaus Steinmetz was named *Rennleiter* (racing team manager). Steinmetz had joined BMW the previous November after working at Abarth in Turin for several years, and was also responsible for chassis modifications and development. The chassis was a monocoque structure designed by Eric Broadley of England and mounted a Hewland 5 FT gear-

box. The engine, based on the production-model 1600 block, was claimed to produce 225 bhp at 9500 rpm. Its 89mm (3.50-in.) bore and 64.2mm (2.53-in.) stroke were chosen to come within the 1600cc displacement limit. Von Falkenhausen decided to try Lucas fuel injection and Bosch transistorized ignition on this featherweight engine (a mere 286 pounds). Paul Rosche designed the bottom end and Otto Stulle was in charge of en-

176

gine testing and development. But the top end was the real mechanical marvel, created by Ludwig Apfelbeck.

Apfelbeck was born in Graz, Austria, in 1903. That's the home of Puch motorcycles, and he worked for that firm for a few years in the mid-1920s. It was motorcycle racer and engineer Rudolf Schleicher who brought him to Munich, where he worked in the motorcycle engine design office beginning in October

1939, after Schleicher had developed a supercharged motorcycle engine. With the outbreak of war, Apfelbeck was transferred to the Berlin-Spandau plant as a test engineer for aircraft engines. After the war, he returned to Graz and tuning racing bike engines. He joined Horex in Bad Homburg about 1948 to design a new family of motorcycle engines, then went to Maico in 1955, where a minicar was under study. When that company

went under three years later, he returned to Graz, then went to a company called Trunkenpolz in the town of Mattighofen, where he created motorcycles based on MV-Agusta engineering as well as the Mecky moped. The following year, his friend Schleicher, still at BMW, arranged for his return to Munich. In 1959, Von Falkenhausen named Apfelbeck chief of the 700 engine project. Later he moved to head the section involved with engines for racing 700s. From there he went on to the four-cylinder family of car engines.

The Formula 2 head design was inspired by a single-cylinder Rudge engine from about 1927 employing four radially disposed overhead valves. The mechanical arrangements necessary to accomplish the same breathing pattern on an inline four were considerably more complex, however. Two chain-driven overhead camshafts were used. The valves were splayed in two planes—longitudinally as well as transversely—and opened via a double-rocker system. A V-shaped rocker arm rode against the cam with one wing, while the other wing acted on a finger-type arm bearing against the valve lifter. Intake valves were placed close to the centerline, diagonally left and right of center. The exhaust valves were closer to the outside, with ports on alternate sides. Apfelbeck's main problem was the sharply domed pistons needed for a sufficiently high compression ratio with the short stroke. That led to a valve angle wider than ideal and a valvetrain with overly long rocker arms that were prone to flexing at high rpm. The result was that the valve timing was seriously upset at 9000-10,000 rpm.

BMW had a dismal season in 1967, and cars powered by the Cosworth-Ford FVA engine (with no more than 225 bhp) cleaned up in Formula 2. Apfelbeck was no longer working at BMW by the start of the '68 season, and Paul Rosche went to work on a different four-valve layout.

Born in Munich in 1934, Rosche had attended local schools. After obtaining his engineering diploma in 1957 he went straight to BMW, where he had been ever since. His revised four-valve head differed from usual practice where the two exhaust valves are positioned on one side of the head and the two intakes on the other. His solution was to put one intake and one exhaust valve on each side, each set serv-

ing half of a pentroof combustion chamber. Unfortunately, BMW had to sit out most of the 1968 season while the engine was being finalized. By September, however, it was putting out a reliable 235 bhp at 10,200 rpm, and Hubert Hahne drove the Lola-BMW to its first victory at Hockenheim the following month. There was still a problem: the timing gear teeth had a habit of chipping off, so the engine was reworked again during the winter of 1968-69. At the same time, Len Terry was called in to fix the Lola chassis, which had not shown entirely satisfactory handling. The Lola-BMW proved more competitive during the 1969 season, but it still wasn't a consistent winner.

For 1970, Rosche reverted to two valves per cylinder (with three spark plugs) for yet another revised engine. This unit produced 240 bhp at 10,000 rpm with full reliability, and it became the most successful Formula 2 powerplant that season. This may have been by dint of sheer numbers, for a higher than usual number of cars competed, though quite a few failed to finish some races. Nevertheless, the factory racked up an impressive record. Hahne drove to victory at Hockenheim, Jacky Ickx did the same at Salzburg and Langenlebarn, Siffert scored at Rouen, and Dieter Quester won outright at Neubiberg and Macao.

In late 1971, newly appointed BMW chairman Eberhard von Kuenheim decided that the company should go racing in a more serious and official manner. BMW had no real racing division at the time, so competition efforts had to be conducted with parts and manpower contributed by various departments. Now there would be a separate competition group, and Von Kuenheim named his new sales director, Robert A. Lutz, to head it. Lutz was born in Switzerland of American parents, and grew up in Zürich. After high school he went to the University of Cali-

fornia at Berkeley, where he earned degrees in science and business administration. After military service as a fighter pilot in the U.S. Marine Corps, he was discharged with the rank of captain in 1959. Though his father was a bank manager, Lutz was much more interested in cars than finances and soon landed a job with General Motors in New York. Before long he was handling overseas assignments, first with Opel in Germany and later with GM France.

Lutz's first important action after arriving in Munich was to organize a separate company, BMW Motorsport GmbH, which was incorporated on May 1, 1972 as an autonomous subsidiary. It would be a manufacturer of racing engines, race-tuning kits, and special body and chassis parts, and would serve as a preparation center for BMW's racing customers. To run the new company, Lutz hired race driver Jochen Neerpasch away from Ford Europe, where he had been racing manager since 1968. Born in 1939, Neerpasch had started his career with Porsche as a racing mechanic at the age of 21, and his early driving experience came in a humble Borgward Isabella that he campaigned on weekends. After a brief stint with the German branch of Volvo, he moved on to Ford, and by 1964 had become a member of the Shelby-Cobra racing team. He also drove a Ford GT-40 in Manufacturers Championship events in 1965-66. He then returned briefly to Porsche, racing the incredibly fast 907 and 908 in track events and hill-climbs in 1968. Later that year he went back to Ford, where he set up a separate competition department and also developed the racing Capris that did so well in the European touring car series.

With the Motorsport arm in place, BMW abandoned its Lola-chassis racers in favor of a collaboration with March in England. The factory team was disbanded, and BMW now acted simply as an engine supplier, with March being the official entrant. Meantime, a rules change for the 1972 Formula 2 season moved the displacement limit up to 2.0 liters (122 cid), so Rosche went to work once more. Still using the basic production block, he selected a long 99.2mm (3.90-in.) stroke and 80mm (3.15-in.) bore and modified the four-valve pentroof cylinder head, this time with the usual layout of intake ports on one side and exhaust ports on the other.

Valves were angled at 40 degrees, and intake valve head diameter was 35.8mm (1.41 in.) compared with 30.3mm (1.19 in.) for the exhausts. The twin camshafts were gear-driven, and the valvegear "crash" limit was 11,500 rpm. On a compression ratio of 11.2:1, maximum output was 304 bhp (DIN) at 9250 rpm and a peak 166 lbs/ft of torque at 8000 rpm. The March-BMWs won most Formula 2 races that year, and continued to reign supreme in 1973-74. BMW Motorsport farmed out construction and service of its F2 engines and competition sixes to Schnitzer in 1976. By that time, over 250 F2 engines had been sold at a price of 32,000 marks apiece.

Though its glamorous Grand Prix effort got most of the attention, BMW's activities in sedan racing were in the Sixties and early Seventies of more important—and more immediate—commercial benefit. Long before the 2002 appeared, the blue-and-white badge was carried by the little rear-engine 700 in numerous rallies and closed-circuit races, mainly against the small-displacement Fiats tuned by engine wizard Carlo Abarth.

*Left and top: BMW Motorsport campaigned a team of racing 3.0 CSLs with highly modified bodywork in 1975. The cars were seen at numerous U.S. circuits in the IMSA/Camel GT series, such as the Laguna Seca event shown here. Above: Robert A. Lutz managed the Motorsport arm from 1972 until he left BMW in 1974.*

The 700 scored early, with Walter Schneider and German Touring Car champion Hans Stück taking four class wins in hillclimbs during 1959 and 1960. The 700 and other BMW racers compiled 33 first-place finishes and 22 seconds during '59, then racked up 33 firsts and 19 seconds the following season.

The 700 continued its winning ways through about 1965, by which time the New Class cars, led by the 1800 TI, had begun building an impressive record of their own. One of the highlights was the 24-hour race at Spa in 1966, won by the team of Hubert Hahne and Jacky Ickx. The season also brought BMW triumphs at Snetterton, the Nürburgring, and Zandvoort. On the rally front, the Pfnier/Kling 1800 TI came home 14th overall in the 1966 running of the famed Monte Carlo event, the best showing for any German team. Two years later, the 2000 TI of Bachman/Struntz came home first in class at the Monte.

The advent of the six-cylinder 2800 CS in 1968 gave BMW another racing contender, and the 3.0 CSL version introduced three years later had been conceived expressly with competition in mind. BMW wasted little time exploring the CSL's racing potential. A special 24-valve cylinder head, created by Alex von Falkenhausen, became one of many components built and sold through BMW Motorsport, and was reportedly good for power readings of up to 300 bhp. Other engine mods seen on racing CSLs included a lighter (50-pound) crankshaft, lighter con rods, and special intake manifold. Competition versions also sported light-alloy water pumps, special clutch bell housings, and five-speed ZF gearboxes instead of the normal Getrag transmission.

The CSL fared rather poorly during its first two seasons, but it began winning regularly in 1973, often with spectacular results. Stück and Chris Amon drove to victory in that year's German Grand Prix for Touring Cars at the 'Ring, and Quester paired with Toine Hezemans to finish second. Hezemans won the European sedan championship that year, and teamed with Quester again to score outright wins at Spa, Zandvoort, and the Paul Ricard circuit. The duo also recorded the CSL's first major international victory by coming home first in class at the 1973 Le Mans 24 Hours. The 1974 season was even better, and 3.0 CSLs piled up enough points in the hands of privateers to win the European Challenge Cup for BMW. The next year, the now winged and spoilered big coupes contested events all over America, including the IMSA Camel GT series. They didn't win that series outright, but Sam Posey, Brian Redman, and Ronnie Peterson won several individual events against the formidable factory-sponsored Porsche 930 Carreras. And BMW again captured the European touring car crown in 1975, thanks to Siggi Muller and Alain Peltier in their Alpina-prepared CSL.

Schnitzer and Alpina both

prepped many of the BMWs that saw action in these years. But although racing was supposed to be the major activity for both firms, they probably did more business with non-racing BMW owners who simply wanted more power and speed from their cars, plus special appearance altera-tions and custom equipment. In 1971, Burkhard Bovensiepen hired a young engineer and uni-versity professor named Fritz Indra to head the engine pro-gram at Alpina. Because so many of its modified Bimmers were used on ordinary roads, Al-pina was now considered a man-ufacturer and thus had to ensure its cars met applicable emissions standards in the various coun-tries where they were sold. That included the U.S., of course, so Indra was hired not so much to wring more power out of BMW engines as to see that Alpina's tweaks were emissions-legal

without sacrificing too many ponies.

Indra left Alpina in 1979 to become chief of engine development for Audi, but not before he had worked up a turbocharged version of the big six. BMW had bored out this block in early 1978 to its maximum 93.4mm (3.68 in.), which gave cylinder center spacing of exactly 100mm (3.94 in.). With the 84mm (3.31-in.) stroke from the 3.2-liter CSL, displacement stood at 3453cc (210.6 cid). Because of its smaller bore, the 3.2 had water jackets that separated all the cylinders, but the bores had to

be siamesed on the 3.5-liter engine. Other changes included larger valves and an exhaust flow rate increased by 15 percent. With Bosch L-Jetronic injection, this M-90 powerplant delivered 217.5 bhp at 5200 rpm and 330 lbs/ft peak torque at 4000 rpm. Indra's turbo engine was even more radical. It employed Pierburg mechanical fuel injection and a K-27 blower from KKK with maximum boost set at 0.85 bar (12.5 psi). The result was 350 bhp—a potent 1.63 bhp per cubic inch.

Munich's motor men also tried their hand at turbocharging, but

used the more robust 3.2-liter block. This engine went into a sports racing coupe dubbed 3.5 CSL, and Ronnie Peterson drove it during the 1976 campaign. While it had the necessary power, the aging coupe chassis was no longer competitive by this time, particularly on shorter, lower-speed circuits. The car was also handicapped— at least next to the racing Porsches—by its front-engine layout and relatively high weight (2426 pounds).

BMW had been thinking about a mid-engine racer, and for several sound technical reasons. A

midships car has more weight above its driving wheels than a front-engine/rear-drive car, which means better traction and less wheelspin in acceleration. The rearward weight bias also improves braking efficiency, because the rear wheels still carry enough weight to perform their share of braking duties even under extreme weight transfer in hard deceleration. The layout also tends to confer a lower polar moment of inertia, which can be utilized to speed up handling response. Combined with the lower center of gravity made possible by the absence of a propshaft, this means higher lateral acceleration and, by extension, faster cornering speeds. A final plus is the shorter driveline, which translates into lower frictional losses. These are the things that count most in racing. The mid-engine configuration has advan- tages for street use, mainly improved forward visibility and, because of the altered weight distribution, lighter steering. However, it has several disadvantages that have prevented it from being used for more than a handful of roadgoing sports cars. The main ones are higher levels of cabin noise and heat, more restricted over-the-shoulder vision, and more restricted access to the engine and running gear compared to a front- or even rear-engine design.

Because of its Formula 2 experience, BMW already knew quite a bit about midships cars. And in 1972 the firm displayed an elegant mid-engine styling study to announce the opening of the new company museum in Munich. It was, of course, the BMW Turbo, a sexy, ground-hugging gullwing coupe with body design by Paul Bracq, the well-known French artist who had taken over as styling director on Wilhelm Hofmeister's retirement in January 1970. The Turbo was far more than a one-off exercise, however. Product chief Bernhard Osswald got personally involved with this project, which he viewed as practical experience in designing a mid-engine car that could, just possibly, see production.

The structural base of the Turbo was a steel-and-aluminum unit body/chassis with a rugged central beam. The engine was a turbocharged version of the 2.0-liter four from the 2002, mounted transversely behind the cockpit and tilted rearwards at 30 degrees (corresponding to its lateral slant angle in the sedan). A four-speed gearbox was mounted in line with the crankshaft, with a spur gear on the output shaft and a short, open, double-jointed shaft to the centrally placed final drive unit. The spur gear gave a permanent 1.23:1 reduction, which enabled the engine to pull a 2.37:1 final drive ratio. The all-independent suspension used MacPherson-strut geometry at both ends. At the rear were the conventional coil springs surrounding the upper portions of the struts, but the front used transverse torsion bars as the springing medium. Steering was by rack-and-pinion, disc brakes with ventilated rotors were fitted all around, and fat tires on 14- x 9.5-in. wheels were specified. Wheelbase was 94.5 inches, and front and rear tracks measured 61.1 and 60.2 inches, respectively. Height was only 43.3 inches, width 54 inches. Overall length, including the handsomely integrated impact-absorbing bumpers, came to 163.3 inches. Curb weight was about 2426 pounds. Factory figures show the Turbo had standing-start acceleration of 15.7 seconds to 100 mph and 6.6 seconds to 100 km/h. Top speed was a claimed 155 mph.

Glamorous and futuristic, the Turbo touched off the inevitable speculation that BMW was about to release a mid-engine production model. The company didn't

really need one, but the Turbo prototype was dusted off for a project that would lead to such a car, the M1. Originally designated E-26, it came out of a project begun in 1976 to produce a competitive mid-engine BMW for GT-class racing. Bob Lutz wanted to homologate the new car in Group 4 for the Manufacturers Championship series. The rules stipulated that for a model to run in this class it had to be built in quantities of at least 400 units within a 12-month period. Such a number was more than the racing community was likely

to absorb in a year, so the decision was made to offer a street version legal for all European markets. There was one snag: the Motorsport subsidiary had nowhere near this level of production capacity despite a recent expansion of its facilities, and the E-26 was too specialized to be built economically at any of BMW's existing plants. Because the International Sporting Code said no car could run until 400 had been built, BMW farmed out assembly to Lamborghini, the exoticar manufacturer in Sant' Agata Bolognese outside

Opposite page: The business end of the roadgoing M1. This page, top: Dieter Quester's 1980 racing M1. Left: The 277-bhp twincam, four-valve six as used in the production M1. Above: Designer Paul Bracq with the Turbo prototype in 1972.

Modena, which had capacity to spare at that time. Styling was also farmed out, to the renowned Giorgetto Giugiaro and his Ital Design firm in Moncalieri (Bracq had left BMW in 1974). Bodies would be made of reinforced fiberglass, assembled by Ital Design from locally produced moldings and painted, then shipped to Lamborghini. Power-

train components would be supplied from Munich, while Lamborghini was supposed to manufacture most of the chassis parts.

Lutz wanted to display the new midships machine at the Geneva show in March 1978, with a competition debut slated for that year's Le Mans 24-hour race in June. Lamborghini was expected to complete develop-

ment in reasonable time, and things looked good as the first test cars took to public roads in the summer of 1977. Lamborghini's contract called for production at the rate of two per week and a total run of 800 units. But delay after delay pushed back Lutz's timetable several times. Finding the Italians' explanations unacceptable,

185

BMW canceled the contract in April 1978. A new plan was hastily devised, and production finally began that September. Ital Design shipped raw bodies to the Baur works in Stuttgart, which mated them to the tubular space frame to form the general structure. Final assembly was then carried out by BMW Motorsport, which also ended up making most of the chassis parts. The hope was that the mandatory 400 units could be built in time for 1979 homologation, but additional problems surfaced and certification wasn't fully completed until the 1981 season.

The M1 designation was chosen to signify a BMW Motorsport project, but it was greeted humorously in England, where M-1 is the main interstate-type highway running from London to the Midlands. The car itself was taken very seriously, for it was a thoroughly professional job. Built on a 100.8-inch wheelbase and 171.7 inches long overall, it looked low and wide, an impression confirmed by the 61-inch front track, 62-inch rear track, 71.8-inch overall width, and squat 44.9-inch overall height. The all-coil suspension geometry was based on modern Formula 1 practice, with long semi-trailing arms plus cross-links that more

*Above: A winged M1 as seen in SCCA Group 4 action. Right: The production M1 (right) poses with the potent 286-bhp M635 CSi, the limited-production 6-series built by BMW Motorsport. Upper right: A view of the M1 cockpit. Dash on the Italian-designed midships car differed quite a bit from that on other BMWs.*

effectively restricted camber changes during spring deflection, a factor that becomes more and more important as tire width increases. Steering was by rack-and-pinion. Four-wheel ventilated disc brakes were employed, mounted inboard on the axle shafts at the rear and outboard in the wheel hubs at the front.

As for appearance, the M1 disappointed some critics, who judged it one of Giugiaro's less inspired efforts. Despite a strong shape, the styling was somehow plainer and less interesting next to the Bracq-designed Turbo. No doubt Giugiaro was trying to avoid copying too much from the show car, but the fussiness in certain areas was less understandable. These included curiously slotted wheels, a dumpy louvered hood, oddly shaped engine cooling slots aft of the rear side windows, and an awkward break line on the upper rear bodysides created by the engine

cover's slight downward wrap. Overall, the M1 was purposeful but not as elegantly sleek or as tightly integrated as the Turbo.

The original E-26 concept envisioned the 4.0-liter V-12 power unit then under study for a new luxury sedan (see Chapter 12).

three-valve head before deciding on the four-valve setup developed in 1974 for the racing CSL coupes. The M-88 had twin overhead camshafts driven by single-stage duplex chain. A two-piece cylinder head was used, with a separate magnesium casting to carry the camshafts, each running in seven bearings. The combustion chamber was of the pentroof type, and the valvegear comprised 240 individual parts. Intake valves were disposed at an 18-degree angle from the vertical, exhaust valves at 20 degrees. Kugelfischer fuel injection, dry-sump lubrication with chain-driven pumps, one pressure pump, and digital electronic ignition by Marelli completed the basic specifications.

The M-88 was produced in three stages of tune. The road version was rated at 277 bhp (DIN) at 6500 rpm with a peak 243 lbs/ft torque at 5000 rpm on 9.0:1 compression. Valve head diameters were 47mm (1.85 in.) for the intakes and 32mm (1.26 in.) for the exhausts. Though the output figures seem mild compared with the competition engines, the "production" M1 nevertheless had splendid go. The typical 0-100 km/h (62-mph) time was only 6.0 seconds, running to 100 mph from rest was a 13.3-second trip, and the standing-start 400 meters (a bit less than a quarter-mile) took 13.8 seconds. Top speed was over 160 mph. The racing engines had 11.5:1 compression and bigger valves, 48.6mm (1.91-in.) intakes and 32.5mm (1.28-in.) exhausts. Group 4 tuning delivered 470 bhp (DIN) at 9000 rpm, with 530 lbs/ft torque peaking at 7000 rpm. For Group 5, displacement was brought back to 3.2 liters and a KKK turbocharger was fitted. Output here was 800 to as much as 850 bhp at 9000 rpm (depending on boost setting) with practically the same torque as the Group 4 unit. The turbocharger's maximum boost range was 1.2 to 1.4 bar (17.6 to 20.6 psi), but waste-

When this idea was shelved, BMW had no choice but to use its big six, though it was considerably modified for the M1. Designated M-88, it was based on the production cast-iron 3.5-liter block, basically a 3.2 bored out to 92.5mm (3.64 in.) but retaining the 86mm (3.39-in.) stroke. The engine was mounted longitudinally, since it was too long for transverse installation to permit a convenient, reliable driveline without excessive frictional losses. Rosche experimented with a

gate settings permitting up to
2.5 bar (37 psi) for brief periods
sent power soaring to about 950
bhp. The Group 5 car was calculated to have a top speed of 217
mph, quite good considering the
body's mediocre 0.41 drag
coefficient.

Regardless of engine, all M1s
were equipped with the same
five-speed all-synchromesh ZF
gearbox and twin-plate Fichtel &
Sachs clutch with hydraulic actuation. Gearbox ratios were indirect: 0.704 in fifth, 0.846 in
fourth, 1.14 in third, 1.61 in second, and 2.42:1 in first. The
final drive was of the hypoid
type with a 4.22:1 reduction, and
the differential was limited to a
40 percent slip.

In 1979, BMW again joined
forces with March, which came
up with a new car designed
around the M1 engine intended
for both Groups 5 and 6 that
season. Unfortunately, the proposed March-BMW was barred
from Group 5 because it had yet
to meet the minimum production
requirement, and its engine was
too large for the 3.0-liter (183-

cid) Group 6 displacement
limit. However, March boss Max
Mosley came up with a clever
ploy to get M1s on the track.
Called PROCAR, it was a special
"celebrity" European racing

series not unlike Roger Penske's
original International Race of
Champions (IROC) in the U.S.
Here, famous Formula 1 pilots
competed against privateers, all
driving identically prepared

*Opposite page, top: A recent much-modified, first-generation 3-series racer. Bottom: BMW clinched the 1983 touring car crown at Spa after a season-long duel with the Jaguar V-12s (seen here at Vallelunga). This page, top left: The March-BMW F2 car for 1981. Top right: Hans Stück drove this 430-bhp CSL in 1974. Above: The famous 1976 CSL turbo racer painted by Frank Stella.*

M1s. This amounted to a racing "side show," as Halwart Schrader describes it, but it did mark the M1's competition debut and, as he notes, served as a sort of informal public introduction following the car's formal unveiling at the Paris salon the previous October.

How the M1 might have fared against real competition is something we may never know. As mentioned, the final homologation hurdles were not cleared until the 1981 season, and by then the car was no longer competitive. The main problem was excess weight, about 1985 pounds compared to only 1544 pounds for the equally powerful Porsche 936s. BMW then ended the M1 affair shortly afterwards, completing about 450 examples of this rare and powerful car that, ironically, never saw the competition it was designed for.

The bombastic Bavarian wasn't quite finished, however, and in 1981 several lightweight cars were built around the M1 powertrain. Schnitzer prepared a Group 5 machine powered by a 3150cc (192-cid) version of the M-88 with 89.2mm (3.51-in.) bore and 84mm (3.31-in.) stroke. Fitted with dual KKK turbochargers, it was claimed to deliver 800 bhp (DIN) at 8000 rpm. Bodywork was a Kevlar structure built by Sager & Hoffman of Steckborn in Switzerland. In April, the March-BMW M1C appeared. It was a cooperative effort between Max Mosley and the engineers of March Engineering, Ltd; BMW Motorsport GmbH; and BMW North America. Motorsport saw it as a prelude to contesting Category C in 1982, a new formula replacing Group 5. An open-cockpit roadster with a monocoque sheet-aluminum chassis, it was powered by a turbocharged 3.5-liter M-88 engine delivering 475-480 bhp. This car was fast, but its career was cut short by machinery that was faster still.

Thus ended the most ambitious program undertaken by BMW Motorsport, at least so far. Apart form the Formula 1 engine (see Chapter 13), the firm has since concentrated on supporting the many private teams campaigning BMW production cars, mainly 3-series sedans and 6-series coupes often modified beyond all recognition.

# EXPANDING ON EXCELLENCE: THE 5-SERIES AND 3-SERIES

*The 1978 European 520/6 posed in a midwinter scene. Power out was 122 bhp (DIN).*

In the spring of 1975, BMW chairman Eberhard von Kuenheim declared: "We cannot economically produce cars smaller than the 1502," and went on to describe the firm's product plans through 1980 as basically a program of "refinement in all areas." Considering BMW was only some 10 years removed from its microcar days at this point, the boss may have sounded a bit smug. But he was perfectly justified: BMW was in a period of unprecedented expansion. The excellent basic design of the New Class had been evolved into a full range of cars with strong international sales appeal, and profits had swelled along with the marque's prestige. To meet the burgeoning demand, the company hired more workers at Milbertshofen and added a second production center, at Dingolfing in Lower Bavaria, as well as a subsidiary in South Africa that began operations in 1974. A modern new proving grounds facility opened at Aschheim in late 1971, followed the next year by a grand new headquarters and museum complex in Munich. By mid-decade, daily output in Germany had reached 1000 units per day, a level undreamed of in the dark days of the late Fifties. With this sort of success, it's no wonder that "refinement"—in other words, more of the same—was the order of the day.

While most of this expansion was accomplished methodically, one part of it deserves a close look. On January 2, 1967, BMW took over the automotive division of Hans Glas GmbH Isaria Maschinenfabrik. For a time, this small automaker was an effective competitor for BMW. The company had been established in 1860 by Maurus Glas in Freising, and its earliest products were farm implements. The concern moved to Dingolfing in 1908. Hans, the grandson of the founder, secured a job with Massey-Harris in Berlin, and in 1910 was transferred to Toronto. He spent the war years in America, and later worked for McCormick, Ford, American Bosch, and the Indian Motorcycle Company. Returning to Germany in 1920, Hans bought back the family enterprise and within a decade had built it into the largest maker of seeding-machines in Europe. The company made a fresh start after World War II, and Anderl Glas, Hans' son, now took over.

In 1951, Glas embarked on production of motor scooters under the trade name Goggo (nickname of the founder's great-grandson). It abandoned the market the very next year to try a new idea: a four-wheel scooter with a car-type body. This became the Goggomobil, a genuine minicar that went into production in May 1955. Karl Dompert, who had been in the Luftwaffe with Anderl Glas, served as chief engineer. The first Goggomobil was a tiny two-door sedan powered by a 13.6-bhp air-cooled parallel twin of 242cc (12.2 cid) originally designed by Felix Dozekal for Adler motorcycles. Then came a 296cc (18-cid) 14.8-bhp version, followed by a 395cc (24.1-cid) model, both also available with coupe bodywork. A more proper car, the T-600, was introduced in late 1957 with a 584cc (35.6-cid) engine producing 20 bhp. Labelled the Isar (after the river that runs between Munich and Dingolfing), it was the first car actually to bear the Glas name. A larger-capacity companion, the Isar T-700, appeared the following year with 688cc (42-cid) and 30 bhp. Both Isars were offered in two-door sedan or wagon form. Styling was curiously American, with such hallmarks as wrapped windshields, two-tone paint jobs, and even Buick-like "sweepspear" side trim that looked a bit silly on these Liliputians. The Isars sold fairly well, though, and production ran to some 87,000 units through 1965.

Glas took a big step up the size and power ladder in September 1961 with the 1004. It was powered by a 992cc (60.5-cid) overhead-cam inline four designed, interestingly enough, by a former BMW engineer, Leonhard Ischinger. This little powerplant is significant in being the first to employ a cogged or toothed belt instead of a chain to drive the overhead camshaft, a feature that has since become nearly universal for ohc engines. Body styles comprised a two-door coupe, sedan/wagon, and convertible. The styling was modern if a bit awkward in some ways, especially the excessive front overhang, but it was neat, pert, and distinctive. A more powerful (64-bhp) TS version arrived in January 1963 along with 1189cc (72.5-cid) variants labelled 1204, with 53 bhp standard and 70 bhp in TS trim. This was followed in September 1965 by the 1304 series, powered by a 1290cc (78.7-cid) enlargement offering up to 75 bhp.

Glas moved up the size and price hierarchy once again with two new models displayed at the 1963 Frankfurt auto show. One was a four-door sedan with handsome lines courtesy of Ghia and intended for the European middle-class 1.5-liter market. The other was a slick little fastback coupe styled by Frua and powered by the 75-bhp engine from the 1304 TS. It went into production in March 1964. The sedan followed in September as the Glas 1700, with a 1682cc (102.6-cid) enlargment of the basic ohc four. This engine also became available in the coupe as the 1700 GT starting in May 1965.

Then came the real eye-opener: a prestige 2+2 with V-8 power. Designated 2600, it was the largest and most expensive car yet seen from Glas, priced at around 25,000 marks and bearing elegant, sophisticated Frua styling reminiscent of the designer's bodywork for the Maserati Mistrale. The 2576cc (157-cid) engine was essentially two of the 1304 fours on a common crankshaft. Bore and stroke were unchanged at 75 x 73mm

*The Glas 2600 GT was kept alive in 1967-68 as the BMW-Glas 3000, shown here. A mere 71 were built before the Dingolfing plant was retooled for BMW production.*

of 50 million marks. Before the end of the year, BMW paid the Glas family 9.1 million marks for the company and its assets. Anderl Glas was temporarily left in the president's chair, with Karl Dompert and Helmut Werner Bönsch as members of the management board. Then, on December 1, 1966, the Glas name disappeared completely from the corporate organizational chart and its factory was renamed the BMW Dingolfing Works. Hahnemann now took complete charge, though Anderl Glas retained the title of director.

The Goggomobil was continued under the new regime and nearly 7000 of them were built in 1968. In May 1967 the Glas 2600 evolved into the BMW-Glas 3000 via a displacement increase to 2982cc (182 cid). Compression went up to 9.2:1, and output climbed to 160 bhp at 5100 rpm. Top speed for the revised model was a claimed 125 mph and 0-100 km/h (62-mph) acceleration was stated as nine seconds. Bönsch saw this car as a logical replacement for the Bertone-bodied 3200 CS, and hoped it would not steal sales from the existing 2000 C/CS. BMW also continued the 1300 GT, but grafted on a twin-kidney front and ditched the trouble-prone Glas mechanicals for the engine, gearbox and rear axle of the 1600 TI. Now called the BMW 1600 GT, it saw nearly 1300 copies in 1967-68. Fewer than 100 of the V-8 2+2s were built. After this, all the former Glas models disappeared. The Dingolfing factory was remodeled for production of BMW parts, and ground was broken for a new assembly plant adjacent to it.

Acquisition of the Dingolfing plant was not enough to satisfy BMW's lusty expansion. Construction of a new multifloor stamping plant with over 172,000 square feet of floor space began at Milbertshofen in August 1967; it was in operation

*continued on page 209*

(2.95 x 2.87 in.) and separate belt drives were used for each overhead camshaft, one per bank. With twin two-barrel carburetors and 9.0:1 compression, this V-8 put out 140 bhp (DIN) at 5600 rpm, which gave the car a claimed top speed of 125 mph. The front suspension was conventional, with coil springs and unequal-length A-frame lateral control arms. The rear suspension was out of the ordinary: a de Dion tube, semi-elliptic leaf springs, and inboard-mounted disc brakes. Curb weight was 2536 pounds.

By 1966, Glas was deep in financial hot water due to high production costs and the enormous drain of its rapid model expansion. Only the little Gog-

gomobils were profitable, and the firm was losing money by the carload. BMW management had been following the firm with great interest. Now, sales director Paul Hahnemann arranged to meet privately with Anderl Glas, who told him that losses for the year would run to 15 million marks. Hahnemann offered help in the form of joint marketing, then began serious negotiations for a takeover. The Bavarian government agreed to BMW's acquisition of the company against a deficit guarantee

*A competition 3.0 CSi prepared by Schnitzer makes a pit stop at Zeltweg (Osterreichring) in Austria.*

A trio of 6-series coupe variations. Opposite page, bottom: the basic production model as offered from 1976 as the 630CS/Csi and the 633CSi (U.S. debut for the latter was 1978). Top: A chin spoiler identifies the 218-bhp 635CSi from 1981. This page: A modified U.S. 630CSi with twin-turbocharged 3.0-liter engine.

BMW's mass-market line, the 3-series, arrived in Europe in 1975 to replace the "02" sedans, and made its U.S. debut the following year. Above: The American 320i. Right: European models nearing the end of the body line. Opposite page, top: A targa cabriolet conversion by Bauer on the European 318. Bottom: A U.S. 320i from 1983 with 1.8-liter engine and the optional "S" equipment package. Through the end of 1978, more than a half million 3-series cars of all types were produced and sold worldwide.

*An all-around look at the editors' test 633CSi from 1983. Although the basic lines of BMW's handsome coupes have remained unchanged since their introduction, the years have brought a number of detail refinements, such as adoption of the Bosch Motronic engine management system and BMW's innovative Service Interval Indicator. Contrary to the designation, the 633's engine displacement is closer to 3.2 liters, precisely 3210cc.*

A second-generation 5-series appeared in 1982 with lines very similar to those of its predecessor even though no major body panels were actually interchangeable. As before, European customers can choose from several different engines ranging from 1.8 to 2.8 liters. American offerings are limited to the high-performance 533i, shown above, with the 3.2-liter "big-block" six and the 2.7-liter 528e powered by the lower-revving economy-oriented "eta" engine.

The popular 3-series was updated in 1983 with this all-new design styled in the BMW tradition. Features include reduced aerodynamic drag, modified suspension, and a revised four-cylinder engine. Shown above, top, and opposite page top is the initial U.S. offering, the two-door 318i. Scheduled for release in 1984 is a new four-door body style and companion 325e variants powered by the six-cylinder "eta" engine. Opposite page bottom: Robots weld 3-series bodies at Milbertshofen.

BMW's long-time relationship with Karosserie Karl Bauer remains as strong as ever. Shown here is that firm's latest cabriolet conversion on the second-generation European 320i. The U.S. 318i sedan is shown for comparison, opposite page bottom. Unlike the former four-cylinder U.S. 320i, the European model is a six-cylinder car with 125 bhp (DIN). A 139-bhp 323i model is also available.

*Right:* First seen in 1981, the AVT (Aerodynamicsher Versuchsträger *or aerodynamics research vehicle) reflects BMW's interest in improving the efficiency of its present and future cars. Below, bottom, and opposite page bottom: Over the years, many aftermarket firms have offered tweaked versions of stock BMW sedans. One of the newest is this modified 5-series called the Hartge H5S. Featured are a 240-bhp (DIN) 3.5-liter six, close-ratio gearbox, and ABS anti-skid braking system.*

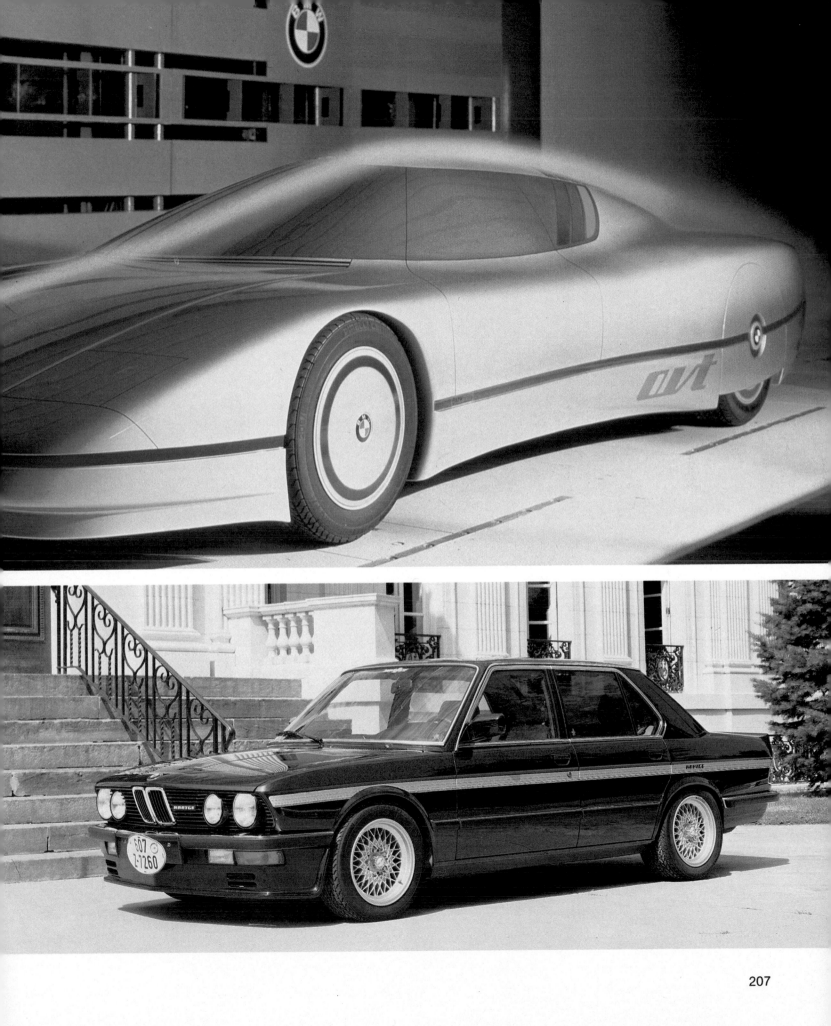

A group of BMW owners test their skills
and their cars in a driver's school at
Continental Divide Raceway in Colorado.

*continued from page 192*

by the end of 1968. And within six months, Hahnemann was toying with thoughts of taking over Lancia in Turin. The Italian automaker was an independent at the time, with the Italcementi group holding majority control. In March 1968 he went to Turin to meet with Italcementi boss Dr. Carlo Pesenti, but returned to Munich without this plum. The main stumbling block was too high a price, though that may have been a deliberate ploy to keep Lancia out of German hands. A year later, Fiat bought the company for a token sum in exchange for assuming Lancia's debts. Hahnemann's timing had been off by about 12 months. It was probably just as well, because it meant more money was left over for capital improvements. In 1970-72, BMW went on something akin to a spending binge, investing 200 million marks each year for plant expansion at Munich, Dingolfing, and Landshut. The company was making 700 cars a day in 1969, and it badly wanted to reach the magic 1000 mark.

To help spur sales, the Dingolfing plant was retooled for car production, and in September 1972 it began turning out the all-new model 520. Developed under the E-20 internal code, it replaced the 1800/2000 New Class as the mid-size offering, and also marked a return to a more traditional model identification system at BMW. The "5" stood for 5-series, denoting rank or body size; the "20" indicated engine displacement in liters multiplied by 10. Accordingly, the new model was powered by the 2.0-liter (122-cid) four from the 2000/2000tii, available in 115-bhp twin-carb form or as the 520i with Kugelfischer mechanical fuel injection and 130 bhp. Both versions featured a new cylinder head with the combustion chambers redesigned along the tri-spherical principle of the six-cylinder engines. Four- and five-

*Top: Another Glas holdover was the BMW 1600 GT, which saw 1255 copies in 1967-68. Above: The 5-series structure and running gear as it appeared in 1972.*

speed manual transmissions and a three-speed ZF automatic were offered, all with floorshift control.

Dimensionally, the 5-series differed only slightly from its New Class predecessors, but Paul Bracq's modern, stylish four-door body was far less boxy in appearance. Wheelbase increased by about three inches (to 103.8), overall length went up by about five inches (to 181.9), and about an inch was taken off the overall height (56.1 inches) and width (66.5 inches). The dimensional increases implied greater weight, and the new cars were heavier by a surprising amount, some 250-300 pounds, the 520 tipping the scales at 2780 pounds, the 520i at 2820. The 5-series also closely followed its predecessors in chassis design,

but there were differences. MacPherson struts were still used in front but were now angled rearwards at 12 degrees, and wheel travel was extended by 20mm (0.75 in.) both front and rear in the interest of increased ride comfort. Rear semi-trailing arms and spring/struts mounted on the hub carriers were retained, as was Gemmer-type worm-and-roller steering made by ZF. However, the 520 did not get four-wheel disc brakes, using drums at the rear instead.

209

Due to its extra weight, the 520 was not a particularly brilliant performer. The twin-carb base model could run from 0 to 100 km/h (62 mph) in 12.3 seconds and had a top speed of 108 mph, while figures for the injected 520i were 11.1 seconds and 114 mph. Average fuel consumption was quoted as 22 mpg. If not exactly the best for either speed or efficiency, at least the 520/520i was still a BMW, and that's what counted for most people. Both models sold well right from the start, and quite a few buyers plunked down the 15,000-16,000 deutsche marks it took to buy one in late 1972. In view of the demand, completion of the second Dingolfing facility (called Plant 2-4) in November 1973 was quite timely. With a capacity of 300 units per day, it was assigned to build the 5-series exclusively, thus freeing up space at Milbertshofen. By early 1974, BMW's total automotive production was perking along at 1100 units per day.

The E-20 bodyshell had been designed from the outset to accommodate the BMW six, though larger-capacity spinoffs didn't arrive until a year after the four-cylinder cars. The first was the 525, appearing in September 1973 carrying the 2.5-liter (151-cid) six from the big 2500 sedan, tuned to deliver 145 bhp (DIN) at 6000 rpm. It was followed in February 1975 by the 528 with the 165-bhp 2.8-liter power unit. Both these models had standard rear disc brakes, and power-assisted steering was offered at extra cost. Responding to the fuel panic brought on by the 1973-74 Arab oil embargo, BMW also released a smaller-displacement four-cylinder version, the 90-bhp 518, in June 1974. This used the 1766cc (107.7-cid) engine from the 1800 New Class four-door and was a direct replacement for it. Though it was only 1500 marks cheaper than the 520 and actually returned poorer mileage, it sold quite well until it was discontinued in 1976.

U.S. buyers had to wait a couple of years for the 5-series, which arrived as a "federalized" car with various modifications for the welter of government safety and emissions regulations then taking effect. Introduced in 1975 as the 530i, it was the first BMW model created expressly for the North American market. Under its hood was a detuned version of the 2985cc (182-cid) six, with Bosch L-Jetronic fuel injection and 8.1:1 compression compatible with low-calorie 91-octane gas. Power output was 176 bhp (SAE net) at 5500 rpm, with peak torque of 185 lbs/ft developed at 4500 rpm. Tailpipe cleanup was accomplished via exhaust-gas recirculation, thermal reactor, and air injection. The mandated safety bumpers and side marker lights were fitted outside, and an afterthought bank of warning lights (fasten seatbelts and reactor and EGR service) was added inside.

*Road & Track* magazine pointed out in its initial 530i test that the new model was actually a replacement for the Bavaria in the U.S. lineup, and its comparisons with the larger sedan are interesting. "Dimensionally, the 530i is only 5.1 in. shorter, 1.7 in. narrower, and about 100 pounds lighter [but] it's about as roomy, has a more refined chassis, and is less expensive; it costs just $9200 with power steering, whereas the Bavaria listed for about $9400 without."

The editors applauded the "superb" seating comfort in the 530i and described its ride as "an excellent compromise of softness and firmness. Harshness over small, sharp disturbances has been reduced to practically nil and pitching over gentle pavement undulations—our biggest criticism of previous BMW chassis behavior—is gone. [It] is without a doubt the best-riding BMW ever and, with the possible exception of the 2.8-and 3.0-liter coupes, the best-handling also. The vastly improved power steering has

quicker response, requires slightly heavier effort that is more to our liking, and transmits better road feel. Now it's more like the Mercedes [system] but not that stiff...Handling ranges from near-neutral in high-speed sweepers to slight oversteer in tight, low-speed turns. In the latter, the inside rear wheel lifts, effectively limiting cornering speed and reducing oversteer to very controllable levels."

As for performance, the 530i turned in respectable times considering its 3315-pound curb weight: 10.2 seconds in the 0-60 mph sprint and 17.5 seconds for the quarter-mile at 78 mph. Fuel economy? Not bad, either: 19 mpg. Overall, *R&T* concluded that BMW "has been able to maintain performance with far superior driveability...The 530i is everything a luxury-sports sedan should be. It's comfortable, practical in the extreme, and with a good measure of performance, ride and handling thrown in. It's no wonder we had little trouble choosing it as one of the world's ten best cars."

The original 5-Series continued through 1981 with mostly minor year-to-year changes. A facelift in 1977 brought a raised twin-kidney grille and a revised hood, plus revamped taillamps and a fuel filler flap relocated from the back panel to the right rear fender. That same year, the carbureted 528 was succeeded by the injected 528i, and a U.S. version with more sophisticated emissions control—three-way catalytic converter and Bosch Lambda sensor—was sent over to replace the 530i for 1979

The mechanical changes for the U.S. 528i were a revelation. Despite a smaller engine with

*Top: Though virtually all-new, the first-generation 5-series was faithful to New Class engineering principles. Below: a selection of 5-series variants over the years (clockwise from top left): The 525 (1974), the original 520/520i (1972), the second-series 1981 European model, the U.S. 530i from 1977, and the six-cylinder European 528i, also from '77.*

seven fewer horsepower, the new model was faster yet thriftier. *Road & Track* reported 0-60 mph times averaging 8.2 seconds, plus a full three-mpg fuel economy improvement ("a solid 22.0 mpg") for its 1979 example. A 1981 car tested by CONSUMER GUIDE® magazine's staff returned a creditable 18.6 mph in mostly city driving, while zipping to 60 mph from rest in 9.4 seconds. Noted an *R&T* staffer: "That BMW six has been unleashed at last; I couldn't find any problems with driveability, starting, acceleration, or anything else." Well, almost. The test report noted that "somehow, the quiet refinement of the BMW six got lost in the translation [to the 528i]. Just how much of the increased noise is due to about 20 pounds less insulation in the car, or the more advanced spark timing, we don't know...but in everyday driving

it has a harshness and roughness no modern BMW six has ever exhibited." Of course, the distinction here is a fine one, and few production engines, including most newer ones, match the BMW six for mechanical smoothness—or its delicious sounds. "A very 'mechanical' car in overall feel," was the CONSUMER GUIDE® magazine verdict, with appeal "for those who value superior dynamic capabilities. Offers meticulous craftsmanship and a good deal of practicality plus an eager, sporty character. Rather exclusive and hardly cheap [about $22,000 basic in 1981] but considering what it can do the 528i isn't outlandishly priced. Recommended for those who appreciate—and can afford—the better things in life."

The 5-series marked the start of the first complete product overhaul at BMW since the New

Class. The mid-range cars were vital from a marketing standpoint but the oldest in design age, which is why the 5-series came first. BMW had obviously learned lessons from its own history. Now it was time to update the volume sellers, the "02" two-doors. Product chief Bernhard Osswald wanted their successors to offer more interior space, a better ride, improved fuel economy, and greater occupant protection in a crash ("passive safety"). With 5-series production humming along at Dingolfing, the Milbertshofen plant was retooled for a new family called the 3-series.

Introduced in July 1975, the new small-car line initially comprised four models: 316, 318, 320, and 320i. Engines were essentially carryovers from the "02" series, though there were a few modifications. The carbureted power units got a new Solex carburetor with automatic choke, while the 320i engine was switched from mechanical injection to the more modern Bosch K-Jetronic solid-state system. Because injection made for easier emissions tuning, only the 320i was exported to the U.S., where it was rated at 110 bhp (SAE net) at 5800 rpm. The European version packed 125 bhp (DIN) at 5700 rpm. All four 3-series models were available with four- or optional five-speed manual transmission supplied by Getrag, and ZF three-speed automatic (3HP 22) was listed at extra cost for all but the 316.

Like their redesigned mid-size linemates, the second-generation two-doors emerged slightly larger and heavier than their predecessors. Compared with the "02" cars, the 3-series gained 2.5 inches in wheelbase (100.9

inches) and 3.5 inches in overall length (171.5 inches in European trim). External body width swelled by 0.8 inch, but interior width expanded by a claimed 1.6 inches. The new Paul Bracq styling was unmistakably BMW, but smoother and more contemporary in flavor. The same applied to the interior, which featured what BMW called "cockpit" design. This referred to a central instrument panel area angled slightly toward the driver to put minor controls closer at hand.

The 3-series also followed 5-series practice in retaining BMW's now-familiar basic chassis layout, again with improvements. Up front were revised engine mounts, and bushings were spaced further apart and "voided" to offer selective resistance rates—soft against torque reactions, hard against fore/aft forces. Also, the MacPherson-

strut geometry now had negative caster offset (scrub radius) for better stability in uneven traction conditions. The front stabilizer bar was modified to do double duty as a drag strut, forming the forward portion of the lower control arm as shown in Earle MacPherson's original patents. Front spring rates were reduced by about 25 percent compared to the "02" cars, while rear spring rates were stiffer by some 40 percent to eliminate pitching movements. The previous worm-and-roller steering gave way to a rack-and-pinion system with 4.05 turns lock-to-lock, and a hydraulic steering damper was fitted on all models but the 316. The front disc brakes were treated to ventilated rotors of six percent greater diameter and 60 percent more friction area. Drums continued at the rear, enlarged by about nine percent. The brake

system's vacuum servo was strengthened by about 20 percent. A final chassis change with definite safety implications was a fuel tank moved from below the trunk floor to between the rear wheel arches so as to avoid damage in a rear-end collision. Dry weights ranged from 3131 pounds for the 1.6-liter car to 3219 for the 320i, modest increases of 20 to 66 pounds over comparable "02" models.

Selling at very attractive prices ranging from 14,000 to 20,000 deutsche marks, the 3-series proved tremendously popular in Europe. BMW car production had hit 184,330 units in calendar 1974. Partly on the strength of the 3-series it jumped to 221,298 the next year. To put that in perspective, Daimler-Benz was running at around 350,000 units annually at the time. So, on the whole, "little" BMW wasn't doing badly at all.

The American-market 320i debuted to mostly very favorable reviews. *Road & Track* liked the snappy performance (12.0 seconds 0-60 mph), near economy-car frugality (21.5 mpg overall), improved ergonomics, and—something the "02" cars had sorely needed—windows-up interior ventilation. Comfort earned special praise: "The ride is superb and sets new standards for small sedans. The 320i has better balanced springing and more suspension travel than its predecessor and it handles rough surfaces even better than the already outstanding 2002." Better still, handling was apparently not sacrificed. "Handling is typical BMW," said the test report. "There's neutral response until the car is pressed hard, then mild final oversteer associated with its semi-trailing arm independent rear suspension... Those who slalom the car or demand the ultimate in road response should order the optional limited-slip differential."

*Road & Track*'s assessments of the 320i remained remarkably consistent over the years, cor-

responding nicely with the
steady sales demand for this
model in the U.S. In 1980 the
editors wrote that "summing up
the 320i is child's play: superb
ride and handling characteristics, crisp gearbox, well thought-
out controls, comfortable seats,
and an engine that's relatively
responsive while meeting emission levels and fuel economy
standards for the next decade . . . The enthusiast who takes
driving seriously will feel very
much at home in the BMW
320i." There were obviously a lot
of those folks around, and in
some of the more affluent parts
of the country these cars became
as thick as flies at a July picnic.
Like the 2002 before it, the 320i
did nothing but enhance BMW's
standing among Americans
searching for the ultimate in
driving satisfaction.

BMW experienced another
round of personnel changes in
the mid-Seventies. Unlike previous years, however, this one was
orderly and created no serious
disruptions. The year 1974 saw
the departure of stylist Paul
Bracq, who went to Peugeot as
chief of interior design two years
later, and Bob Lutz, who moved
to Ford Europe. Taking over
for Lutz was Hans-Erdmann
Schönbeck, who had impressed
the German auto industry as
sales director at Audi since

1969. Bernhard Osswald retired
at the end of 1975. His replacement was Karlheinz Rad-
ermacher, who wasn't a "car
man" in the product sense but a
first-class engineer. He was also
relatively young, just 44 at the
time, and had held several high-
ranking positions in German industry. He came to BMW in October 1973 as a deputy board
member for research and
development—an "understudy"
for Osswald, in fact. At the same
time, BMW appointed a new
styling chief, Claus Luthe, also
44. Widely known for his professional craftsmanship more
than artistic inspiration, he had
worked for NSU, where he
translated the styling sketches
for that company's Wankel-
engine Ro-80 sedan into accurate engineering drawings. He
was named styling director in
1967 and developed the K-70
model. Following the Volkswagen takeover in 1969, he
was made head of the Audi-NSU
design section.

Meanwhile, BMW's prodigious
expansion continued at break-
neck pace. Capital investment
during 1974 totalled 166.5 million marks, most of it for 3-
series tooling. The next year,
spending was 130 million; in
1976 it totalled 250 million. For
1977 the company slated 300
million marks for capital im-

provements. Hiring naturally
paralleled this freewheeling
spending. As one example, em-
ployment at Glas had been just
2377 at the time of the BMW
takeover. Just 10 years later, the
Dingolfing factory had more
than 10,000 workers.

Quick though it was, the 3-se-
ries seemed to beg for more
horsepower, just like the 1600-2
before it. A number of tuning
firms obliged speed-crazy customers with all manner of bolt-
on performance modifications for
the BMW four, but this wasn't
enough for some folks, who
craved extra smoothness as
much as extra go. BMW had
been thinking along the same
lines, but it had no engines sized
between its largest 2.0-liter four
and its smallest 2.5-liter six,
which was physically too large
for the 3-series engine bay. This
situation prompted formation of
a project team to develop a new
"small-block" six. Working under
project code M-60, this group
was headed by Karlheinz Lange,
with Gustav Ederer as supervisor.

Initially there was some de-
bate about whether the M-60
should be a big four, a V-6, or
an inline six. As time passed,
though, the last was increasingly
favored. Chief among the reasons is the inherent balance of
the inline six, which suffers no
negative periods in its torque-

producing cycle. In other words, it's smoother than a big four or a V-6 throughout the rpm range. For the 2.0-2.5-liter displacement envisioned, Lange knew that a straight six tends to weigh more than an inline four of the same size and that its longer crankshaft tends to have more flex. But compared to a V-6, he knew an inline unit was more amenable to a low-cost overhead camshaft installation, permitted a wider choice of carburetion setups, and presented no installation problems as far as crank length was concerned for the cars it would go into. An inline five was not even considered. While this configuration's inherent balance problems can be solved—as Audi and D-B were proving—the costs are high, and calculations indicated that a straight five wouldn't weigh that much less than a straight six of comparable capacity.

What emerged from all this was a brace of new small-displacement inline sixes. Following the example of Ford of England, Lange settled on a short-stroke design with 80mm (3.15-in) bore. With a 66mm (2.60-in.) stroke, displacement worked out to 1990cc (121.4 cid)—exactly the same as the old four—while 76.8mm (3.02-in.) crank throws yielded 2.3 liters (141 cid).

The architecture of the M-60 differed in several ways from that of the big-block six, though the new engines retained aluminum cylinder heads and cast-iron blocks with deep crankcases. All cylinders in the little sixes are separated by water jackets no thicker than a blanket. With the 91mm cylinder spacing there is only 4mm left for metal on each side and 3mm for water between the cylinders. Instead of a forged-steel crankshaft, a low-cost cast-iron crank

is used, running in seven main bearings of 60mm diameter. The single overhead camshaft is driven by cogged belt, and there are two valves per cylinder, splayed at 22 degrees each way and all having the same 10.3mm (0.40-in.) lift. Intake valve head diameter is 40mm (1.57 in.) compared with 34mm (1.34 in.) for the exhausts. Pistons are flat-topped and slipper-skirted. The piston and rod assemblies are optimized for light weight, and rocker arms are made of aluminum with a steel insert at the cam contact face. Weight-saving was emphasized throughout, so the M-60 block weighs only 104.7 pounds, which isn't that much more than the 2.0-liter four's 93.7 pounds. For comparison, the M-52 big-block weighs 130 pounds. As installed, the 2.0-liter M-60 weighs 375 pounds, the 2.3 unit 388 pounds. By contrast, the 1800/2000 fours weigh 309-331 pounds and the big sixes weigh 452-485 pounds depending on displacement and carburetion.

The M-60 debuted in September 1977 for two new 3-series models designated 320/6 and 323i, plus a 5-series variant, the 520/6. As installed, the

2.0-liter unit delivered 122 bhp (DIN) at 6000 rpm with 9.2:1 compression and single Solex 4A-1 carburetor. The 323i packed 143 bhp (DIN) at 6000 rpm thanks to its Bosch K-Jetronic injection and 9.5:1 compression. This move made the 5-series line exclusively six-cylinder. The four-cylinder 320/320i disappeared from Europe, but the latter was continued for the American market in deference to emissions and fuel economy standards. Unhappily, U.S. buyers have so far been denied a six-cylinder 3-series, though this will change for the 1985 model year, but a small number of the first-series cars were brought into compliance and sold through the American distributor for Alpina.

With the advent of the M-60, engine production at BMW was soon split almost equally between fours and sixes, a situation that hadn't existed since before the war. Von Kuenheim began thinking about dropping the fours altogether, but Dr. Radermacher convinced him this would be unwise.

BMW's long-time body supplier, Baur of Stuttgart, created and built a cabriolet version of the 3-series. Like the later 1600/2002 models, this one wasn't a full convertible but a "targa" type with an integral rollover bar or "hoop" where the sedan's B-pillars would normally be. Ahead of this was a solid lift-off panel, and a folding cloth section was used behind. This design looked more awkward, but it was probably more practical. A few of these cars also came to the States, though not through BMW North America.

Over at Ingolstadt, up-and-coming Audi had enjoyed good success with its large front-drive 100 series. In 1975 it bowed a more luxurious, redesigned successor that was sold in the U.S. as the 5000. This car represented a direct challenge to the 5-series as well as the smaller Mercedes-Benz models, and it intrigued Bernhard Osswald,

who instituted a front-wheel-drive research program at BMW. The 2.0-liter M-60 six was reworked for transverse installation, and a new driveline was tested in several 5-series prototypes. But, after weighing all the pros and cons, Radermacher decided to stay with rear drive.

BMW continued to break production records in the mid-Seventies, reaching 275,022 units in 1976, then slightly over 290,000 for 1977. The target for 1978 was 310,000, a figure that was actually exceeded by over 10,000 units. Despite Audi's increasing competitive threat, BMW saw the three-pointed star as its main rival. As Von Kuenheim commented to Thomas C. Lucey of the *International Herald Tribune* in an April 1977 interview: "Our direct competitor, Mercedes-Benz, expands its capacity, and we do it too." In October of that year, the BMW board voted a 3-million-mark budget for more flexible production equipment with an eye to upping annual output to 350,000 units by 1982.

The 5-series was looking rather old-fashioned by 1980, and some press critics began to wonder if BMW hadn't become mired in its own tradition. It hadn't, of course, as Osswald's front-drive experiments suggest, but the 5-series was overdue for an update after eight years. BMW had, in fact, been preparing a successor since early 1975. This was the E-28 project that resulted in a second-generation design, which started coming off the Dingolfing lines in June 1981. It was greeted with disbelief. Though it was virtually an all-new car—only the central body structure was carried over from the previous model—Claus Luthe's restyling was so subtle that the new 5-series could easily be mistaken for the old one. Said *Road & Track*: "We've argued for years against change for the sake of change, but there's a limit and BMW is probing it . . ."

Nevertheless, the second-generation 5-series was substantially changed in almost every area: engines, suspension, ventilation, weight distribution, styling and body engineering, transmissions, steering and brakes all came in for attention. Its dimensions were all very similar to the older models', the main differences being a half-inch reduction in overall height and a corresponding gain in overall width. Despite their familiar looks, the new models were more aerodynamic, and the drag coefficient was pulled down from 0.445 to 0.382-0.384 (depending on model) by clever attention to details affecting air flow. The engine compartment was given an undertray, a front spoiler was made standard, the decklid was raised, the hood was rolled smoothly down at its leading edge, the front fenders were more tapered, air turbulence in the engine compartment was reduced, C-post vents were moved to near-vertical, and roof drip rails were eliminated on the A- and C-pillars. BMW also took about 90 pounds out of the main structure through computer analysis of load-bearing profiles, which revealed areas of highest stress. That made it possible to reduce the thickness of some body panels by up to 13 percent. Nearly 30 pounds were saved under the hood by more extensive use of lightweight materials and by paying closer attention to the location of engine accessories. Another 55 pounds were saved in the drivetrain, and 50 pounds were taken out of the interior. In all, the new 5-series ended up about 200 pounds lighter than its predecessor. That was a big step considering curb weights now ranged from 2560 pounds for the four-cylinder 518 to 2910 pounds for the six-cylinder 528i.

The new 5-series was available in Europe with a choice of four different powerplants, all essentially carryovers from the final lineup of first-generation models. However, all were reworked for more economical operation. Taking them in order from smallest to largest, the 1.8-liter four for the 518 got higher compression (9.5:1), a new two-barrel carburetor with automatic choke, and transistorized ignition. Coinciding with adoption of Bosch L-Jetronic fuel injection, the 2.0-liter small-block six for the 520i had compression raised to 9.8:1, and a Getrag five-speed manual transmission was added as a new option as a further aid to economy. With an output of 125 bhp (DIN), the 520i could run up to 126 mph, while fuel consumption as measured in the ECE urban cycle improved to 18.8 mpg and to 36.2 mpg at a steady 56 mph (90 km/h). Electronic injection was extended to the 2.5-liter six for the new 525i, which also boasted more torque (158 lbs/ft) via tighter 9.6:1 compression. The European 528i also got a five-speed manual gearbox as standard, with closer-ratio gearing that cut 0-100 km/h (62-mph) acceleration from 9.3 to 8.9 seconds. Fuel economy at a steady 74.5 mph (120 km/h) improved to 27.3 mpg.

Of course, none of these variants came to the U.S. Instead, BMW shipped over a special economy model called the 528e, created expressly for our government's ever-rising corporate average fuel economy (CAFE) targets. Power was supplied by a bored-and-stroked 2693cc (164.3-cid) version of the M-60 small-block incorporating the firm's newly developed "eta" technology (described in Chapter 14). It was well down on power compared to the previous American-market 528i, plunging from 169 bhp (SAE net) at 5500 rpm to 121 bhp at 4250 rpm. Worse, the new engine had a rev limiter to protect its lighter-weight valvegear. Torque was unchanged at 170 lbs/ft, though it peaked lower, at 3250 rpm versus the previous 4500 rpm. With all this, the 528e must have seemed a disappointment to performance fans, but these folks only had to wait a year, be-

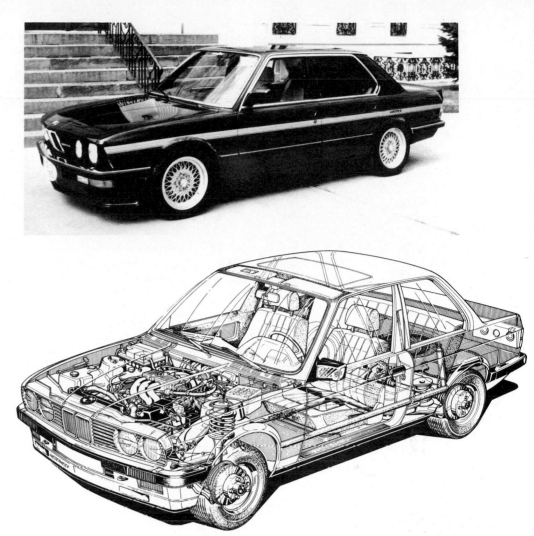

cause BMW reinstated the big-block 5-series for 1983. This was the 533i, powered by the 3210cc (196-cid) engine from the big 6- and 7-series models and an American-market exclusive. It packed 181 bhp (SAE net) at 6000 rpm and 195 lbs/ft torque peaking at 4000 rpm. Predictably, it was faster and thirstier than the 528e, but at least American buyers now had the luxury of choice. *Road & Track* magazine's test results make an illuminating comparison:

|  | 528e | 533i |
|---|---|---|
| Final drive (:1) | 2.93:1 | 3.25:1 |
| Trans/gears | man/5 | man/5 |
| 0-60 mph (sec.) | 10.3 | 8.3 |
| 0-¼-mi. (sec.) | 17.5 | 16.4 |
| 0-¼-mi. (mph) | 79.0 | 85.5 |
| Fuel economy (mpg) | 24.0 | 19.0 |

Suspension changes in the

*Top: The Hartge H5S, a high-performance limited-edition 5-series conversion. Center: An inside look at the second 3-series. Above: The 2.0-liter M-60 six.*

Top: The second-generation 3-series was bolstered in late 1983 by the first-ever four-door version of the smallest BMW. Right: The European 318i two-door. Above: A 1983 European 320i cabriolet by Baur.

new 5-series did not directly affect fuel consumption, of course, but brought a big benefit in cornering stability. The earlier cars were known to be twitchy and prone to sudden oversteer in hard cornering near the limits of adhesion. The new ones still oversteered ultimately but remained much more controllable under higher lateral loading, and the transition from understeer to over-steer was smoother and more manageable. Contributing to this improvement was the double-jointed front suspension geometry adapted from the 7-series (see Chapter 12) in which the spring leg axis does not coincide with shock absorber angle. The choice of suitable anchorage points reduced steering roll radius from 2.5 to 0.45 inches, which in turn reduced the scrub radius (still positive). Perhaps more significant was the new rear suspension, with revised geometry and less unsprung weight. The semi-trailing arms on the 518, 520i and 525i retained the 20-degree angle (relative to the transverse plane) previously used. For the 528i and the U.S. 528e and 533i, the angle was reduced to 13 degrees, a rear stabilizer bar was fitted, and an intermediate "Trac Link" was added to reduce camber, track, and toe-in changes. Also, the arms' pivot points were raised slightly to keep the rear roll center at the desired height, and bushings were revised to work with the new Trac Link arrangement. The effect, said Road & Track, was less rear-end sensitivity: "Throttle liftoff, for instance, still changes the attitude of the

533i, but it's a gradual change that would bother only the ham-fisted."

Bringing the story of the small BMWs up to date is the second-generation 3-series, launched in Europe in the spring of 1983 and arriving in the U.S. later that year as a 1984 model. Once again, the emphasis of this project, code E-30, was on preserving traditional BMW design elements, augmented with praccal high technology. Key personnel included Karlheinz Lange for design and Hans Joachim Kraft as chief of legal compliance, safety and emission control. Styling, again the work of Claus Luthe, was too close to that of the previous 3-series for some tastes and, despite extensive wind tunnel work, the coefficient of drag (Cd) worked out to an unimpressive 0.38 for the four-cylinder models and 0.39 for the sixes. The familiar two-door sedan body style was retained, and a new four-door was added for Europe in September 1983 and for the U.S. at mid-model year 1984.

A revamped model group reflected a number of technical changes in the new 3-series—not to mention BMW's delightfully inconsistent model nomenclature. The initial U.S. offering was the more accurately named 318i, which retained the 1766cc (108-cid) injected four used in the American 320i since 1980. Engine specifications were largely unchanged. For mid-1984, BMW introduced a second 3-series model, the six-cylinder 325e, available in both two- and four-door form. Despite its numerical designation, this version was powered by the 2.7-liter "eta" six as used in the 528e. For Europe, the 1.6 four was scratched and a new 316 model was issued with a 90-bhp (DIN) version of the 1.8. The previous 318 gave way to a 318i, sporting Bosch L-Jetronic injection and 105 bhp (DIN). Output on the 2.0-liter six rose to 125 bhp at 5800 rpm for the European 320i, which also switched to L-

Jetronic and got a compression increase (to 9.8:1) plus improved torque (now 125 lbs/ft). The topline 323i acquired the BMW/Bosch Motronic engine management system, which combines L-Jetronic with breakerless electronic ignition, good for a rated 139 bhp (DIN) at 5300 rpm and a maximum 151 lbs/ft torque at 4000 rpm.

There were other engine revisions for the new 3-series. A lighter ribbed crankcase was adopted, and a stiffening flange was added between the engine and gearbox to reduce vibration transfer to the cabin. Lower-tension valve springs and narrower camshaft bearings reduced internal friction, and the fours got lighter pistons to minimize secondary imbalance forces. Idle speed on injected engines was lowered to 850 rpm and a fuel shut-off was added, effective on deceleration at 1200 rpm. Also, the 316 and 318 acquired a new four-speed Getrag gearbox with Borg-Warner synchromesh, while the larger-displacement models received a new ZF five-speed.

Chassis alterations were equally extensive, aimed at reducing the earlier 3's capriciousness in extreme cornering situations. Wheel/tire size was upped an inch to 14 inches, and front suspension geometry was modified along the lines of the new 5-series. The rear geometry was modified in detail. The coil springs were no longer concentric with the struts but mounted directly on the semi-trailing arms. The arm angle was reduced as on the 5-series to lessen toe-in changes under roll and to allow longer spring travel. Rotor diameter of the front disc brakes was enlarged to 10.2 inches for all models, and the 323i got rear discs instead of drums. A laudable safety plus was first-time availability of the Bosch ABS anti-lock brake system for the 320i and 323i, a feature that has, unfortunately, so far not come to the U.S.

The new 3-series represented

a significant upgrading of the small BMWs, so prices were predictably much higher—up to the 24,000-30,000 mark range in Germany. The U.S. 318i was some $4000 costlier in base form than the last 320i—about $16,500—and it didn't take many options to push that well past $18,000. Said *Road & Track*: "It's a good car to be sure, one with most of the rough edges polished off. . .On the other hand, it fails to make a strong impression [and] leaves us wondering if BMW has set its price too high." CONSUMER GUIDE® magazine's auto editors had no such doubts, calling the 318i "overpriced." We thought "more power would be appropriate" in light of that, though we also rated this newcomer as "more refined than the 320i and still packing a spunky engine [10.2 seconds in our 0-60 mph test], fine handling, and good brakes."

High prices don't seem to deter BMW sales, however. And, in fairness, the steady price escalation in the Seventies wasn't entirely the company's fault. A strong German economy and unfavorable exchange rates between the dollar and deutsche mark for most of the decade were major factors. In retrospect, we can judge the firm's steady move upmarket a success. The first-generation 3-series had accounted for some 60 percent of total sales, and chairman Eberhard von Kuenheim predicted that some 2 million of the new ones would be sold before the next design change. The 5-series had about 30 percent of the pie, and daily production rose from 450 to 600 units with the second-series models.

The remaining 10 percent of sales belonged to the 6- and 7-series cars. They were bold, dramatic evidence of the upmarket shift, a statement of BMW's intent to become a major force in the luxury market worldwide. These glamorous and exciting machines are the subject of our next chapter.

# EXCITING ELEGANCE. THE 6-SERIES AND 7-SERIES

No matter how modern a car may seem at first, it eventually stops looking new. BMW's first-generation six-cylinder coupes were no exception. Introduced in 1968, they remained eminently satisfying, mechanically up to date driving machines well into the Seventies, but their Wilhelm Hofmeister styling had become a bit dated by mid-decade. Aware of how fickle fashion can be, Bernhard Osswald had initiated work on a new coupe design in 1973, and the program was ultimately carried through by his successor, Karlheinz Radermacher. What emerged was arguably the most elegant BMW since the classic Type 507.

Bowing as the 6-series at the Geneva show in March 1976, the new coupes were longer, lower, wider, and heavier than their predecessors. The main attraction was an all-new bodyshell with handsome, contemporary, very clean lines penned by the artistic Paul Bracq. Familiar BMW hallmarks were retained, such as the twin-kidney nose, broad hood and rear deck, rounded contours, and tall, glassy greenhouse, but the 6-series was fresh, taut, almost masculine, well-proportioned and not at all faddish. It may not go down as a timeless design, but it still looks good today, some eight years after it came on the scene. Karmann continued as body supplier for the new coupes, but final assembly now took place at BMW's Dingolfing facility, not at the coachbuilder's Osnabrück works.

Underneath the new body was

what amounted to the 5-series sedan chassis, with components retuned for this installation and its altered weight distribution. Basic dimensions were a 103.4-inch wheelbase, 187.2-inch overall length (192.7 for U.S.-market models), 67.9-inch overall width, and height of 53.7 inches. Compared to its predecessor, then, the 6-series was 3.74 inches longer, 2.17 inches wider, and 0.2-inch lower. It was also heavier, by some 200-250 pounds depending on equipment.

The 6-series was initially offered in three versions, two for Europe, one for the U.S. The carbureted 630 CS had what was essentially the 3.0 CS engine, but instead of dual two-barrel carbs it had a single Solex 4A-1 four-barrel instrument. Though compression was unchanged at 9.0:1, maximum output climbed to 185 bhp at 5500

rpm. With Bosch L-Jetronic fuel injection, this model was sold in the U.S. as the 630 CSi beginning in 1977. Power output was 176 bhp (SAE net) at 5500 rpm. The next year, BMW sent over a federalized edition of the up-market European offering, the 633 CSi, powered by a 3210cc (196-cid) variant of the big-block six with 88.9 x 86.1mm (3.50- x 3.39-in.) bore and stroke, Bosch injection and breakerless electronic ignition. Compression ratio was 9.0:1 in European form, good for a rated 200 bhp (DIN) at 5000 rpm. The U.S. model used a lower 8.4:1 squeeze compatible with low-octane fuel, but the resulting power drop was not severe and rated output was 177 bhp (SAE net) at 5500 rpm. Standard across the board was an improved four-speed Getrag manual gearbox (designated 262/9) and the ZF three-speed 3HP 22 automatic was optional. The standard four-speed gave way to a Getrag five-speed overdrive unit for 1981, and a new four-speed ZF automatic with lockup torque converter replaced the three-speed unit for 1984.

In chassis and suspension design the 6-series was closely related to the 5-series sedans and not all that different from the previous coupes. The major change was a much-modified rear suspension, with the spring legs now mounted on the hub carriers instead of having separate mountings for the coil springs and shocks. ZF worm-and-roller steering was used as before, but had a faster ratio and a modified servo pump that progressively reduced the amount of power assist as road speed increased. Four-wheel disc brakes were also retained, but the rotors were now ventilated all-round.

Though its wheelbase was only fractionally shorter than that of the 5-series sedan, the 6-series was more a 2+2 than a full four-seater. The smartly tailored exterior styling was matched by an impressive new instrument panel boasting

"cockpit" design, a wide center console, the usual large and legible BMW instrumentation, and a new gadget called Active Check Control. The latter was a comprehensive bank of warning lights that blinked on when critical fluid levels were low or when an external light bulb burned out. It also kept tabs on the brake system. The ACC would shortly find its way into other BMWs except the 3-series. Interior appointments included a telescoping steering column, a two-way lever for adjusting driver seat height and angle, rich upholstery, and the by-now traditional set of tools built into a drop-down compartment on the underside of the trunklid.

Once again a new BMW sent road test writers scurrying for superlatives. *Road & Track* magazine's comments were typical, as in this excerpt from its 1977 test of the 630 CSi: "This engine is without a doubt the most sophisticated production in-line six in the world. Although the effects of retarded ignition timing and exhaust-gas recirculation rob it of some of its around-town response, when driven hard it frees up, smooths out, and goes nearly as well as the 3.0 CS we tested in 1973." That meant 9.7 seconds in the 0-60 mph dash and 17.5 seconds to run the quarter-mile (at 81.0-mph terminal speed). A year later, *R&T* termed the more powerful and better equipped 633 CSi "the perfect example of engineering improvements and comfort refinements that make a great GT car even more pleasurable." The magazine's 0-60 mph time came down to 8.4 seconds and its quarter-mile figures improved to 16.8 seconds at 84.5 mph, yet fuel economy was only one mpg less (17.0 mpg overall) than for the earlier car. The 6-series' high handling and roadholding levels, well-nigh perfectly judged steering, comfortable yet well-controlled ride, and excellent ergonomics also earned high marks. High price was still a sore spot. The coupe arrived in the U.S at $23,600, and by 1983 the figure had escalated to near 40 grand. This was quite a premium over the more practical, mechanically similar 5-series sedan—a 50 percent premium to be exact. *R&T* put the issue directly: "Whether the coupe's distinctive styling and slightly better overall performance are worth [the extra money] is something only your ego and your pocketbook can decide."

Under pressure from Eberhard von Kuenheim, BMW got into a "race" with Mercedes-Benz to see who could produce the fastest four-seat coupe in Europe. The 633 CSi wasn't quite as quick as the V-8-powered 450 SLC 5.0 from Stuttgart, so the engineers in Munich decided to slot in their 3.5-liter (213.5-cid) M-90 engine and dress up the 6-series body with aerodynamic aids such as a front air dam and a rear spoiler. BMW may have overlooked the rear seating in the Porsche 928 when it claimed that its new 635 CSi, introduced at mid-year 1978, was Germany's fastest four-seat coupe— or possibly it felt that the Porsche's aft cabin failed to meet the definition of a proper rear seat. Be that as it may, the 635 CSi had a claimed top speed of 140 mph and a blistering 7.3-second 0-100 km/h (62 mph) capability. For comparison, the European 630 CS could do the 0-100 km/h trek in 8.9 seconds and the 633 CSi was a full second faster than that.

The M-90 engine had a bigger 93.4mm (3.68-in.) bore but a shorter 84mm (3.31-in.) stroke. Exact displacement was 3453cc (210.6 cid). With 9.3:1 compression and Bosch L-Jetronic fuel injection, peak power output was 217.5 bhp (DIN) at 5200 rpm. The M-52 unit in the 633 CSi delivered its maximum torque at 4250 rpm, an engine speed considered too high for best tractability in normal street driving. The carbureted engine produced its peak torque at a more tolerable 3500 rpm. For the M-90, torque was raised by nearly 10 percent but peaked further down the scale, at 4000 rpm.

The 635 CSi employed a five-speed Getrag gearbox with direct-drive fifth and final drive ratio of 3.07:1. Suspension design and geometry were altered to handle the extra power and increased performance. Spring rates were increased, shock absorbers revalved, stabilizer bars reinforced, and anti-tilt blocks were added to the front spring/struts to reduce the car's roll angle in fast bends. Tire size remained as for the 633 CSi (195/70VR-14), but rims were widened from 6.0 to 6.5 inches for better stability near the limit of adhesion. High-speed stability was enhanced by the front air dam and rear spoiler. They looked stylish and could be dismissed as mere fashion gimmicks, but both were actually very functional, carefully developed in wind tunnel tests. Together they reduced lift by 15 percent without adding to the drag coefficient.

Born in the shadow of the mid-engine M1, the 635 CSi was not immediately tried out in competition. In 1981, however, three Group 2 cars prepared by Ruedi Eggenberger's garage in Switzerland for drivers Grano, Kelleners, and Cecotto ran in European Touring Car Championship events. Despite their 370-bhp engines, they bowed to the more powerful and faster Porsches. Group A regulations took effect in 1983, which decreed specifications much closer to factory stock, and many BMW entrants saw their chance for a crack at the championship title. Alpina tuned the 635 CSi to 285 bhp at 6100 rpm, and Eggenberger used it in this form for his Group A assault. Schnitzer also prepared a brace of 635s for Dieter Quester and Hans Stück Jr., while Juma prepared cars for Hans Heyer and several other contestants. With so many entries, it was no surprise when BMW clinched the Group A championship at the 24-hour race at Spa-Francorchamps in Belgium. Heyer repulsed a challenge by the Jaguar V-12 contingent to win a grueling enduro that saw only 22 cars cross the finish line out of 57 starters. Quester came home second.

Encouraged by this experience, BMW decided to produce a virtually race-ready coupe for 1984 on a very limited basis. Developed by Horst Rech and R. Bratenstein, it was presented as the M635 CSi (M for Motorsport) at the Frankfurt show in September 1983. The engine was a modified M-88 unit with dual overhead camshafts and four valves per cylinder, and slanted 30 degrees from the vertical as installed. Other features included a new heavy-duty five-speed gearbox and Michelin TRX 220/55VR-390 tires. Revised intake and exhaust systems coupled with 10.5:1 compression and Bosch Motronic wizardry yielded nine more horsepower than the M1 engine: 286 bhp (DIN) at 6500 rpm. Maximum torque of 250 lbs/ft was developed at 4500 rpm, remarkably low for a competition engine. BMW claimed the M635 CSi could accelerate from 0 to 100 km/h (62 mph) in 6.4 seconds and reach 158 mph tops.

Only a year after the 6-series debuted, BMW rejuvenated its big sedans. The need here was less acute than with the two-doors, mainly because the basic styling of the 2500/2800/Bavaria/3.0 was holding up extremely well, even though it also dated from 1968. Over a quarter million of these cars (252,559 to be exact) were built over an eight-year production run and they were highly profitable, playing a big part in financing BMW's expansion. Though it may seem odd to an outsider, BMW actually began planning the replacement for the big sedans as soon as they went into production.

This new program, designated E-23, was entrusted to Bernhard Osswald, who was responsible

for concept, design, testing, and development—not to mention keeping track of 3-series, 5-series, and 6-series efforts. His prime objective was to improve comfort, silence, and safety compared to the existing models. He chose a wide-awake all-round engineer as project manager, Walter Stork, who had joined BMW in 1966 to take charge of advanced engineering and chassis development. Born in Wiesbaden, Stork went to work for Opel in 1952, then moved to Detroit, where he was assistant chief engineer at Pontiac Division from 1953 to 1957. He then transferred to the GM Engineering Staff, where he remained until 1966. Wilhelm Hofmeister had made preliminary styling sketches for E-23, and Dr. Joachim Elsholz supervised body design and engineering for the new model. The first mockup

*Top left: The most sporty and powerful member of the European 6-series lineup, the 635 CSi is powered by the 218-bhp (DIN) M-90 engine and can reach nearly 140 mph flat out. Just visible here is the modest trunklid lip spoiler. Also note the deep front air dam. Top right: Even more formidable is the M635 CSi, a limited-production special from BMW Motorsport able to hit 100 km/h from rest in 6.4 seconds. Center left and right and bottom: The big 7-series sedan in its initial 1977 form. Engine choices comprised 2.8-, 3.0- and 3.2-liter sixes. Only the last came to the U.S.*

223

*A beautiful piece of machinery itself, this is the 24-valve version of BMW's 3.5-liter six as used in the M635 CSi. Its maximum 286 bhp (DIN) is reached at a high 6000 rpm. Torque output is 250 lbs/ft at 4500 rpm.*

was shown to management in June 1970, the structural design went on the drawing board in September, and crash tests began the following spring.

The first E-23 prototypes went on test as modified Bavarias in early 1971 at the newly completed Aschheim proving grounds on the Speichersee. The main object of interest was a modified front suspension designed by Wolfgang Matschinsky, assisted by Eugen Gebler. The new wrinkle was double-jointed spring legs with the MacPherson struts resting on two lower pivots, one at the outer end of each lower control arm and the other at a point where the ends of the stabilizer bar were attached to the arms. The intersection of straight lines drawn from these two links marked the effective lower swivel point, which moved

according to steering angle. The amount of offset in the steering axis thus varied according to how sharp the turn was. This arrangement brought several advantages, including increased anti-dive effect and greater compactness, which enabled the use of larger brakes. It also allowed a reduction in front spring rates without ill effects on steering or handling, and a doubling of front wheel caster action, which improved straightline stability at speed, minimized the effects of road irregularities, and speeded up steering self-centering. A short while later, Christian Dietrich and Emil Winkler came in to assist Gebler and Matschinsky on E-23 chassis engineering. The independent rear suspension was a straight redesign of the existing big-car layout, but a good deal of research and testing was still needed for the front end. Meantime, an improved power steering system was developed in collaboration with ZF.

Approval to proceed with construction of E-23 production pro-

totypes came in September 1972, just as the 3.0 CSL was introduced. The 5-series began rolling off the lines at the same time, which freed up designers to reinforce Stork's group and thus speed program completion. The new car's basic dimensions had already been decided. Compared with the Bavaria and its relatives, wheelbase was stretched from 106 to 110 inches and length grew 6.3 inches to 191.3 overall. The E-23 was also given a wider stance, with front track extended from 56.9 to 59.45 inches and rear track broadened from 57.7 to 59.8 inches.

Another group of cobbled-up prototypes, using Bavaria parts where practical or expedient, was tested beginning in the spring of 1973. Then came the fuel crisis in October and all product development at BMW was suspended for re-evaluation. Improved fuel economy now became a top priority for E-23, but it would still have to be a true BMW, with performance at least equal to that of its predecessors.

The engineers scrambled. Karlheinz Lange assigned Gustav Ederer to devise a new range of more economical engines based on the big six. Among his assistants was Gustav Vorberger, who had become BMW's expert on supercharging and turbocharging and contributed new ideas in combustion chamber and manifolding design. Two other engineers named Jeude and Starmühler were also on the team. Bertold Mayr and G. Thiele made fresh studies on methods for reducing gaswasting internal friction. The basic engine was thus "economized" for the E-23, which would be offered with all three existing displacements. The 2.8- and 3.0-liter units were fitted with Solex four-barrel carburetors and delivered 170 and 184 bhp (DIN), respectively, both at 5800 rpm. L-Jetronic was specified for the 3.2-liter unit, rated at 197 bhp at 5500 rpm.

Meantime, Paul Bracq was

working on a new body design, and it was ready in May 1974. Structural engineering began immediately, proceeding in parallel with chassis and powertrain development. Finally, all phases of the E-23 effort were united in a final prototype, completed in late fall of 1975. By this point, the new big car was being openly referred to within the company as the 7-series. A batch of pre-pilot cars was built before the end of the year and assigned to the proving grounds, then the design was frozen in early 1976 and tooling orders went out. Though Osswald had officially retired at the end of 1975, he was on hand as a consultant to shepherd the E-23 through its last pre-natal stages. Dr. Radermacher finalized such details as model designations and equipment and trim levels before the end of 1976 in coordination with the marketing and sales staffs directed by Hans-Erdmann Schönbeck and Herbert Kothe.

Announced in May 1977, the 7-series began rolling off the Dingolfing assembly line the following month. The three initial models—728, 730 and 733i—incorporated several last-minute improvements, some derived from the 6-series. Among these were a central, engine-driven hydraulic pump providing power assist for both steering and the standard all-disc brake system. No important revisions were made in the familiar transmissions, but there was a completely new final drive made by BMW itself. Ratios were 3.64:1 on the 728 and 3.45:1 on the 730 and 733i. Despite strict weight control throughout the development program, the new cars weighed more than their predecessors: 3375 pounds dry for the 728, 3485 for the 730, and 3530 pounds for the 733i.

Did the 7-series meet performance targets? Perhaps not at first, but the new models were at least as quick as the previous big sedans. The 728 needed 10.1 seconds for the 0-100 km/h

(62-mph) dash and could reach 122 mph. The 730's figures were 9.6 seconds and 125 mph, and the 733i came in at 8.9 seconds and 129 mph. Average fuel consumption ranged between 19.9 and 20.4 mpg.

The 7-series was widely applauded, and sales got off to a fast start. Only a year after introduction, the new line was being built at the rate of 3300 a month, which was comparable to the monthly output of the W116 Mercedes-Benz S-Class at Sindelfingen. The big Merc, of course, was the natural rival for the 7-series, and *Road & Track* was quick to match them up in a 1978 comparison test along with Jaguar's XJ-12L. The 733i (the only version offered in the U.S.) was predictably down on power compared to its European counterpart, mainly due to a lower 8.4:1 compression (also specified for the American-market 633 CSi) and add-on emissions controls. Compared to the federalized 450SEL it was down on torque (196 lbs/ft at 4000 rpm in SAE net measure) though not much on power (177 bhp at 5500 rpm). But the BMW was the only one of this trio available with a manual gearbox, "and it really means something in the acceleration," said *R&T*. "It undercut [at 8.6 seconds] the 0-60 mph times of the Mercedes by 0.7 sec. and even the V-12 Jaguar by 0.2 sec. Add the automatic to the 733i and it slips to a full second slower than the 450SEL and 1.5 seconds behind the Jaguar. The automatic changes the entire image of the 733i, making it more sedate, even though the ZF is a crisp-shifting transmission that likes to be manually [shifted] to extract maximum performance." Because of its less torquey engine, the 733i "needs the manual gearbox, that and the fact that the engine doesn't feel that well matched to the automatic . . ."

As for the rest of it, *R&T* described the 7-series "as just a larger extension and refinement of the same traits we've enjoyed

in BMWs for years." They rated its ride a nice compromise between Mercedes hardness and the Jaguar's comparative softness. Despite recording the highest numbers on the skidpad, the 733i split the difference in handling, too. "It leans," said the editors. "That tends to put a number of drivers off as they feel a bit uncertain with body roll, but make no mistake, because the 733i handles. It's just a question of learning how far the car will lean because when it's at that farthest point, it will stick and transmit back a much more balanced feel than you would expect."

The 733i came out on top in the *R&T* "comparo," slightly ahead of the Mercedes, but with a more decisive margin over the XJ-12. The editors' verdict: "The new 733i and the 450SEL are very comparable in so many ways, their differences often being less a matter of better or worse than just two different approaches to the same end. There is, however, one difference we feel is quite important: price. As much as we like the 450SEL, we don't feel it's $6360 better than the BMW." They were talking in 1978 dollars, remember, when the 733i's initial price was a bit over $21,000. Unhappily, it has since gone up to around $34,000, but if there is such a thing as a "bargain" in this rarified class, then the big BMW must be it. Which brings up a telling point: by the end of the Seventies, BMWs had evolved to the point where they were usually compared with their vaunted Mercedes rivals, yet were much more shrewdly priced relative to overall size, displacement, power, and performance. They still are, yet continue to enjoy a similar level of prestige.

Two years after its debut, the 7-series came in for its first round of revisions. These were pretty much restricted to Europe and were aimed mostly at improving both performance and fuel efficiency. Compression on all engines was bumped up to 9.3:1, the carbureted 3.0-liter was discontinued, the 2.8-liter version acquired L-Jetronic injection to become the 728i, and the 733i was renamed 732i (which it should have been in the first place). An exciting newcomer was the 735i, powered by a 3430cc (209.3-cid) M-90 engine with bore and stroke of 92 x 86mm (3.62 x 3.39 in.). Rated at 218 bhp (DIN) at 5200 rpm and 229 lbs/ft torque peaking at 4000 rpm, this executive express could hit 135 mph flat out and run the quarter-mile in about 15.5 seconds from a dead stop. Engine availability was likewise shuffled in the coupe line, as the 630 and 633 were replaced by the 184-bhp 628 CSi. Model designations stayed the same for the American market, even though both the 633 CSi and 733i used the 3210cc power unit. For 1981, the U.S. versions acquired the five-speed manual gearbox previously available in Europe, replacing the four-speed.

A second wave of 7-series changes was instituted in September 1983. Fuel consumption was reduced by some 20 percent on the 728i and by some 15 percent on the 735i, mainly through a weight loss of about 250 pounds, and a mildly reworked front end that shaved the drag coefficient by some 13 percent (from 0.44 to a more respectable 0.383). Compression ratio on the 3.5-liter six was bumped to 10.0:1. Also contributing to economy was availability of ZF's new 4HP 22 four-speed overdrive automatic with lockup torque converter for both the 6-series and 7-series. This change also showed up on the 1984 American models as well as the 5-series sedans. A 1982 alteration affecting only the U.S. 633 CSi and 733i was adoption of the Bosch Motronic digital ignition/fuel injection system. This allowed a compression increase to 8.8:1, which yielded an extra 4-7 horsepower, to 181 bhp (SAE net) at 6000 rpm.

Concurrently with the re-

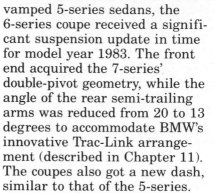

vamped 5-series sedans, the 6-series coupe received a significant suspension update in time for model year 1983. The front end acquired the 7-series' double-pivot geometry, while the angle of the rear semi-trailing arms was reduced from 20 to 13 degrees to accommodate BMW's innovative Trac-Link arrangement (described in Chapter 11). The coupes also got a new dash, similar to that of the 5-series.

Dreams die hard, but sometimes they live long enough to become reality. One of the most persistent dreams in Munich ever since the war involved a *Grosser* BMW, a luxurious, high-performance supercar equal in prestige and ability to anything made anywhere in the world. Hanns Grewenig had dreamed of it in the early postwar years. In the Sixties it became the vision of Helmut Werner Bönsch and Paul Hahnemann, who wanted a competitor for what some critics judged "the world's best sedan," the Mercedes 300SEL 6.3. Eberhard von Kuenheim picked up the dream in the Seventies, and again a Mercedes was the target, the W116 S-class. The 7-series had closed the gap with D-B's finest, though not completely. But perhaps a special 7-series could be the *Grosser* BMW that company leaders had dreamed of for so long—the car with which the Bavarians would at last triumph over their Swabian rivals

as builders of the world's best-performing production automobile. Thus was born the turbocharged 745i, truly a grand BMW in every way.

The genesis of the 745i goes all the way back to February 1965, when Alex von Falkenhausen was instructed to draw up proposals for a very high-powered engine even larger than the M-20 six then under development. With due regard to manufacturing costs, he proposed a V-8 built from two of the existing fours, the blocks angled at 90 degrees to fit a common crankshaft. A displacement range of 3.6-5.0 liters (220-305 cid) was envisioned for this M-36 project, and Dieter Henning was made chief draftsman. Unfortunately, he ran into a snag right away. To achieve the upper displacements without going overboard on stroke length, it would be necessary to increase cylinder spacing—which made it impossible to utilize either the existing blocks or their machining lines. The V-8 would also need bigger valves and different valvegear, which ruled out sharing off-the-shelf cylinder heads. But the project was not halted despite these costly drawbacks. Cylinder centers were placed 124mm (4.88 in.) apart, compared with 100mm (3.94 in.) in the big six, so that the V-8 could be bored out as far as 100mm. The new engine was to have

been built in at least four sizes. A 3.6-liter was planned with a bore of 90mm (3.54 in.) and a 71mm (2.80-in.) stroke. There would also be 4.0- (242-cid) and 4.5-liter (273-cid) versions built with the same crankshaft and short 71mm stroke in combination with bigger bores of 95 and 100mm (3.74 and 3.94 in.), respectively. For the 5.0-liter edition, Henning stretched stroke to 97mm (3.82 in.) and used the 100m bore. Only the 4.5- and 5.0-liter units were actually built and tested. BMW followed American practice by fitting a two-plane crankshaft to cancel out most of the unbalanced secondary coupling forces, and six accurately machined counterweights took care of the primary forces. Each cylinder bank had its own chain-driven overhead camshaft operating splayed overhead valves via rocker arms. An extremely long chain drove both camshafts from a sprocket at the front of the crankshaft. Cast iron was chosen for the cylinder block. Despite the use of light alloy for the heads and intake manifold, the 5.0-liter engine was quite weighty: 639.5 pounds including clutch, fuel injection system and exhaust headers.

Physically, the basic V-8 was 34.25 inches long and 27.6 inches high. This was surprisingly close to the envelope of the M-20 six and meant that any

of the four versions could easily substitute for it. The prototype 5.0-liter engine with Bosch B-Jetronic fuel injection and 9.5:1 compression was rated at 275 bhp (DIN) at 5800 rpm and 263 lbs/ft torque at 3500 rpm. It was tested in a coupe, which turned in rocket-like 0-100 km/h acceleration of less than six seconds and topped out at an astounding 155 mph. Fitted with a Rochester four-barrel downdraft carburetor and 9.0:1 compression ratio, the 4.5 delivered 250 bhp at 5500 rpm and maximum torque of 246 lbs/ft at 4200 rpm.

But the V-8 was not to be, and the project was terminated before the end of 1972. BMW's official explanation listed four reasons. First, the new engine lacked smoothness, not significantly superior to the six in this regard. Second, its power-to-weight ratio was poor in view of the modest displacement increase. Third, the V-8 would not be an easy installation job despite appearances to the contrary. The basic engine would fit alright, but there was little room left over for accessories without restricting the steering angle. The fourth reason was likely the deciding factor: high cost. With all its unique parts but only modest potential production volume, the V-8 was just too expensive on a unit basis to justify the considerable tooling investment involved.

The V-8 idea was not so much killed as it was preempted by another project. BMW had started design work on the M-60 small-block six in 1970-71, and it became clear at some point that the 2.3-liter (140-cid) version could become the basis for a 4.6-liter V-12. Like the V-8, it could be built by simply bolting two of the sixes together on a common crankshaft, and it promised the same attractive cost savings and assembly line efficiencies. It also promised something else: comparative exclusivity. Even prestigious Rolls-Royce didn't have a V-12, and the only other such engines in regular production at the time were the silky 5.3-liter (323-cid) Jaguar unit and Ferrari's magnificent 4.0-liter (244-cid) powerhouse. Significantly, Mercedes-Benz didn't have one either, and Von Kuenheim especially liked the idea for this reason. Osswald found the V-12 more attractive than the V-8 as an installation package since it was narrower, its cylinder banks angled at 60 degrees instead of 90 degrees.

With that agreed, design and development for the V-12 were duly entrusted to Karlheinz Lange. The six's crossflow head and overhead camshaft would be retained, making this a twincam powerplant. Lange chose a linerless cast-iron block with an upper crankcase extending well below the crankshaft centerline. The crankshaft was a seven-main-bearing design with six journals spaced at 120 degrees, each journal accommodating two connecting rods machined to their full width. Crank throws were shorter than in the six, reducing stroke from 76.8 to 74mm (2.91 in.). An 80mm (3.15-in.) bore yielded displacement of 372cc per cylinder for an aggregate capacity of 4463cc (272.3

227

cid). Dry-sump lubrication was selected to keep the engine's center of gravity as low as possible, in line with ground clearance requirements. There was a gear-type oil pump driven by roller chain, and an external oil cooler with thermostatic control was added. The alternator and water pump were driven by V-belts. The induction system was designed with equal-length runners for all cylinders. Air was ducted from a body-mounted air cleaner through an airflow-mass measuring device, then split into two symmetrical plenum chambers. The headers were crossed over; in other words, the left-side chamber fed the right cylinder bank and vice versa, an arrangement adopted much later at Chevrolet for its "Cross-Fire" injected V-8 on the 1982 Corvette. The proposed V-12 also had something like a forerunner to the Bosch Motronic system. It consisted of the basic L-Jetronic setup with electronic control units adapted to handle spark timing as well as fuel injection on the basis of the same input data from a set of sensors. Two camshaft-driven six-lug distributors fired the plugs in sequential order.

The prototype V-12 weighed in at 606 pounds with accessories, which compares favorably with the 4.5-liter version of the aborted V-8. It thus had a more favorable power-to-weight ratio considering its maximum 275 bhp (at 5700 rpm) was the same as for the 5.0 V-8. Compression was specified as 9.3:1. Peak torque was 268 lbs/ft developed at 4500 rpm, a speed that seemed high for a luxury-car engine, but fully 90 percent torque was available from as little as 2000 rpm. Minimum fuel consumption as seen on the dynamometer was 198 grams (0.437-pound) per horsepower/hour at 2500 rpm, rising to 300 grams (0.66-pound) per hp/hour at 5000 rpm. Installed in prototype 7-series cars, the V-12 returned overall averages of around 16.8 mpg. And it had performance aplenty:

top speed was around 140 mph and 0-100 km/h (62-mph) acceleration took only about 7.5 seconds. The V-12 thus met or exceeded all of BMW's expectations for performance, response, driveability, and smoothness.

A V-12 BMW would have been simply smashing. Unfortunately, fate intervened in the form of the 1973-74 energy crisis, and this splendid engine fell victim to Munich's new emphasis on fuel economy before the design could be finalized. By the start of 1978, the V-12 had been shelved. The spotlight now turned to a new supercar project drawing heavily on BMW Motorsport experience. Lange had calculated that turbocharging would enable the big-block six to equal the performance of the stillborn V-12—but with only about two-thirds the fuel consumption. He assigned his trusted assistants (Fischer, Niggemeyer, Ziermann, and Windisch) to come up with such an engine. The 745i was on its way.

Lange's team worked quickly, and in May 1980 a turbo-six prototype was ready for test drives by a few journalists invited to the Aschheim proving grounds. "What is BMW trying to do?" we began our report on this session. "Do they think they can turn back the clock or make the energy shortage go away simply by building a luxury sedan with more power and speed than anything else on the market? No. BMW says it is merely expanding its model range upwards." Indeed, the company had a considerable stack of market research suggesting there was an opening for a car of this sort. What sort? The driving experience explains it all. Cruising at 130 km/h (81 mph) was almost like fair-weather flying—quiet, comfortable, and smooth. The car even seeemed rather slow, so we stepped on it. Instantly the automatic transmission downshifted to second, the lusty engine sort of catapulted us ahead and—only seconds later—we were doing 200 km/h (125 mph).

The upshift to top gear, incidentally, occurred at 90 mph. The standing-start 400 meters (quarter-mile) was accomplished in 15.6 seconds. Top speed was a sizzling 138 mph.

As almost every car enthusiast knows, West Germany has no speed limits on its *Autobahnen*, and it is not uncommon to see cars going 100-125 mph. Not many cars are capable of such speeds, and among those that are there is a great sense of competitive pride on the part of their owners—and their manufacturers. It isn't a rivalry in absolute top speed but rather the ability to run at sustained high speeds with maximum comfort, quietness, stability, and safety, as well as quick mid-range acceleration with a full load of passengers and luggage. These are the cars built with due regard to cost and an increasingly watchful eye on fuel consumption but with no compromise in engineering. The 745i definitely belongs in this elite group.

The 745i designation derives from a formula for the displacement equivalence of a turbocharged engine. Here, the blower is calculated to be worth a 40 percent gain in displacement over the normally aspirated 3.2-liter engine, so the turbo version is therefore regarded as equivalent to 4.5 liters (3.2 x 1.4 = 4.48) in output. Compared with the unblown BMW 3.5, the pressurized power unit has a smaller 89mm (3.50-in.) bore, for a more compact combustion chamber, and a longer 86mm (3.39-in.) stroke, for greater low-range torque. This is, in fact, a blown version of the 3210cc big-block six familiar in the U.S. It's much modified, however, with cam profiles, fuel metering, spark timing, and other factors optimized for broad torque output over a wide rpm band rather than merely top-end power. The 745i thus packs 30 percent more torque than the 735i throughout the rev range, and its curve is flatter, too. Several important modifications assure reliability under the higher stress levels associated wih turbocharging. For example, connecting rod bearings have shells with higher wear resistance, and the exhaust valvcs are made of Nimonic, a high-temperature alloy commonly used in gas turbines. The engine oil has its own external cooler, and the circulation system is revised to assure pressure lubrication of the critical turbocharger shaft bearings.

The turbo unit itself is a K-27 series from KKK. An intercooler for controlling charge-air temperature is fitted, along with the usual wastegate to guard against overboost. An additional refinement is a "recirculation" device intended to maintain high turbine speed on a closed throttle, thereby minimizing the throttle lag inherent in many turbo installations. It also helps smooth out the sudden rise in torque when the turbo comes "on boost." Maximum boost is fixed at a fairly low level, only 0.6 bar (about 9 psi). However, that's achieved as early as 2000 rpm and is maintained all the way to the 6300-rpm redline, which accounts for the broad-shouldered torque output. The 3.2 engine's internal compression ratio is eased to 7.0:1 in order to keep overall compression within the knock-resistance limit of the premium gasoline sold in Europe, and Bosch L-Jetronic injection is retained. The result is maximum output of 252 bhp (DIN) at 5200 rpm and 284.5 lbs/ft torque at 2600 rpm.

Like Mercedes-Benz with the 300SEL 6.3, BMW standardized automatic for the 745i, the 3-speed ZF 3HP 21 from the same family of transmissions found on other 7-series models. The final drive ratio was stretched from 3.25:1 on the 735i to 3.07:1 for a higher top speed, as well as fewer engine revs for a given road speed in the interest of quieter cruising. With this gearing, fuel mileage at a constant 75 mph works out to 17.4

*Top: The U.S. 733i for 1982. Above: An attractive 7-series wagon conversion is currently offered by Euler of Frankfort.*

mpg, compared with 21.6 mpg for the lighter, higher-compression 735i. The turbo isn't really working at that speed, of course, but when it does get going it delivers absolutely fantastic push. Acceleration times are 7.9 seconds in the 0-100 km/h (62-mph) test and a brisk 18.6 seconds from rest to 100 mph.

Two different suspensions were evaluated for the 745i, the basic 7-series settings and a "sports" package. Both gave a relatively firm, well-cushioned ride with little body roll and total freedom from pitch. The

sports setup had different shock absorber calibrations and a reinforced anti-roll bar, but both types had 6½J-14 magnesium wheels shod with Michelin TRX 220/55VR-390 tires that give a phenomenal sidebite. Traction was superb in straightline acceleration, but wheelspin could be provoked by being brutal with the accelerator when coming out of very tight bends. The brakes were nothing short of superb. The ventilated front discs were a full 25mm wide (just short of an inch) and so well cooled that you would run out of continuous downhill roads even in the Alps before you could get them to fade. For extra safety in the wet, the Bosch ABS four-wheel anti-lock brake system was standardized.

Taken as a whole, the 745i is not easy to sum up in a few words. It's something of a hot rod, to be sure, but it's really more of a fast luxury tourer, with power-everything, automatic climate control, and BMW's recently introduced on-board computer that will calculate your average speed, fuel consumption, estimated time of arrival, and other trip information, all at the touch of a few buttons. ("It could probably also do the Sunday *Times* crossword puzzle while you're waiting at a red light and balance your checking account every time you switch on," we reported after our Aschheim trip.)

Another way to look at the 745i is to cast around for similar

*Deiter Quester in the racing M635 CSi prepared by Schnitzer for the 1983 season and sponsored by BMW Parts. Note beefy tires and unusual line body graphics.*

cars. There are really only two that come to mind: the current Mercedes 500SEL and Maserati's equally formidable Quattroporte. But, like so many Bimmers before it, the 745i really has no rivals because of its unique personality. Our colleague Thom Bryant put it this way for *Road & Track* readers: "The problem...is that this is a car that is so very hard to drive normally. It wants to go quickly and few enthusiast drivers can resist the temptation to join in the fun. A stab of the accelerator, and other cars just seem to have applied their brakes as you scurry away—quietly, gracefully, but very quickly. And that is why European owners are willing to shell out more than $40,000 to get their hands on the 745i—it is simply a marvelously entertaining car to drive."

The 745i went into limited production later in 1980, shortly after our initial test drive. BMW had planned to build 10 a day, but the market did not want that many. Fortunately, the company did not let it die, and in September 1983 issued a heavily revised version with an even *larger* engine. Bore was taken out to 86mm (3.39 in.), which raised displacement to

3430cc (209 cid). Advances in electronics produced the new Motronic II engine management system, which allowed internal compression ratio to be increased to 8.0:1. Progress in turbocharger technology has brought a more responsive adaptation of turbocharger action to power requirements. As a result, air temperature at the intercooler entry is now 131 degrees F lower than before and the turbo can run up to 30,000 rpm slower. Maximum power is unchanged for the revised model, but it now peaks at 4900 instead of 5200 rpm. Peak torque speed has also been reduced, from 2600 to 2200 rpm, though again there is no change in output. Equally important is adoption of the 4HP 22 four-speed automatic transmission (with electronic/hydraulic actuation) developed jointly by ZF and BMW. It offers the driver a choice of "economy" or "performance" automatic shift points as well as a full manual-shift mode. Chassis improvements involve minor revisions to suspension geometry at each end, plus a new hydropneumatic self-levelling system with electronic control at the rear. The excellent ABS anti-lock brakes continue as standard.

It remains to be seen whether these changes are sufficient to stimulate sales of today's ultimate BMW. However, the 745i is now about 12 percent thriftier and not a tick slower than before, so it certainly won't lose any fans. The official ECE fuel economy figures show 27.8 mpg at 56 mph (90 km/h), 22.6 at 74.5 mph (120 km/h), and 14.2 mpg in the Standard-15 urban test cycle. Whoever said "you can't have your cake and eat it too" obviously never drove a 745i.

What's next? Shortly before his sudden departure from BMW, Dr. Radermacher told us that an all-new 7-series body with advanced aerodynamics was in the works. Now *that* would be an "ultimate driving machine" worth waiting for.

# THE FORMULA 1 ENGINE: THE ULTIMATE DRIVING MACHINE

*Nelson Piquet (car 1) and Ricardo Patrese (car 2) in the '82 Brabham-BMW BT-50s.*

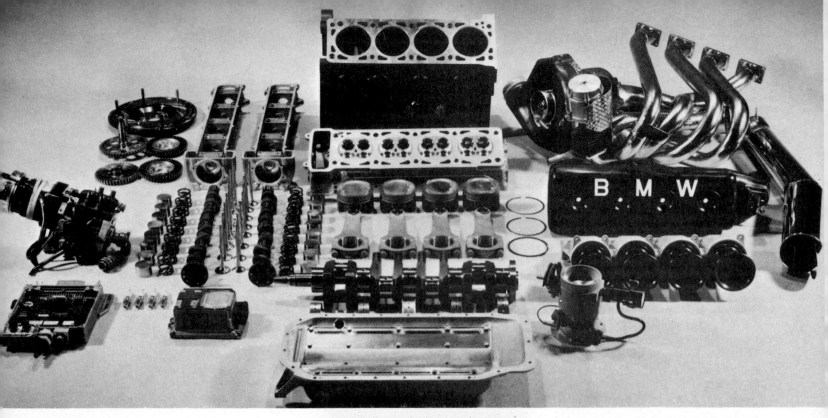

Nelson Piquet won the 1983 Grand Prix driving championship with a BMW-powered Brabham. The most extraordinary fact behind this accomplishment is that the engine that propelled him to the title was not a supersophisticated multicylinder affair but a relatively simple four based on a humble production powerplant. Here surely was proof—if any be needed—that BMW remained not only a builder of great engines but a builder of enormous engineering skill going back more than half a century.

The story begins naturally enough at BMW Motorsport. The racing arm had developed a 16-valve turbocharged competition version of the production 1.6-liter four, and the idea that this could be adapted for Formula 1 use occurred to several people, including Motorsport boss Jochen Neerpasch and engineer Paul Rosche. During 1979 they briefly entertained the notion that the McLaren team might use BMW power for the 1980 season, but despite the division's independence from the parent concern, it was BMW chairman Eberhard von Kuen-

heim who vetoed any collaboration along these lines.

Neerpasch then began informal talks with race car constructor Guy Ligier, who had recently switched to the Ford-Cosworth V-8, abandoning the old Matra V-12 that dated from 1967. The automobile branch of Matra (a company primarily involved in aerospace) was then partly owned by Chrysler France. At the start of 1979, Peugeot S.A. purchased Chrysler's European operations and the French subsidiary was renamed Automobiles Talbot,

marking the return of a nameplate with a great racing heritage. Peugeot had watched Renault make good on its bid for a victory at Le Mans, then saw its arch rival challenge the Grand Prix circuits. The new Talbot management was interested in doing the same, mainly to bolster their firm's image while getting a lot of free publicity in the process. But Talbot did not have the wherewithal to field a Formula 1 effort, and began casting around for a shortcut. Matra seemed to be the key, because it would reopen the door to Ligier.

Ligier was never enamored of the Ford-Cosworth V-8, the engine favored by most Formula 1 constructors. With a promise of fresh money from Talbot, he agreed to design a new GP car, and the Matra people dusted off their old 3.0-liter V-12 as an interim measure. Meanwhile, an all-new 1.5-liter turbocharged

power unit would be readied, perhaps in time for the 1982 season. But Peugeot had a lot of questions about this plan. Talbot cars were proving hard to sell and its newly acquired division was losing a lot of money. What Peugeot wanted to know was who was going to pay Matra, how much would it cost to sponsor the Ligier team, and what tangible good any of this would do for Talbot sales.

Then Neerpasch entered the picture. BMW could supply the engine, he said, and it could certainly be adapted to the Ligier JS-17 chassis during the course of 1980. It sounded good, but the prideful French wanted no part of a German-made engine. The solution was to build the BMW powerplant in France. Neerpasch agreed. Talbot duly purchased the engineering drawings, hired Neerpasch as a consultant, and contracted with BMW Motorsport for development assistance, which secured the services of Paul Rosche as well. Talbot also signed with Matra for technical aid in electronics and aerodynamics, areas where Ligier was weak. Neerpasch moved to Paris to take

over as program chief effective April 1, 1980. Dieter Stappert was appointed as his successor at Motorsport, and financial management of BMW's competition branch was entrusted to Rosche and Dr. Henning Scheu.

Neerpasch gave up an interesting, well-paid position for this daring step into the "twilight zone" of France's auto industry. BMW sales director Hans-Erdmann Schönbeck said at the end of 1980: "We were sorry to lose Jochen Neerpasch. Thanks to his efforts, we made contact with Talbot." Neerpasch probably left because the M1 racing program was nearly dead, and the challenge of taking on new responsibilities for Talbot must have seemed attractive.

In June 1980, representatives of Guy Ligier S.A. and Peugeot S.A. (on behalf of Talbot) signed a letter of intent stipulating the partners' responsibilities for the 1981 racing campaign. For commercial reasons the new F1 car would be known only as a Talbot—not Talbot-Ligier, Talbot-Matra, or Talbot-BMW. However, Automobiles Talbot was absorbed by Peugeot in late December and ceased to exist as

a separate corporate entity. At first, Peugeot officials said this would not affect the racing program, but Eberhard von Kuenheim soon decided that engine development had to remain totally with BMW in Germany— which effectively cancelled the letter of intent. No contract was ever signed. A Talbot-sponsored Ligier did appear in early 1982 with a modernized Matra V-12, but Peugeot shifted its competition towards rallying shortly afterwards, and Talbot's Formula 1 dreams went down the drain.

None of this mattered much to BMW Motorsport, which had arranged to be the engine supplier for the Brabham team. Race fans remember Jack Brabham as the fearless Australian pilot who became two-time world champion in 1959-60 at the wheel of a Cooper-Climax. He was still driving for Cooper in 1961 when he founded Motor Racing Developments, a firm involved with designing and merchandizing performance kits for popular production cars as well as designing new race cars and preparing machines for customers. Brabham won the world title

again in 1966, driving one of his own machines powered by a Repco V-8 engine. In 1968 he sold MRD to his chief engineer, Ron Tauranac, and returned to Australia. The firm was purchased three years later by Bernie Ecclestone, a versatile businessman with interests in real estate, finance, and promotion, who continued production of Brabham race cars. For a time, the Brabham team cars ran with Alfa Romeo engines, which proved far too troublesome and had no real horsepower advantage, so the team ultimately fell in line with most of its rivals and began using the Ford-Cosworth V-8. But Ecclestone and his chief engineer, a young and talented South African

named Gordon Murray, had never stopped looking for an alternative.

It wasn't long before Schönbeck approached Ecclestone to suggest the turbocharged BMW four as the alternative they were looking for. Murray was eager to try it, but Ecclestone was cautious since Formula 1 rules limited displacement on turbo engines to 1.5 liters, versus 3.0 liters for normally aspirated engines. He agreed to tests despite his doubts, and the first trials of a Brabham BT-49 with the BMW engine were made on October 13, 1980, at the Silverstone circuit in England. The shakedown continued during the spring of 1981 while the team ran the Cosworth-powered BT-50, which

was not a success. This encouraged Ecclestone to send two BMW-powered cars to South Africa in October for the Kyalami Grand Prix. They were very fast in practice, so their grid positions were excellent: one car on the front row, one on the second. Unfortunately, engine failures put both Brabhams out of the race. It was a costly lesson. Ecclestone now told Schönbeck that he would suspend running the BMW engine until Munich's engineers could make it more reliable. Countless modifications and reinforcements were duly made that winter and into the spring of 1982. A revised car was entered at Monaco in May, but it was far outclassed, and driver Piquet was even lapped

Opposite page: Piquet nips an opponent in a left-hander at the 1983 Detroit Grand Prix. He came in fourth overall. Left: The turbocharged BMW F1 engine as run in the Brabham BT-50 in 1981. Bosch digital electronic controls are housed in the box just right of the engine. Above: A close-up of Piquet at work in the BT-52 during an unidentified 1983 event.

by a Brabham-Ford. But the engine held up. It now apparently had the necessary robustness to withstand the rigors of racing against the world's elite. BMW engineers suggested that if the car was slow, perhaps it wasn't the engine's fault, and said the BT-50 brakes weren't really up to the job.

Ecclestone and Murray agreed to work on the Brabham chassis before using the BMW engine again. The result was the new BT-51. It made an inconspicuous debut at the Detroit Grand Prix on June 6, 1982, where it proved too slow for Piquet even to qualify. But he roared back just a week later, driving the same car to victory in the Canadian Grand Prix at Montreal. At Zelt-

weg in August the Brabham-BMWs set the fastest lap times in practice, but neither Piquet nor Ricardo Patrese finished. Nevertheless, the new car obviously had tremendous potential: it looked like a world-beater.

BMW instituted another round of engine revisions while Murray, assisted by David North, designed the BT-52. This new car featured a monocoque structure built up as a laminate of carbon fiber and aluminum alloy. By January 1983 the engine had passed its final reliability test, 7200 km (4470 miles) of track work in a BT-50 chassis. The rest is history. Piquet ran the fastest lap and won that year's Brazilian Grand Prix. In April he finished second in the French

GP at the Le Castellet (Paul Ricard) circuit. Another second-place performance at Monaco in May boosted him to second place in the points standings behind Renault's Alain Prost. Piquet was again runner-up in the British Grand Prix at Silverstone in July, and teammate Patrese took third in the German event at Hockenheim in August.

Prost was still the front-runner for the title, and added to his commanding lead by winning the Austrian Grand Prix at Zeltweg. Piquet finished third, but he came home first at Monza in September, then captured the European Grand Prix at Brands Hatch two weeks later. These wins put Piquet a mere two points behind Prost, so the battle for the championship came down to the season finale, the South African Grand Prix at Kyalami. The winner was Patrese, but a third-place finish by Piquet gave him enough points to beat Prost for the driver's championship.

Said Horst Rech, the BMW Motorsport engineer who supervised development of the GP engine: "We must have a technical edge to win races." The edge he refers to has four main ingredients: a special KKK turbocharger with dual-channel housing, an air-to-air intercooler, a Kugelfischer-type mechanical injection pump made by Bosch, and a second-generation Bosch digital electronic engine management system that includes capacitive-discharge ignition.

BMW was satisfied quite early in the game that the 1.5-liter turbo engine would be superior to an unblown 3.0-liter for power. "In the past," Rech admitted, "the turbo engine has shown serious disadvantages in the areas of slower throttle response and higher fuel consumption. It was also more susceptible to mechanical damage, since the critical operating states were more difficult to bring under control." The main limiting factors are the turbo's boost setting and the maximum tolerable degree of cylinder filling. Pushing one or the other beyond the engine's physical limits will result in costly breakdowns, and building in a bigger safety margin usually means less power potential,

which lessens your chances of winning. Cylinder dimensions were pushed to the limit to get the largest bore and the shortest stroke possible. Thus, the Formula 1 unit had 89.2 x 60mm (3.51- x 2.36-in.) measurements instead of the production 316 engine's 82 x 71mm (3.23- x 2.80-in.). Aside from the crankshaft, pistons, gear cover and water pump, components from BMW's Formula 2 engine could be used with only a few minor modifications for the F1 powerplant. "That enabled us to shorten the development time," Rech pointed out. However, the F2 had a maximum 320 bhp, while the F1 target was 700-750 bhp. So far that target has not been achieved, the main problem being internal compression ratio, which has had to be kept down to 6.7:1 with the 40-42-psi boost pressures employed. Rech is trying to find ways to push the C.R. to 7.0 or 7.2:1 and ultimately to 7.5:1.

The cylinder head from the Formula 2 engine needed little modification for its F1 application. An aluminum casting, it has four valves per cylinder

splayed at an angle of only 20 degrees from the cylinder axis and closed by dual-coil springs. Intake valve head diameter is 35.8mm (1.41 in.) and exhaust valve heads measure 30.2mm (1.19 in.). Valve timing has not been disclosed, but Rech admits there is considerable overlap. Because of this, a timed, high-pressure fuel injection system is used to prevent unburned mixture from being ejected into the exhaust system, thus protecting the turbine from overheating. The Kugelfischer pump operates at an injection pressure of more than 440 psi, and provides the maximum fuel quantity required throughout a 100-degree crankshaft angle range. The usual cone-cam arrangement for fuel metering in the normal Kugelfischer system is replaced here by a spiral that is moved by an

*Below: Another look at Piquet's form as seen at the 1983 Detroit GP. Opposite page, top: A port-side view of the F1 engine showing the front cover, exhaust system and turbocharger. Bottom: From the starboard side. High-pressure fuel injection system operates at 440 psi. Boost pressure is 40-42 psi.*

electric-servo motor into the position calculated by the engine's electronic control unit. The spiral can run from one end of its travel to the other in only 0.04-second.

A racing engine generally operates at either full throttle or closed throttle, very seldom in between. But engine conditions change rapidly. For instance, a GP driver typically averages 0.2-second to make a gear change that may take a full second for the average driver in a road car, and this puts special demands on the electronics that meter the fuel and time the spark. Thermal stress loads are a big problem in this connection, which is why an intercooler was fitted. It brings down the temperature of air entering the turbo to about 320 degrees F from about 430 F as discharged. Maximum exhaust temperature is about 2000 degrees. Dry-sump lubrication is employed, with a three-phase scavenge pump that permits the oil to carry its full share of cooling duties.

Ready to race, the BMW GP engine weighs only 364 pounds, including its complete induction and exhaust systems. The exhaust manifold and turbocharger account for 44 pounds, and the cylinder head weighs a mere 11 pounds. By mid-1983, it was delivering 580-600 bhp at 10,500 rpm and 331 lbs/ft of torque at 8500 rpm. This output is sufficient to be highly competitive against the turbo V-6 Renault and Ferrari cars as well as the brigade of GP contenders running the unblown 3.0-liter Cosworth-Ford V-8.

"We discovered," explains Horst Rech, "that this engine, in several instances, allowed far smaller tolerances than the Formula 2 engine, let alone a production engine working under lower loads. This means that the secret of a dependable Formula 1 racing engine does not lie in the use of exotic materials but in the manufacture of proven components with extreme precision and meticulous testing of their dimensional stability and quality. With our insistence on ultra-tight tolerances, we have driven some of the most renowned suppliers to the brink of desperation."

One aspect of BMW's efforts in Formula 1 is fascinating to ponder: the prospect that some of the racing technology will be applied to road cars we can all drive. Aside from publicity, a big reason why car companies spend money on racing is that it adds a dimension to engineering development that no amount of laboratory work can duplicate. While it's impossible to say just how soon any of the GP work will show up in production BMWs, we do know this: it won't go to waste.

# EFFICIENCY EXPERTS: ETA MAGIC AND DIESEL POWER

Factory cutaway emphasizes the lightweight valvegear of the high-compression eta six used in the European 525e.

In response to the energy crisis of 1973-74, the United States Congress passed a significant piece of legislation, the Energy Conservation Act. One of its provisions would have a profound effect on every car company seeking to do business in this country: CAFE, which stands for corporate average fuel economy. In brief, the new law imposed mileage goals for the industry. They would be computed on a "sales-weighted" basis, which meant that the fuel economy for all the cars sold by a given manufacturer in any model year had to average out as equal to or greater than the target figure. CAFE applied to foreign and domestic producers alike, and a hefty financial penalty was written in just to keep everyone honest ($5 per vehicle sold for each 0.1 mpg over the target). The law would take effect with the 1978 model year, and the initial 18-mpg standard would rise in steps to 27.5 mpg by model year 1985.

BMW was one company that took CAFE to heart immediately, and during 1974 it began looking into any and all possible ways for improving the fuel efficiency of its existing models. This program involved not just powertrains but every part of every car system. The plan was to measure and evaluate each proposed improvement and to incorporate those that were feasible and had favorable cost/benefit tradeoffs. It was an enormous undertaking involving a good deal of basic research in internal engine friction, the power consumption of accessories, methods of obtaining faster warmup, and countless other aspects of maximizing energy. Out of all this would come BMW's first diesel engine as well as a totally new approach to making high performance more compatible with high efficiency in gasoline engines.

An early proposal that received close attention was the idea of shutting off one or more cylinders under part-load conditions. In other words, the number of working or "active" cylinders would be matched to the engine's power requirements at any given time. This notion promised two advantages. First, the cylinders being fired would be filled with fresh gas right to the top, which would keep throttling losses to a minimum. Secondly, the greater resulting charge density would assure a higher degree of energy conversion and, therefore, more efficient combustion. Ford and Pontiac were working along these very lines in 1974-76, as was the Eaton company, which developed a "valve selector" that mechanically shut down selected cylinders in response to commands from an electronic control unit. Cadillac adopted this device for what it called a "modulated-displacement" version of its large 6.0-liter (368-cid) V-8. Unhappily for those who bought it, the "V-8-6-4" powerplant proved extremely troublesome, with frequent complaints of sudden stall-out and poor driveability. Though these problems had little to do with the variable-displacement mechanism, Cadillac withdrew the engine from its passenger-car line after only one year, 1981, in the face of class-action lawsuits brought by disgruntled owners.

BMW arrived at a more advanced approach to this principle: a system that would allow the engine to run on either all or half its cylinders. Based on the injected 2.3-liter (140-cid) M-60 unit, the prototype modular engine incorporated a fuel supply and ignition cutoff on cylinders 1, 2 and 3, which allowed smooth operation—with even firing intervals—on cylinders 4, 5 and 6. No valvegear modifications were made, but the intake manifold was split to route fresh air through the "slave" cylinders when idle. In addition, these cylinders breathed high-pressure exhaust gas in the idle mode, supplied by an advance-outlet valve, giving them a significant source of power to minimize pumping losses when switched to active operation. The exhaust gases also kept the engine's front section warm to avoid an increase in friction and wear. The switching was governed by an electronic control system in accordance with engine speed and load, and engineers made sure that the "slave" cylinders cut in or out smoothly. When the driver stepped on the accelerator after a period of running on three cylinders, there was just a slight surge to indicate full six-cylinder operation, a sensation that could be compared with the opening of the secondaries in a four-barrel carburetor. Prototype engines ran in test cars with fully acceptable driveability—when everything was working properly. With mediocre reliability, disappointing fuel economy gains, and high anticipated production costs, the modular engine was a dead duck, and BMW abandoned the project at the end of 1980.

By this time, the firm was focusing on a very different concept that became known by the Greek letter eta, which is the mathematical symbol engineers use to denote efficiency. BMW designers realized full well that overall efficiency does not depend merely on achieving the fullest use of a fuel's stored heat energy at a given rpm. Rather, it depends more on matching all powertrain elements so that the engine runs at the speed where it is least wasteful for the longest possible proportion of driving time. That's what the eta engine is all about. And although nobody has ever accused BMWs of being truck-like, the eta concept does, in fact, derive directly from truck engineering. The basic design principle is a simple one: increase displacement until you have the necessary torque, then restrict rpm to minimize internal friction losses. Many diesel trucks have turbochargers nowadays to help achieve this balance, but the turbo can't do a comparable job in a spark-

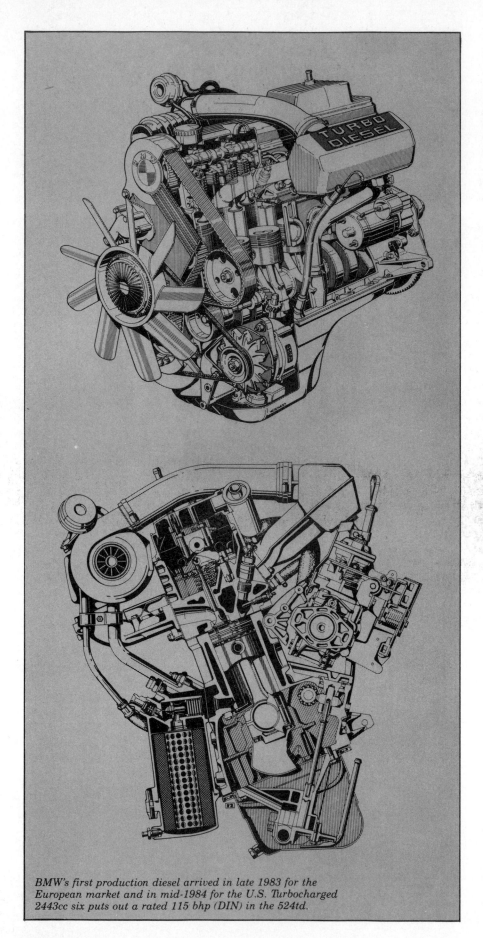

BMW's first production diesel arrived in late 1983 for the European market and in mid-1984 for the U.S. Turbocharged 2443cc six puts out a rated 115 bhp (DIN) in the 524td.

ignition engine because its air/fuel ratio is fixed at about 15:1 while a diesel runs unthrottled and therefore operates with a high proportion of excess air in its cylinders. Of course, BMW did not try to engineer its middleweight passenger cars like a diesel truck, so the eta project involved mostly independent reasoning and research. Even so, it's interesting to note that parallel developments were going on in the truck field, where nothing counts more than cost-per-mile.

The M-20 "big-block" six was chosen as the basis for the eta experiments. The underlying consideration in this choice was the fact that frictional losses increase exponentially with engine speed by a factor of two, but increase only in direct proportion with engine size. The eta would have a more restricted rev range, so its so-called "valve vibration speed," the rpm at which the valves no longer follow the cams but start to vibrate at random, would be lower than for an ordinary engine. This allowed the use of lower-tension valve springs in order to reduce frictional losses between the rocker arms and cams. The lower rpm limit also provided the opportunity to eliminate a few camshaft bearings to cut friction still further, so the eta has four bearings instead of the M-20's usual seven, and piston rings with less pre-tension were specified for the same reason. To optimize cylinder filling at low engine speeds, the intake valves close at an early point, which also reduces valve overlap. Long intake manifolds make a significant contribution to good low-rpm filling by providing a large "dynamic post-charge effect," as it's called. This means that the fresh mixture column moves in front of the open intake valves in such a way that a particularly large amount of gas is able to get into the cylinders.

The eta engine was the brainchild of a team supervised by Karlheinz Lange and consisting of Richard Hofmann, Emil Heck,

Rainer Bauer, and Heinrich Aumüller. It was revealed to the press in October 1978, but the first production version wasn't built until September 1981. This was a "low-compression" (9.0:1) engine devised with an eye to the low-octane unleaded gasoline available in the U.S. and Japan, but it lacked one of the concept's inherent basic advantages. BMW had discovered in the engine lab that an 11.0:1 compression ratio was the optimum for premium-grade fuel. A tigher squeeze would not provide a noticeable gain in fuel economy, and anything less tended to increase emissions. But 11.0:1 compression was used in areas where high-octane leaded is still sold, and this eta engine debuted in April 1983 for the new European 525e. Because octane ratings can vary widely, BMW deemed it prudent to specify the Bosch Motronic digital engine management system, which features microprocessor control for both fuel metering and spark timing to keep them in proper relation to one another. The system also cuts off fuel flow on deceleration (down to 1200 rpm) and governs idle speed (brought down to 700 rpm at normal operating coolant temperatures). The Motronic system also features a rev limiter that shuts off the ignition and fuel supply at 5000 rpm, thus making over-revving impossible.

The 525e appeared about a year and a half behind its U.S. counterpart, the 528e (see Chapter 11). However, both models use the same 2.7-liter (165-cid) power unit. Based on the block of the 528i, the eta six has bore and stroke dimensions of 84 x 81mm (3.30 x 3.20 in.). Maximum output in European tune is 125 bhp (DIN) at 4250 rpm, with peak torque of 177 lbs/ft at 3250 rpm.

Obviously, the eta concept could not be fully exploited without gearing matched to the engine's characteristics, which implied an overdrive manual transmission pulling a very tall

final drive. Accordingly, a Getrag five-speed gearbox with direct-drive fourth and 0.81 overdrive fifth was made standard in combination with a 2.93:1 final drive ratio for both the 525e and 528e. Optional at extra cost is the new four-speed 4HP 22 automatic from ZF (also offered in the 6- and 7-series) with lockup torque converter clutch and electronically controlled shifts (via Bosch-designed circuitry). The 525e can loaf along at 65 mph on a mere 2000 rpm in fifth gear—speeds equivalent, the chart says, to 33.6 mpg. Yet the car will pull cleanly from 800-900 rpm in any gear, and delivers strong torque from 1100 rpm upwards.

Factory data confirm the European model's outstanding steady-speed fuel mileage as measured in the standard ECE tests: 39.8 mpg at 56 mph (90 km/h), 31.0 at 74.5 mph (120 km/h), and 20.6 mpg in the urban cycle. This thriftiness would do credit to a small-displacement econocar, but the 525e can also accelerate from 0 to 100 km/h (62 mph) in 10.7 seconds, cover 400 meters (about a quarter-mile) from a standing start in

*The author's first exposure to the BMW turbodiesel six came in late 1978 with this modified production model, labelled 520. Production didn't begin until 1983.*

17.4 seconds, and see upwards of 110 mph. And remember, we're talking about a 2760-pound five-passenger luxury sedan, which puts this achievement into its proper perspective.

Despite its complex subtleties, the eta concept may very well set the pattern for economy engineering at other auto companies in the years ahead. Based on our experience, we can say they would do well to copy this BMW innovation. It represents, in our view, a triumph of common sense and appropriate use of technology over mere gimmickry that is used more for its advertising value than any real contribution to efficiency. And in this respect, at least, the eta engine is perfectly in keeping with BMW tradition.

While the eta concept was being developed, BMW was also looking into diesel power. The company had never offered a diesel passenger car up to this point, mainly because it hadn't

Above: The author poses with an early European 525e. The basically similar American-market 528e appeared for the 1982 model year. Top: The 525e engine bay. Eta six is derived from the M-60 small-block power unit, packs 125 bhp.

might improve its sales with a diesel engine in the lineup, perhaps by a like amount.

Though project personnel were probably unaware of it, this was not BMW's first attempt at a diesel car. In fact, the firm had built and tested one as early as 1935. It was powered by a 1911cc six-cylinder gasoline engine converted to compression ignition and fitted with a truck-type Bosch injection pump. The cylinder head was of the Lanova type, which meant direct fuel injection into the cylinders, with a compressed-air injector mounted opposite the fuel nozzle and a glow plug (for cold starts) mounted near the center of the combustion space. This design was the invention of Franz Lang (Lanova is a combination of Lang and "nova," Latin for "new"), who had worked at MAN with Dr. Rudolf Diesel himself shortly after the turn of the century and later established his own consulting business. Lanova licenses were sold to Henschel & Sohn of Kassel in Germany, to the Dennis Brothers of Guildford in England, and to Mack Trucks in Allentown, Pennsylvania. Buda Motor of Harvey, Illinois, also bought a license, as did the Electric Power Boat Company in New York and Güldner Motoren GmbH. BMW purchased manufacturing rights to the Lanova head as well, and its experimental diesel was rated at 70 bhp, considerably more than Daimler-Benz was getting from its 2.6-liter four. The engine was installed in a Type 319 sedan for test but, for a variety of reasons, it never got to market.

By 1975 some 40 years of technical refinement had gone into diesel car engineering, and the market was not only well established but growing rapidly. Engineering chief Karlheinz Radermacher told Karlheinz Lange to come up with a new diesel suitable for BMW. That was a real challenge, because it would have to have performance characteristics consistent with the BMW image. That meant it

needed one. But one result of the first energy crisis was a big upsurge in demand for diesel cars, which led to a new batch of compression-ignition models from several manufacturers. One of them, as we know, was General Motors, which saw the diesel primarily as a way to improve the mileage of its large, heavy family models without resorting to downsizing. BMW no doubt realized much the same thing, but its interest in diesels probably stemmed at least as much from their sales potential as their greater economy. BMW may also have been a bit envious of long-time rival Daimler-Benz, which had pioneered diesel passenger cars in the late Thirties. By 1975, diesels accounted for 40 percent of Mercedes-Benz sales. It didn't take a marketing genius to figure out that BMW would not only have to be free of all the typical "oiler" vices but would also have to possess the responsiveness demanded by the firm's largely enthusiast clientele. There were many difficult choices to make. Should it be a "pure" diesel, that is a ground-up engine where every part is designed for diesel operation? Or should it be simply a conversion of an existing gasoline engine? The latter was tempting because of the greatly reduced engineering and manufacturing costs it implied, and the idea did not necessarily have any drawbacks—provided the gasoline engine you started with was strong enough to withstand the higher stress levels of compression ignition. Lange thought the M-60 small-block six, with its 92mm bore-center spacing and 2.0-2.7-liter (121-165-cid) displacement range, would have the required strength. To meet performance targets, he would turbocharge it. To meet demands for quiet running and low exhaust emissions, he would employ indirect fuel injection via a Ricardo-type swirl chamber as used by Peugeot, Perkins, and Volkswagen, to name a few.

After three years of experimental work, BMW let the press have a look at how far it had progressed with its turbodiesel in October 1978. This author attended a press briefing, held at Lenggries in Upper Bavaria, to test-drive a prototype and interview project staff. The driver who stopped in front of me stepped out of what looked and sounded like a standard BMW 520. "Are you sure that's a diesel?" we asked. Grinning broadly, the BMW engineer opened the hood. There it was, an oil-burner idling as smoothly and quietly as a Jaguar V-12. When it was my turn to drive, we stayed on the byways for a while before venturing out on the *Autobahn*. There's a lot more to judging diesel-car performance than making a couple of timed acceleration runs, so we trickled along in third gear for a

spell through village traffic and found strong pull right down to idle speed with none of the usual diesel knock. Returning to the open road, we simply floored the accelerator: the car took off with a smooth hum, quickly gaining speed without snatch or stumbling. This particular car had a five-speed manual transmission, and we held third until the revs ran out—which was at fully 70 mph. Fourth was good for 90 mph and fifth, with 18 percent overdrive gearing, took us to 105 mph. When we found half a mile of straight, wide road, we got out the stopwatch and made some timed runs. This four-door sedan went from 0-100 km/h (62 mph) in 11.5 seconds using only first through third gears. Heading back, we clocked 100 mph from standstill in 35 seconds. Top speed was 112 mph, the engine spinning without fuss up to 5000 rpm.

The specification sheet supplied with the car listed maximum output as 115 bhp (DIN) at 5000 rpm and a peak 140 lbs/ft torque at 2500 rpm. Fuel consumption? Well, that was the big question, especially as swirl chambers don't have the same efficiency as direct injection. But Karlheinz Lange noted that part-load operation accounts for some 90 percent of the average motorist's driving time, in which case the new diesel could realize a 20-25 percent fuel saving compared with a gasoline car of comparable size and performance. Maximum fuel economy, absolute reliability, and simpler, more cost-effective engineering solutions for certain design aspects: these would be the three main fronts for further development of the BMW turbodiesel.

Production plans were being laid when we drove that prototype car at Lenggries, but there was already a problem. Though the new diesel would share a number of parts with BMW's existing gasoline engines, the firm had no factory space for building it. Setting up a brand-new plant is a costly proposition,

particularly when you're only guessing about the size of the market for the goods you'll be producing, so BMW decided to take in a partner. It was Steyr-Daimler-Puch AG, the Austrian maker of trucks, tractors, mopeds, and military vehicles. In December 1978, the two firms signed a pact for joint diesel engine development, production, and marketing. This was not BMW's first tie-up with Steyr. In the early Fifties this duo had seriously considered joint production of a new 1.2-liter car, but the project fell through, mainly due to Steyr's link with Fiat as that company's Austrian importer.

To seal the deal, a new company called BMW-Steyr Motoren GmbH was formed in March 1979, each partner having half-ownership. It would produce and sell the new diesels not only for the partners but also—and more importantly—for outside customers. A new factory with annual capacity of 200,000 units was erected in the town of Steyr. Ford in Dearborn expressed great interest in the venture, and signed a letter of intent to purchase 190,000 six-cylinder engines over a three-year period. The order was later reduced to 71,000 due to a sudden drop in diesel-car sales in the U.S., but the new engine did arrive as promised, appearing for mid-1984 as an option in the plush Continental sedan and Mark VII coupe. While the turbodiesel six was being tooled, development began on a four-cylinder unit and a normally aspirated diesel six. At the same time, Steyr engineers went to work adapting direct injection to the BMW design, based on a concept from AVL, the engine laboratories owned by Hans List in Graz.

The future for the joint engine company seemed to hold nothing but smooth, long-term collaboration and plenty of mutual profit. But during the summer of 1981, BMW became increasingly dissatisfied with the Austrians' delays in getting the plant tooled up. At the same time, the AVL-based engine, which BMW was planning to use in some of its future models, was failing to meet expectations in dynamometer tests and was falling hopelessly behind schedule. The following January, BMW offered to buy out Steyr's interest in the company, but the Austrians held out until the Germans had nearly doubled their original figure. BMW became sole owner in March 1982. Steyr-Daimler-Puch retained full rights to the AVL concept, by then extensively revised, as BMW had no further interest in it. As for the factory, it was gradually integrated with BMW's other manufacturing facilities, and production of the M-60 gasoline engine family was transferred at mid-year to the plant in Steyr.

BMW pushed quietly ahead with its 2.4-liter (146.4-cid) turbodiesel six. Bearing the M-105 designation, it finally got into production in March 1983 and debuted in June for the 524td, the world's fastest diesel-powered production automobile. The M-105 employs a cast-iron cylinder block and, unusually for a diesel, an aluminum head. It's comparatively light for a diesel, too, weighing 408 pounds complete. Crankshaft, connecting rods, bearings and pistons come from the M-60, modified for diesel operation, and capacities of the cooling system and oil pump are similarly upgraded. Compression ratio is 22:1, high enough to assure easy starting but not so high as to compromise reliability. Bore and stroke measure 80 x 81mm (3.15 x 3.19 in.) for swept volume of 2443cc. Maximum power output is 115 bhp (DIN) at 4800 rpm and peak torque is 115 lbs/ft at 2400 rpm.

Dry technical facts don't give a complete picture of the new engine. For example, its torque curve is so flat that 90 percent of maximum torque is available all the way from 1800 up to 4250 rpm—and half of the full rated power is delivered at 2000 rpm!

The engine will give useful pull from as low as 1200 rpm, and the pump governor holds maximum revs to 5000. What this generous torque spread does for the 524td is simply amazing. You can step on it in fourth gear and get satisfying go from almost any speed above 16 mph. Even in fifth, the car will scoot away from as little as 22 mph.

In common with the gas engines, the M-105 has a crossflow head, with intake and exhaust passages on opposite sides. The valves in the diesel hang vertically rather than being splayed, but the head layout has advantages for both valve size and porting layout. The swirl combustion chamber shape was designed so that it represents no more than 50 percent of the compressed volume, and the injection nozzle is mounted tangentially to the contour of the chamber. The Bosch VE distributor-type injection is driven by the same wide, cogged belt that drives the overhead camshaft. BMW is experimenting with electronic injection system control, but for now the 524td has mechanically controlled fuel metering and timing. The exhaust system was designed specifically with an eye to optimum turbocharger efficiency. The headers from cylinders 1-2-3 and 4-5-6 are branched into separate pipes that feed individual ports on the turbine housing. The turbocharger comes from Garrett AiResearch and reaches its maximum 0.8-bar boost (11.8psi) at 2200 rpm. Later, a KKK unit will be used as an alternate. The compressor mounts on the exhaust manifold and, because of the crossflow head, its output is ducted across the top of the cam cover to a plenum chamber on the intake side, with fairly long individual runners to the intake ports.

Transmissions available on the 524td comprise the standard Getrag five-speed overdrive manual (0.81:1 fifth) or the four-speed ZF automatic with 0.73:1 top

gear. Both transmissions are mated to a 3.15:1 final drive ratio, which gives a top speed of 112 mph for the manual and 109 mph for the automatic. What's more, at an 81-mph cruise the engine is just loafing at about 2500 rpm. As for acceleration, the 524td is not startlingly fast for a BMW, but it is outstanding for a diesel car. It'll scamper to 100 km/h from rest in 12.9 seconds with the five-speed or in 13.6 seconds with automatic. Diesel cars, of course, appeal more for economy than performance. By staying in the upper gears and keeping the revs down you can achieve mileage numbers in the 524td that would be the envy of many lighter models—including some diesels. The factory's official steady-speed figures for the five-speed show 45.2 mpg at 56 mph (90 km/h), 33.6 mpg at 74.5 mph (120 km/h), and 26.1 mpg in the ECE urban test. BMW claims the identical numbers for the automatic except for a slightly poorer 24.7 mpg in the city cycle.

With its state-of-the-art turbodiesel and eta engines, BMW reaffirms its engineering leadership while setting new standards of automotive efficiency for the Eighties. Even more impressive is the fact that it has achieved amazing mileage improvements with little loss of performance in cars that are arguably a bit too large and heavy by today's rapidly changing standards. In recent years, some critics have taken BMW to task on this point with monotonous regularity. The company is too conservative, they cry, too hidebound by its own traditions, and is increasingly out of step with industry trends. We suspect the people in Munich would answer such charges with a simple smile and the offer of a test drive in one of the new turbodiesel or eta-engine cars. There's nothing wrong with tradition as long as it works, and BMWs still work, by golly—supremely well. Let's hope we never lose that in our headlong rush towards tomorrow.

*Future shape? The AVT aerodynamic research car in BMW's Aschheim wind tunnel, 1981.*

# BMW TODAY: STATUS AND OUTLOOK

Let's face it: BMW is a phenomenon. For a quarter century now, the history of this company has been marked by steady growth and seemingly unstoppable success, a record of prosperity and achievement that is the envy of every other automaker in the world, one largely unaffected by international currency fluctuations, governmental regulations, or Middle East petroleum power politics. Today BMW cars have never been more popular, the marque's prestige has never been greater or more universal, and production has never been higher (a record 400,000 units in calendar 1983). With all this, BMW's 25-year ex-

pansion shows no sign of slowing down, and the firm faces the future with supreme confidence as it busily prepares for it.

BMW is currently engaged in a wide variety of projects, both short- and long-term. A symbol of the firm's continuing strength was the opening of a new wind tunnel facility at the Aschheim proving grounds in the late Seventies, built at a cost of 22 million marks. Shortly after it was completed, the management board voted to construct a new research and development center on the site of the U.S. Army's former "Alabama" barracks on the north side of Munich. It will be inaugurated in 1986, though

it is not expected to be finished until 1992. Total investment in the new center will run to over a billion marks, and this doesn't even include budgeted spending for new-model development during the period.

BMW has also set aside large sums—about 1.5 billion marks— to boost its production capacity. The goal is a 40 percent gain, which will push combined output up from the current 1600 to some 2250 units a day. A key element in this program is a brand-new factory going up outside the town of Regensburg, about 75 miles northeast of Munich. The decision to build the new plant came in 1979. Initial plans called for a facility smaller than the Dingolfing operation with a workforce of about 12,000. Cost for the first phase of construction was estimated at 450 million marks. The final plans, approved in November 1982, are far more ambitious and aim for a maximum daily output of 600. Construction is well under way, and the new factory is expected to come on stream in 1986. However, the work force may fall short of 12,000 because BMW plans to increase its use of automation for processes where it makes economic sense, in line with advances in technology. We can be fairly sure that BMW will not rush to robotics simply to keep production costs down or to enhance its corporate image, and certainly not for jobs better left to humans. After all, this is a firm with a heritage of quality.

Incidentally, BMW is fortunate in that one of its suppliers is a leader in robotics. Known as KUKA (Keller und Knappich, Augsburg), it is a subsidiary of the IWKA (Industrie-Werke Karlsruhe) combine owned by the Quandt group. KUKA played a key role in modernizing the Milbertshofen plant in 1980-82, where the 3-series cars are now built at the rate of 800 per day, and the company continues to study possible new applications for robotics at BMW as one of its major activities.

The ownership of BMW still rests firmly with the Quandt group (small stockholders account for less than 30 percent of the total shares). Patriarch Herbert Quandt relinquished his seat on the supervisory board at the age of 70. He died in July 1982 at his home in Bad Homburg only a few days before his 72nd birthday. Succeeding him was the 54-year-old Hans Graf von der Goltz.

Another recent personnel change rocked BMW to its very core and clouded the type and timing of future product developments. In a surprise move that made front-page headlines

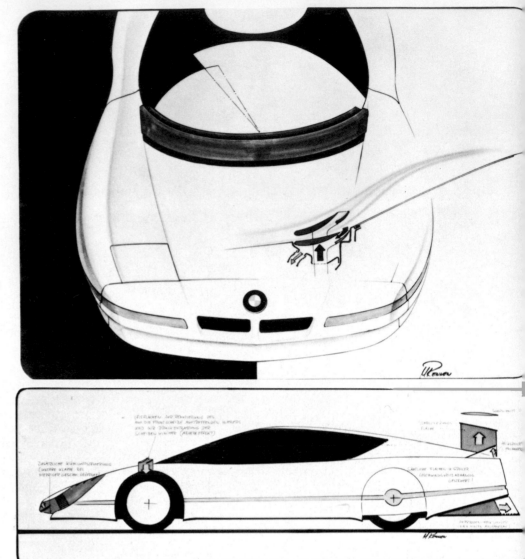

*Above and opposite page: A series of BMW design sketches highlight wind-cheating body features of the experimental AVT shown on the previous page. Note the small moveable rear spoilers, underbody air exits in the rear valence, smoothly rounded nose, and wipers hidden under a flip-up panel a la 1968-72 Corvette.*

in trade journals and business publications all over the world, Dr. Karlheinz Radermacher resigned as head of automotive engineering on May 6, 1983. (He was named chief of the ZF technical center in Friedrichshafen four months later.) Radermacher had come under increasing criticism over the years for BMW's failure to update its cars in line with industry design trends. They had unquestionably fallen

behind in some ways simply because they were not fundamentally changed during the Radermacher years, but it's difficult to know whether this was entirely his doing. Keep in mind that he had no prior experience as the head of an automotive engineering staff when he came to Munich. Said the technical director of a rival German automaker (not Daimler-Benz): "I don't think Radermacher is to blame. I suspect the problem was Kuenheim. He had a Mercedes fixation. It was the only yardstick he would measure the BMW against." One thing is certain: Radermacher left after quarreling with the chairman. Some observers, including several close to the company, have

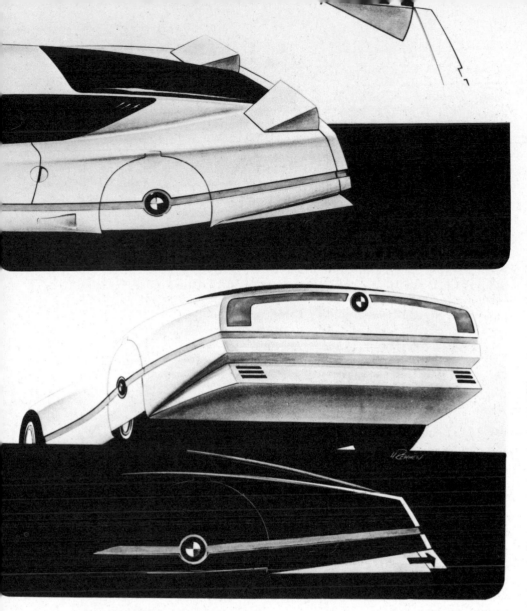

speculated that Radermacher *was* to blame. Others believe he was actually a "knight in shining armor" who fought to preserve the individuality of BMW's cars, but was politically stymied by the Quandt group's representative on the management board. In other words, BMWs, particularly the top-end offerings, became much more like certain Mercedes-Benz models over the years not because of Radermacher's efforts but in spite of them.

Lending credence to the "pro-Radermacher" view is the choice of his replacement. It would have been natural to promote from within the company, and there was an eminently qualified candidate in the person of Franz

Behles. Joining BMW in the summer of 1981 as head of proving ground studies and new-model testing, Behles came from Audi, where engineering boss Ludwig Kraus had promised him the top job. But when Kraus left, Volkswagen gave the post to Ferdinand Piëch, the grandson of Dr. Ferdinand Porsche. Behles seemed set for a similar promotion at BMW. He certainly had the credentials. He had first worked at BMW in 1952-53 as a motorcycle engineer, then went to Stuttgart and tackled a wide variety of assignments for Daimler-Benz. Transferring to Auto Union in 1963, he was named head of the Audi design office and spent 10 years with the firm, mainly in development

of front-wheel-drive models including the second-generation Audi 100/5000.

When Behles returned to BMW, he got into some stormy arguments with colleagues Radermacher, Stork, Kraft, and others over the relative merits of front drive versus rear drive. Not surprisingly he favored fwd at first, but after a time he became convinced that rear drive was best for the performance-oriented cars that had become a BMW hallmark. By the time Radermacher resigned, Behles looked very much like an heir apparent who had no intention of rocking the company boat. Even so, he was passed over. The reason was more or less an open secret at company headquarters: he had sided with Radermacher in that decisive dispute with Von Kuenheim. Given Behles's experience—and assuming the "pro-Radermacher" theory is correct—we can logically conclude that both engineers disagreed with the chairman precisely over future product plans—specifically, whether new models would continue to be conventionally traditional or become more radically contemporary. Remember, too, that Behles had worked at D-B for nine years, and had managed to avoid too much similarity between his Mercedes efforts and his later Audi designs. If nothing else, the showdown taught both engineers the lesson of that well-worn axiom, "the boss may not always be right, but he's always the boss."

BMW management hesitated a relatively long time over Radermacher's replacement. The choice was finally made in October 1983 and it was a bit of a surprise: Hans Hagen, a well-known engineer in the truck field but one with no experience in the auto industry. A student in mechanical engineering at the Munich Technical University in the early Fifties, Hagen had worked briefly at Machinenfabrik Flottmann before returning to the University to earn degrees in combustion-engine and vehicle engineering. Joining MAN in 1964, he was assigned to coordinate research and development work for that firm's line of heavy trucks, and by 1970 had been promoted to chief engineer for advanced design. He was promoted again, in 1977, to head truck technical affairs, and was appointed overall technical director four years later.

What will tomorrow's BMWs be like? That's a difficult question to answer at this writing as Hagen has been on board only a short time. Nevertheless, we can make a few general predictions based on current developments. First, we will certainly see more examples of practical electronics in the BMWs of the late Eighties and early Nineties. A hint of the future may be seen in two recent innovations, the Service Interval Indicator and the instantaneous fuel economy gauge, both now standard equipment on all U.S.-market models. As the knowledgeable Ron Wakefield described it in *Road & Track* magazine's *1983 Sports & GT Guide,* the SII "tailors the car's maintenance schedule to the way it is driven. A microcomputer [linked with the engine's electronic management system] processes odometer mileage on the basis of how often the engine is operated cold and run at high speeds. On the basis of this processed mileage...LEDs light up green, yellow or red to inform the driver when service is due or not. According to how the BMW is driven, the SII can stretch the nominal 7500-mile interval for minor service to as much as 9000 miles (if there are few cold starts and little high-speed operation) or shorten it to as little as 6250. Similarly, the major service can be due every 18,000 miles, every 12,500 miles, or anything in between." The economy gauge is analog, not digital, and displays the car's fuel economy at any given moment based on the rate of fuel flow as calculated by the electronic fuel

injection system.

A less practical but no less fascinating example of electronic wizardry is BMW's trip computer, introduced to America with the 733i and now available as an option on all U.S. models except the 3-series. It consists of a calculator-style key pad and digital display mounted on the dash. Depending on model, it can be used to perform either 10 or 15 separate operations. These include the usual time, speed, and distance calculations handled by most other "on-board" car computers, but BMW's can also be used as a "speed minder" (sounding a gong when the driver exceeds a pre-set velocity) and as an anti-theft device (the car won't start unless a preselected code number is correctly entered). Oh, yes: it also tells you the time and outside temperature. Though it's enormous fun to play with, the trip computer has a serious side, and some of its capabilities were built in expressly to encourage a more economy-minded driving style.

Besides being more "electronic," future BMWs will also be more aerodynamic. The growing interest in low-drag body design as an aid to improved fuel economy has led many journalists to chide BMW for staying with its bluff, traditional styling even as other carmakers produce more wind-cheating shapes. The firm is aware of the need, but it also considers the distinctive, well-established BMW look to be a definite sales asset. Since 1978, the company has devoted an increasing amount of attention and money to aerodynamic research, and that seems sure to accelerate with the opening of the Aschheim wind tunnel. A number of experimental streamliners are already being tested, and the company recently showed one to the public. Called AVT (for *Aerodynamischer Versuchsträger,* aerodynamic research vehicle), it's a wild-looking thing that wouldn't seem out of place on a race track.

Given BMW's conservative attitude toward change, we won't see anything like the AVT on the road for quite a few years, if ever. But you can expect production styling to begin moving toward a much less extreme version of this basic shape. The major elements are likely to be more rounded contours, shorter and more sharply sloped hoodlines, less abrupt transitions from hood to roof and roof to rear deck, extended lower bodysides matching deeper front and rear skirts, flush glass, full-disc wheels, and perhaps the return of the near-full covers for the rear wheel openings used on certain 1930s BMWs.

Finally, look for future BMWs to incorporate new materials as they become available and/or more reasonable in cost. We know that several new engines are on the drawing boards right now, others are undergoing dynamometer testing, and plans are in the works to extend the "eta" concept to new engine families. Meantime, a host of supplier companies are developing or are already providing a variety of new high-tech components ranging from ceramic engine parts to composite brake pads.

Automaking has changed profoundly since the initials BMW first appeared on a car, and so has the company they stand for. BMW has been through two "lives"—one prewar, one postwar—has twice come perilously close to extinction, has known utter ruin and hard-won triumph. Today, BMW is taking steps that will only enhance its reputation for engineering excellence and top-notch craftsmanship, even as it moves to the forefront of technological innovation and forward-thinking design. The signs are that BMW is ready to meet the challenges of the future as successfully as it has met the challenges of its past. But no matter how much its cars may change they will always be BMWs, Bavaria's driving machines. And that's something we can all look forward to.

# BRIEF SPECIFICATIONS AND PRODUCTION

*The 1982 European-spec 5-series: the 'family' BMW.*

| Years Built | Model | Body Style | Cyl. | cc | bhp (DIN) | Top Speed (mph) | weight (lbs) | Production* |
|---|---|---|---|---|---|---|---|---|
| 1929-32 | 3/15 Dixi | 2 seat | 4 | 743 | 15 | 47 | 1036 | |
| 1929-32 | 3/15 Dixi | convertible | 4 | 743 | 15 | 47 | 1036 | |
| 1929-32 | 3/15 Dixi | sedan 2d | 4 | 743 | 15 | 47 | 1179 | |
| 1929-31 | Wartburg | roadster | 4 | 743 | 18 | 53 | 882 | 18,976 |
| 1929-31 | 3/15 Dixi | convertible | 4 | 743 | 15 | 47 | 1179 | |
| 1929-31 | 3/15 Dixi | delivery | 4 | 743 | 15 | 47 | 1091 | |
| 1931-32 | 3/15 Dixi | coupe | 4 | 743 | 15 | 47 | 1179 | |
| 1932-34 | 3/20 | sedan 2d | 4 | 782 | 20 | 50 | 1433 | |
| 1932-34 | 3/20 | 2-seat | 4 | 782 | 20 | 50 | 1433 | |
| 1932-34 | 3/20 | 4-seat | 4 | 782 | 20 | 50 | 1433 | 7,215 |
| 1932-34 | 3/20 | convertible | 4 | 782 | 20 | 50 | 1433 | |
| 1932-34 | 3/20 | delivery 2d | 4 | 782 | 20 | 50 | 1433 | |
| 1933-34 | 3-wheel | delivery | 1 | 200 | 6 | 25 | 761 | |
| 1933-34 | 3-wheel | delivery | 1 | 400 | 12 | 37 | 783 | 600 |
| 1933-36 | 303 | sedan 2d | 6 | 1173 | 30 | 56 | 1808 | |
| 1933-36 | 303 | sunroof sedan | 6 | 1173 | 30 | 56 | 1808 | |
| 1933-36 | 303 | convertible | 6 | 1173 | 30 | 56 | 1808 | 2,300 |
| 1933-36 | 303 | sport convertible | 6 | 1173 | 30 | 56 | 1808 | |

\* Available factory data does not distinguish between model year and calendar year production for individual models within the newer BMW series. Combined worldwide sales for calendar years 1978-82 are as follows: 3-series: 1,001,521; 5-series: 524,078; 6-series: 32,292; 7-series: 164,299.    \*\* SAE net . 1: U.S. sales. 2: 1982-83 U.S. model sales.  3: 1983 U.S. model sales. 4: U.S. sales as of 12/31/83 (source: BMW of North America).

| Years Built | Model | Body Style | Cyl. | cc | bhp (DIN) | Top Speed (mph) | weight (lbs) | Production* |
|---|---|---|---|---|---|---|---|---|
| 1934-36 | 309 | sedan 2d | 4 | 845 | 22 | 50 | 1653 | |
| 1934-36 | 309 | sunroof sedan | 4 | 845 | 22 | 50 | 1653 | |
| 1934-36 | 309 | touring 2d | 4 | 845 | 22 | 50 | 1653 | 6,000 |
| 1934-36 | 309 | convertible | 4 | 845 | 22 | 50 | 1653 | |
| 1934-36 | 309 | sport convertible | 4 | 845 | 22 | 50 | 1653 | |
| 1934-37 | 315 | sedan 2d | 6 | 1490 | 34 | 62 | 1830 | |
| 1934-37 | 315 | sunroof sedan | 6 | 1490 | 34 | 62 | 1830 | |
| 1934-37 | 315 | touring 2d | 6 | 1490 | 34 | 62 | 1830 | |
| 1934-37 | 315 | convertible | 6 | 1490 | 34 | 62 | 1830 | 9,765 |
| 1934-37 | 315 | sport convertible | 6 | 1490 | 34 | 62 | 1830 | |
| 1934-36 | 315/1 | roadster | 6 | 1490 | 40 | 74 | 1653 | |
| 1934-36 | 319/1 | roadster | 6 | 1911 | 55 | 81 | 1720 | |
| 1935-37 | 319 | sedan 2d | 6 | 1911 | 45 | 71 | 1874 | |
| 1935-37 | 319 | sunroof sedan | 6 | 1911 | 45 | 71 | 1874 | |
| 1935-37 | 319 | touring 2d | 6 | 1911 | 45 | 71 | 1874 | 6,646 |
| 1935-37 | 319 | convertible | 6 | 1911 | 45 | 71 | 1874 | |
| 1935-37 | 319 | sport convertible | 6 | 1911 | 45 | 71 | 1874 | |
| 1936-37 | 329 | convertible | 6 | 1911 | 45 | 68 | 1940 | |
| 1936-37 | 329 | sport convertible | 6 | 1911 | 45 | 68 | 1764 | 1,179 |
| 1936-41 | 326 | sedan 4d | 6 | 1971 | 50 | 71 | 2480 | |
| 1936-41 | 326 | convertible 2d | 6 | 1971 | 50 | 71 | 2425 | 15,936 |
| 1936-41 | 326 | convertible 4d | 6 | 1971 | 50 | 71 | 2425 | |
| 1937-38 | 320 | sedan 2d | 6 | 1971 | 45 | 68 | 2205 | |
| 1937-38 | 320 | convertible 2d | 6 | 1971 | 45 | 63 | 2205 | 4,185 |
| 1937-40 | 325 | 4WD staff car | 6 | 1971 | 50 | 50 | 3913 | 3,259 |
| 1937-39 | 328 | roadster | 6 | 1971 | 80 | 93 | 1830 | 462 |
| 1937-41 | 327 | convertible | 6 | 1971 | 55 | 78 | 2425 | |
| 1938-41 | 327 | coupe | 6 | 1971 | 55 | 78 | 2425 | 1,304 |
| 1938-41 | 327/28 | convertible | 6 | 1971 | 80 | 87 | 2425 | |
| 1938-41 | 327/28 | coupe | 6 | 1971 | 80 | 87 | 2425 | 569 |
| 1939-41 | 321 | sedan 2d | 6 | 1971 | 45 | 68 | 2204 | |
| 1939-41 | 321 | convertible | 6 | 1971 | 45 | 68 | 2204 | 3,692 |
| 1939-41 | 321 | sport convertible | 6 | 1971 | 45 | 68 | 2204 | |
| 1939-41 | 335 | sedan 4d | 6 | 3485 | 90 | 90 | 2866 | |
| 1939-41 | 335 | convertible 2d | 6 | 3485 | 90 | 90 | 2866 | 410 |
| 1939-41 | 335 | convertible 4d | 6 | 3485 | 90 | 90 | 2866 | |
| 1952-54 | 501 | sedan 4d | 6 | 1971 | 65 | 84 | 2954 | 2,125 |
| 1954-55 | 501 A | sedan 4d | 6 | 1971 | 72 | 87 | 2954 | |
| 1954-55 | 501 B | sedan 4d | 6 | 1971 | 72 | 87 | 2954 | |
| 1954 | 501 A | coupe | 6 | 1971 | 72 | 87 | 2954 | 3,327 |
| 1954 | 501 A | convertible 2d | 6 | 1971 | 72 | 87 | 2954 | |
| 1954 | 501 A | convertible 4d | 6 | 1971 | 72 | 87 | 2954 | |
| 1955-58 | 501/6 | sedan 4d | 6 | 2077 | 72 | 90 | 2954 | |
| 1955-58 | 501/6 | coupe | 6 | 2077 | 72 | 90 | 2954 | 3,459 |
| 1955-58 | 501/6 | convertible 2d | 6 | 2077 | 72 | 90 | 2954 | |
| 1954-58 | 501 V8 | sedan 4d | 8 | 2580 | 95 | 99 | 3153 | |
| 1958-61 | 2.6 | sedan 4d | 8 | 2580 | 95 | 99 | 3153 | 5,914 |
| 1961-62 | 2600 | sedan 4d | 8 | 2580 | 100 | 100 | 3175 | |
| 1954-58 | 502 2.6 | sedan 4d | 8 | 2580 | 100 | 99 | 3175 | |
| 1954-58 | 502 | coupe | 8 | 2580 | 100 | 99 | 3175 | |
| 1954-58 | 502 | convertible 2d | 8 | 2580 | 100 | 99 | 3175 | |
| 1954-58 | 502 | convertible 4d | 8 | 2580 | 100 | 99 | 3175 | 3,117 |
| 1958-61 | 2.6 Luxus | sedan 4d | 8 | 2580 | 100 | 99 | 3175 | |
| 1961-64 | 2600 L | sedan 4d | 8 | 2580 | 110 | 102 | 3175 | |

* Available factory data does not distinguish between model year and calendar year production for individual models within the newer BMW series. Combined worldwide sales for calendar years 1978-82 are as follows: 3-series: 1,001,521; 5-series: 524,078; 6-series: 32,292; 7-series: 164,299. ** SAE net. 1: U.S. sales. 2: 1982-83 U.S. model sales. 3: 1983 U.S. model sales. 4: U.S. sales as of 12/31/83 (source: BMW of North America).

| Years Built | Model | Body Style | Cyl. | cc | bhp (DIN) | Top Speed (mph) | weight (lbs) | Production* |
|---|---|---|---|---|---|---|---|---|
| 1955-58 | 502 Super | sedan 4d | 8 | 3168 | 120 | 106 | 3240 | |
| 1958-61 | 3.2 | sedan 4d | 8 | 3168 | 120 | 106 | 3240 | 2,537 |
| 1961-62 | 3200 L | sedan 4d | 8 | 3168 | 140 | 109 | 3240 | |
| 1957-61 | 3.2 Super | sedan 4d | 8 | 3168 | 140 | 109 | 3307 | 1,328 |
| 1961-63 | 3200 S | sedan 4d | 8 | 3168 | 160 | 118 | 3285 | |
| 1956-59 | 503 | coupe | 8 | 3168 | 140 | 118 | 3307 | 412 |
| 1956-59 | 503 | convertible | 8 | 3168 | 140 | 118 | 3307 | |
| 1956-59 | 507 | roadster | 8 | 3168 | 150 | 137 | 2932 | 253 |
| 1962-65 | 3200 CS | coupe | 8 | 3168 | 160 | 124 | 3307 | 603 |
| 1955-62 | Isetta 250 | | 1 | 245 | 12 | 53 | 795 | 161,728 |
| 1956-62 | Isetta 300 | | 1 | 298 | 13 | 53 | 795 | |
| 1957-59 | 600 | | 2 | 582 | 19.5 | 64 | 1213 | 34,813 |
| 1959-64 | 700 | coupe | 2 | 697 | 30 | 78 | 1411 | 19,896 |
| 1959-62 | 700 | sedan 2d | 2 | 697 | 30 | 75 | 1411 | 62,141 |
| 1961-62 | 700 Luxus | sedan 2d | 2 | 697 | 30 | 75 | 1411 | |
| 1960-63 | 700 Sport | coupe | 2 | 697 | 40 | 84 | 1433 | 9,346 |
| 1963-64 | 700 CS | coupe | 2 | 697 | 40 | 84 | 1433 | |
| 1961-64 | 700 | convertible | 2 | 697 | 40 | 84 | 1510 | 2,592 |
| 1962-65 | 700 Luxus | sedan 2d | 2 | 697 | 30 | 75 | 1499 | 92,416 |
| 1962-63 | 700 LS | sedan 2d | 2 | 697 | 30 | 75 | 1499 | |
| 1964-65 | 700 LS | coupe | 2 | 697 | 40 | 84 | 1521 | 1,730 |
| 1962-64 | 1500 | sedan 4d | 4 | 1499 | 80 | 92 | 2337 | 23,807 |
| 1964-66 | 1600 | sedan 4d | 4 | 1573 | 83 | 96 | 2359 | 10,278 |
| 1963-71 | 1800 | sedan 4d | 4 | 1773 | 90 | 101 | 2403 | 134,825 |
| 1965-71 | 1800 Auto. | sedan 4d | 4 | 1773 | 90 | 98 | 2403 | 3,922 |
| 1964-66 | 1800 TI | sedan 4d | 4 | 1773 | 110 | 109 | 2469 | 18,417 |
| 1965 | 1800 TI/SA | sedan 4d | 4 | 1773 | 130 | 116 | 2315 | 200 |
| 1965-68 | 2000 C | coupe | 4 | 1990 | 100 | 107 | 2646 | 443 |
| 1966-70 | 2000 C Auto. | coupe | 4 | 1990 | 100 | 104 | 2690 | 3,249 |
| 1965-70 | 2000 CS | coupe | 4 | 1990 | 120 | 115 | 2646 | 9,999 |
| 1966-72 | 2000 | sedan 4d | 4 | 1990 | 100 | 104 | 2579 | 108,743 |
| 1966-72 | 2000 Auto. | sedan 4d | 4 | 1990 | 100 | 102 | 2624 | 17,038 |
| 1966-68 | 2000 TI | sedan 4d | 4 | 1990 | 120 | 112 | 2535 | 6,482 |
| 1966-70 | 2000 TI Lux | sedan 4d | 4 | 1990 | 120 | 112 | 2579 | 17,440 |
| 1969-72 | 2000 tii | sedan 4d | 4 | 1990 | 130 | 115 | 2579 | 1,952 |
| 1966-71 | 1600-2 | sedan 2d | 4 | 1573 | 85 | 101 | 2072 | 210,451 |
| 1967-68 | 1600 TI | sedan 2d | 4 | 1573 | 105 | 109 | 2116 | 8,835 |
| 1967-71 | 1600 | convertible | 4 | 1573 | 85 | 101 | 2161 | 1,682 |
| 1971-72 | 1600 Touring | sedan 3d | 4 | 1573 | 85 | 101 | 2271 | 4,379 |
| 1971-75 | 1602 | sedan 2d | 4 | 1573 | 85 | 101 | 2161 | 56,351 |
| 1971-75 | 1802/A | sedan 2d | 4 | 1766 | 90 | 104 | 2161 | 83,351 |
| 1971-74 | 1800 Touring | sedan 3d | 4 | 1766 | 90 | 104 | 2271 | 4,075 |
| 1967-68 | 1600 GT | coupe | 4 | 1573 | 105 | 115 | 2138 | 1,255 |
| 1967-68 | 3000 V8 | coupe | 8 | 2982 | 160 | 121 | 2976 | 71 |
| 1968 | Goggomobil | | 2 | 247 | 13.6 | 50 | 959 | 10,883 |
| 1968-75 | 2002 | sedan 2d | 4 | 1990 | 100 | 107 | 2183 | 302,349 |
| 1969-75 | 2002 Auto. | sedan 2d | 4 | 1990 | 100 | 105 | 2227 | 34,558 |
| 1968-71 | 2002 ti | sedan 2d | 4 | 1990 | 120 | 115 | 2183 | 16,448 |
| 1971-75 | 2002 tii | sedan 2d | 4 | 1990 | 130 | 118 | 2227 | 38,703 |
| 1971-75 | 2002 | convertible | 4 | 1990 | 100 | 107 | 2993 | 2,517 |
| 1971-74 | 2000 Touring | sedan 3d | 4 | 1990 | 100 | 107 | 2271 | 14,980 |
| 1971-74 | 2000 Touring Auto. | sedan 3d | 4 | 1990 | 100 | 105 | 2315 | 989 |
| 1971-74 | 2000tii Touring | sedan 3d | 4 | 1990 | 130 | 118 | 2315 | 5,783 |
| 1973-74 | 2002 turbo | sedan 2d | 4 | 1990 | 170 | 131 | 2381 | 1,672 |

* Available factory data does not distinguish between model year and calendar year production for individual models within the newer BMW series. Combined worldwide sales for calendar years 1978-82 are as follows: 3-series: 1,001,521; 5-series: 524,078; 6-series: 32,292; 7-series: 164,299.   **SAE net. 1: U.S. sales. 2: 1982-83 U.S. model sales. 3: 1983 U.S. model sales. 4: U.S. sales as of 12/31/83 (source: BMW of North America).

| Years Built | Model | Body Style | Cyl. | cc | bhp (DIN) | Top Speed (mph) | weight (lbs) | Production* |
|---|---|---|---|---|---|---|---|---|
| 1975-77 | 1502 | sedan 2d | 4 | 1573 | 75 | 98 | 2161 | 71,564 |
| 1968-77 | 2500 | sedan 4d | 6 | 2494 | 150 | 118 | 2998 | 75,976 |
| 1969-77 | 2500 Auto. | sedan 4d | 6 | 2494 | 150 | 118 | 3042 | 17,387 |
| 1974-75 | 2.5 CS | coupe | 6 | 2494 | 150 | 125 | 3086 | 844 |
| 1968-75 | 2800 | sedan 4d | 6 | 2788 | 170 | 124 | 2998 | 28,998 |
| 1968-75 | 2800 Auto. | sedan 4d | 6 | 2788 | 170 | 124 | 3042 | 11,162 |
| 1975-77 | 2.8 L | sedan 4d | 6 | 2788 | 170 | 121 | 3175 | 3,423 |
| 1975-77 | 2.8 L Auto. | sedan 4d | 6 | 2788 | 170 | 121 | 3219 | 1,613 |
| 1968-71 | 2800 CS | coupe | 6 | 2788 | 170 | 128 | 2987 | 6,924 |
| 1969-71 | 2800 CS Auto. | coupe | 6 | 2788 | 170 | 128 | 3031 | 2,475 |
| 1971-77 | 3.0 S | sedan 4d | 6 | 2985 | 180 | 127 | 3131 | 29,826 |
| 1971-77 | 3.0 S Auto. | sedan 4d | 6 | 2985 | 180 | 127 | 3175 | 21,718 |
| 1971-77 | 3.0 Si | sedan 4d | 6 | 2985 | 200 | 130 | 3175 | 19,724 |
| 1971-77 | 3.0 Si Auto. | sedan 4d | 6 | 2985 | 200 | 130 | 3219 | 2,586 |
| 1971-75 | 3.0 CS | coupe | 6 | 2985 | 180 | 132 | 3086 | 5,017 |
| 1971-75 | 3.0 CS Auto. | coupe | 6 | 2985 | 180 | 132 | 3131 | 5,071 |
| 1971-75 | 3.0 CSL | coupe | 6 | 3153 | 206 | 137 | 2800 | 1,096 |
| 1971-75 | 3.0 CSi | coupe | 6 | 2985 | 200 | 137 | 3086 | 8,142 |
| 1975-77 | 3.0 L | sedan 4d | 6 | 2985 | 180 | 124 | 3241 | 2,529 |
| 1975-77 | 3.0 L Auto. | sedan 4d | 6 | 2985 | 180 | 124 | 3285 | 2,992 |
| 1974-76 | 3.3 L | sedan 4d | 6 | 3295 | 190 | 127 | 3351 | 381 |
| 1974-76 | 3.3 L Auto. | sedan 4d | 6 | 3295 | 190 | 127 | 3395 | 1,241 |
| 1976-77 | 3.3 Li | sedan 4d | 6 | 3205 | 197 | 127 | 3351 | 477 |
| 1976-77 | 3.3 Li Auto. | sedan 4d | 6 | 3205 | 197 | 127 | 3395 | 924 |
| 1982-date | 315 | sedan 2d | 4 | 1573 | 75 | 95 | 2227 | |
| 1975-82 | 316 | sedan 2d | 4 | 1573 | 90 | 100 | 2293 | |
| 1983-date | 316 | sedan 2/4d | 4 | 1766 | 90 | 109 | 2183 | |
| 1975-83 | 318 | sedan 2d | 4 | 1766 | 98 | 104 | 2293 | |
| 1975-83 | 318 Auto. | sedan 2d | 4 | 1766 | 98 | 104 | 2337 | |
| 1983-date | 318i | sedan 2/4d | 4 | 1766 | 105 | 114 | 2205 | |
| 1983-date | 318i (USA) | sedan 2/4d | 4 | 1766 | 101** | 113 | 2360 | |
| 1983-date | 318i Auto. (USA) | sedan 2/4d | 4 | 1766 | 101** | 110 | 2380 | |
| 1975-77 | 320 | sedan 2d | 4 | 1990 | 109 | 107 | 2337 | |
| 1975-77 | 320 Auto. | sedan 2d | 4 | 1990 | 109 | 107 | 2381 | |
| 1975-77 | 320i | sedan 2d | 4 | 1990 | 125 | 113 | 2381 | |
| 1977-83 | 320/6 | sedan 2d | 6 | 1990 | 122 | 114 | 2601 | |
| 1977-83 | 320/6 Auto. | sedan 2d | 6 | 1990 | 122 | 114 | 2649 | |
| 1983-date | 320i | sedan 2/4d | 6 | 1990 | 125 | 122 | 2315 | |
| 1983-date | 320i Auto. | sedan 2/4d | 6 | 1990 | 125 | 119 | 2335 | |
| 1977-83 | 323i | sedan 2d | 6 | 2315 | 143 | 119 | 2535 | |
| 1983-date | 323i | sedan 2/4d | 6 | 2315 | 139 | 125 | 2381 | |
| 1983-date | 323i Auto. | sedan 2/4d | 6 | 2315 | 135 | 116 | 2401 | |
| 1983-date | 325e | sedan 4d | 6 | 2693 | 125 | NA | NA | |
| 1974-81 | 518 | sedan 4d | 4 | 1766 | 90 | 101 | 2778 | |
| 1977-81 | 518 Auto. | sedan 4d | 4 | 1766 | 90 | 96 | 2822 | |
| 1981-date | 518 | sedan 4d | 4 | 1766 | 90 | 102 | 2558 | |
| 1972-77 | 520 | sedan 4d | 4 | 1990 | 115 | 109 | 2778 | |
| 1972-77 | 520 Auto. | sedan 4d | 4 | 1990 | 115 | 106 | 2822 | |
| 1972-77 | 520i | sedan 4d | 4 | 1990 | 130 | 114 | 2822 | |
| 1977-81 | 520/6 | sedan 4d | 6 | 1990 | 122 | 112 | 2976 | |
| 1977-81 | 520/6 Auto. | sedan 4d | 6 | 1990 | 122 | 112 | 3020 | |
| 1981-date | 520i | sedan 4d | 6 | 1990 | 125 | 115 | 2690 | |
| 1981-date | 520i Auto. | sedan 4d | 6 | 1990 | 125 | 111 | 2720 | |
| 1983-date | 524td | sedan 4d | 6 | 2443 | 115 | NA | NA | |

\* Available factory data does not distinguish between model year and calendar year production for individual models within the newer BMW series. Combined worldwide sales for calendar years 1978-82 are as follows: 3-series: 1,001,521; 5-series: 524,078; 6-series: 32,292; 7-series: 164,299.    \*\*SAE net. 1: U.S. sales. 2: 1982-83 U.S. model sales. 3: 1983 U.S. model sales. 4: U.S. sales as of 12/31/83 (source: BMW of North America).

| Years Built | Model | Body Style | Cyl. | cc | bhp (DIN) | Top Speed (mph) | weight (lbs) | Production* |
|---|---|---|---|---|---|---|---|---|
| 1973-81 | 525 | sedan 4d | 6 | 2494 | 145 | 119 | 3042 | |
| 1973-81 | 525 Auto. | sedan 4d | 6 | 2494 | 145 | 119 | 3086 | |
| 1981-date | 525i | sedan 4d | 6 | 2494 | 150 | 122 | 2844 | |
| 1981-date | 525i Auto. | sedan 4d | 6 | 2494 | 150 | 118 | 2864 | |
| 1981-date | 525e | sedan 4d | 6 | 2693 | 125 | NA | NA | |
| 1975-77 | 528 | sedan 4d | 6 | 2788 | 165 | 123 | 3120 | |
| 1975-77 | 528 Auto. | sedan 4d | 6 | 2788 | 165 | 123 | 3164 | |
| 1977-81 | 528i | sedan 4d | 6 | 2788 | 176 | 129 | 3197 | 10,435[1] |
| 1977-81 | 528i Auto. | sedan 4d | 6 | 2788 | 176 | 129 | 3241 | 9,275[1] |
| 1981-date | 528i | sedan 4d | 6 | 2788 | 184 | 132 | 2911 | |
| 1981-date | 528i Auto. | sedan 4d | 6 | 2788 | 184 | 128 | 2931 | |
| 1981-date | 528e (USA) | sedan 4d | 6 | 2693 | 121** | 121 | 2953 | 8,260[2] |
| 1981-date | 528e (USA) | sedan 4d | 6 | 2693 | 121** | 114 | 2973 | 10,968[2] |
| 1974-77 | 530i (USA) | sedan 4d | 6 | 2985 | 176 | 124 | 3300 | |
| 1974-77 | 530i Auto. (USA) | sedan 4d | 6 | 2985 | 176 | 120 | 3344 | |
| 1982-date | 533i (USA) | sedan 4d | 6 | 3210 | 181** | 134 | 3125 | 3,042[3] |
| 1982-date | 533i Auto. (USA) | sedan 4d | 6 | 3210 | 181** | 130 | 3145 | 976[3] |
| 1979-80 | M535i | sedan 4d | 6 | 3453 | 218 | 136 | 3150 | |
| 1979-date | 628 CSi | coupe | 6 | 2788 | 184 | 132 | 3153 | |
| 1979-date | 628 CSi Auto. | coupe | 6 | 2788 | 184 | 129 | 3173 | |
| 1976-79 | 630 CS | coupe | 6 | 2985 | 185 | 131 | 3252 | |
| 1976-79 | 630 CS Auto. | coupe | 6 | 2985 | 185 | 131 | 3296 | |
| 1977-78 | 630 CSi (USA) | coupe | 6 | 2985 | 176** | 125 | 3360 | 837[1] |
| 1977-78 | 630 CSi (USA) | coupe | 6 | 2985 | 176** | 119 | 3380 | 814[1] |
| 1976-81 | 633 CSi | coupe | 6 | 3210 | 200 | 134 | 3296 | |
| 1976-81 | 633 CSi Auto. | coupe | 6 | 3210 | 200 | 134 | 3340 | |
| 1979-date | 633 CSi (USA) | coupe | 6 | 3210 | 181 | 129 | 3350 | 3,783[4] |
| 1979-date | 633 CSi Auto. (USA) | coupe | 6 | 3210 | 181 | 125 | 3370 | 3,351[4] |
| 1978-date | 635 CSi | coupe | 6 | 3453 | 218 | 138 | 3351 | |
| 1983-date | M635 CSi | coupe | 6 | 3453 | 286 | 158 | 3400 | |
| 1977-79 | 728 | sedan 4d | 6 | 2788 | 170 | 122 | 3417 | |
| 1977-79 | 728 Auto. | sedan 4d | 6 | 2788 | 170 | 122 | 3461 | |
| 1979-date | 728i | sedan 4d | 6 | 2788 | 184 | 125 | 3263 | |
| 1979-date | 728i Auto. | sedan 4d | 6 | 2788 | 184 | 121 | 3283 | |
| 1977-79 | 730 | sedan 4d | 6 | 2985 | 184 | 125 | 3527 | |
| 1977-79 | 730 Auto. | sedan 4d | 6 | 2985 | 184 | 125 | 3571 | |
| 1979-date | 732i | sedan 4d | 6 | 3210 | 197 | 129 | 3307 | |
| 1979-date | 732i Auto. | sedan 4d | 6 | 3210 | 197 | 125 | 3327 | |
| 1977-79 | 733i | sedan 4d | 6 | 3210 | 197 | 129 | 3593 | |
| 1977-79 | 733i Auto. | sedan 4d | 6 | 3210 | 197 | 129 | 3683 | |
| 1979-date | 733i (USA) | sedan 4d | 6 | 3210 | 181** | 123 | 3440 | 5,210[4] |
| 1979-date | 733i Auto. (USA) | sedan 4d | 6 | 3210 | 181** | 119 | 3640 | 10,974[4] |
| 1978-date | 735i | sedan 4d | 6 | 3430 | 218 | 135 | 3307 | |
| 1978-date | 735i Auto. | sedan 4d | 6 | 3430 | 218 | 128 | 3327 | |
| 1980-83 | 745i Auto. | sedan 4d | 6 | 3210 | 252 | 142+ | 3506 | |
| 1983-date | 745i Auto. | sedan 4d | 6 | 3530 | 252 | 142+ | 3506 | |

\* Available factory data does not distinguish between model year and calendar year production for individual models within the newer BMW series. Combined worldwide sales for calendar years 1978-82 are as follows: 3-series: 1,001,521; 5-series: 524,078; 6-series: 32,292; 7-series: 164,299.   \*\*SAE net. 1: U.S. sales. 2: 1982-83 U.S. model sales. 3: 1983 U.S. model sales. 4: U.S. sales as of 12/31/83 (source: BMW of North America).

# INDEX

*The 1983-model 323i (left) and 316, top and bottom of the German lineup.*